FOURTH EDITION

Inequality
and Stratification
Race, Class, and Gender

ROBERT A. ROTHMAN

Professor Emeritus
University of Delaware

Prentice
Hall

Upper Saddle River, New Jersey 07458

Library of Congress Cataloging-in-Publication Data

Rothman, Robert A., (date)
    Inequality and stratification : race, class, and gender / Robert A. Rothman.—4th ed.
      p. cm.
    Rev. ed. of: Inequality & stratification. 3rd ed. c1999.
    Includes bibliographical references and indexes.
    ISBN 0-13-033669-6 (pbk.)
      1. United States—Social conditions.   2. Equality—United States.   3. Social
structure—United States.   4. Social classes—United States.   5. Social status—United States.
6. Minorities—United States.   I. Rothman, Robert A., (date) Inequality & stratification.   II.
Title
HN57 .R577 2002
305'.0973—dc21   2001019901

VP, Editorial Director: Laura Pearson
AVP, Publisher: Nancy Roberts
Managing Editor: Sharon Chambliss
Editorial/production supervision and interior design: Mary Araneo
Director of Marketing: Beth Gillett Mejia
Prepress and Manufacturing Buyer: Mary Ann Gloriande
Cover Art Director: Jayne Conte
Cover Designer: Bruce Kenselaar

This book was set in 10/12 Times by A & A Publishing Services, Inc.,
and was printed and bound by Maple Press. The cover was
printed by Phoenix Color Corp.

ISBN   0-13-033669-6

Pearson Education LTD., London
Pearson Education Australia PTY, Limited, Sydney
Pearson Education Singapore, Pte. Ltd
Pearson Education North Asia Ltd, Hong Kong
Pearson Education Canada, Ltd., Toronto
Pearson Educación de Mexico, S.A. de C.V.
Pearson Education — Japan, Tokyo
Pearson Education Malaysia, Pte. Ltd
Pearson Education, Upper Saddle River, New Jersey

To Nancy: For Everything

Contents

PART TWO:
STRATIFICATION
IN INDUSTRIAL SOCIETIES   37

PART THREE:
PATTERNS OF INEQUALITY   91

PART FIVE:
INHERITANCE AND MOBILITY   212

CHAPTER ELEVEN
Patterns of Social Mobility   213

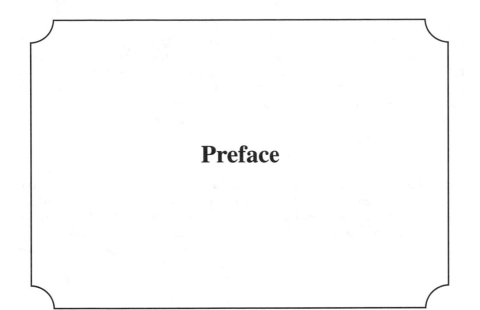

Preface

There can be no doubt that one of the major developments of the end of the twentieth century was the emergence of digital technology. Computers proliferated, as did cell phones, DVD players, and a host of other electronic devices. Electronic mail forever changed the way people communicate, and the Internet reshaped how we shop, listen to music, write research papers, and search out medical information. It also contributed to the creation of a global economy. The digital revolution has had as well a significant impact on the distribution of wealth and the structure of inequality, simultaneously opening new opportunities for many but handicapping those lacking the skills of the twenty-first century.

This edition systematically explores the implications of the digital revolution in industrial nations. It incorporated up-to-date information and research in keeping with the expansion and elaboration of the subject. Although the American experience remains its central emphasis, the scope of the work has been broadened to include more attention to other industrial systems of social stratification.

The basic format introduced in the third edition has been retained. Part One provides a broad overview and introduction to the field. Part Two is an expanded discussion of the evolution and institutionalization of industrial class systems. The three chapters that focus on the basic elements of inequality—economics, prestige, and politics—define Part Three. Part Four includes separate chapters on life chances and lifestyles as well as class consciousness. Social mobility is the subject of Part Five. However, the format is flexible enough to allow faculty to reorder the chapters to fit their personal preferences.

This edition, like earlier ones, is written with the undergraduate student in mind. It is intended to provide the fundamentals of social stratification for undergraduates in a concise and readable format. **Key Concepts** are highlighted with bold type in the text and listed at the end of chapters to facilitate review. The book may be used in different ways: as a basic text for stratification courses; in newer sociology courses that focus on the intersection of class, race, and gender courses in stratification; or as one component of courses such as introductions to sociology, social problems, race and minorities, or gender studies. The format is convenient to combine with any of several useful anthologies.

Any book that attempts to lay out the fundamentals of an area as complex and broad as stratification cannot elaborate all the areas of debate and controversy. Therefore, more advanced students are directed to the material contained in footnotes and annotated Suggested Reading sections for the resources needed to explore these issues in more depth and detail. Consistent with the emphasis on the digital revolution, a listing of useful web sites can be found at the end of each chapter.

I would like to thank the following reviewers for their comments and suggestions: Don Anspach, University of Southern Maine; Marcia L. Bellas, University of Cincinnati; Sheryl Grana, University of Minnesota, Duluth; and Cathy D. Martin, Louisiana Tech University.

Robert A. Rothman

PART ONE

The Nature of Inequality and Stratification

Industrial societies are distinguished by several prominent social divisions—social classes based on position in the economic system of production and distribution, sex and gender, and racial and ethnic categories. Many of the most significant rewards and advantages available to people are shaped by these three factors. The consequences of class, race, and gender are most pronounced in areas such as the distribution of earnings and wealth, judgments and evaluations of social prestige, access to political power, and life chances related to health and illness, crime and justice, and educational opportunities. The system of classes, races, ethnic groups, and genders and the distribution of inequalities are supported and maintained by the culture and social structure of the society. Chapter 1 develops the basic ideas and concepts central to the sociological analysis of inequality and stratification. Chapter 2 reviews the major theoretical conceptualizations and interpretations of the origins of industrial social systems that dominate current theory and research.

CHAPTER ONE

Inequality
and Social Stratification

THE FORMS OF INEQUALITY

The scope of inequality in the contemporary world is obvious. Discrepancies—sometimes vast discrepancies—in wealth, material possessions, power and authority, prestige, and access to education, health care, and simple creature comforts dominate the social life of societies. At the extremes are the homeless and the super-rich, the esteemed and the degraded, the powerful and the powerless, and many levels between them. There are many forms of inequality, but since the nineteenth century sociologists have tended to focus on three major forms—economic, social, and political—an analytic practice first suggested by the pioneering German sociologist Max Weber.

Economic Inequalities

Disparities in wealth and material resources are usually the most visible form of inequality. Industrial societies contain millions of people whose daily lives are a struggle against calamity. Forty-four million Americans have no health insurance (Toner, 1999). One child in ten lives in poverty in the major industrial nations—Australia, Britain, Canada, Ireland, Israel, and Italy (Pear, 1996). In America, it is one child in five! Hundreds of thousands of the destitute are homeless, compelled to wander the streets and fill the shelters in Los Angles, London, and Moscow.

While many struggle for survival, others in the same society enjoy the benefits of great wealth. Professional athletes, entertainers, corporate executives, and e-business entrepreneurs earn millions of dollars each year. Others, fortunate enough to have been born into prosperous families with names such as duPont or Rockefeller or Walton (Wal-Mart), never need to worry about the source of their next meal or confront the fear of being unable to pay the rent. On the contrary, some of the very rich indulge unbelievably ostentatious and extravagant lifestyles. One couple flies their palm trees from Southampton, NY, to Palm Beach, FL, in the winter months to keep them warm (Yazigi, 1999). Wealthy tobacco heiress Doris Duke always felt it necessary to fly her two pet camels with her on trips to Hawaii (Clancy, 1988). Ranged between such extremes are smaller gradations of monetary inequality, often measured by the size of homes, the kind of cars people drive, or the quality of the schools their children can afford to attend.

Social Status

A second important form of inequality is social status. **Social status** is the social standing, esteem, respect, or prestige that people command from other members of society. It is a judgment of the relative ranking of individuals and groups on scales of social superiority and inferiority. Social status is a relevant prize because people are highly sensitive to the evaluations of others, valuing the admiration and approval of their peers as is readily evident when they attempt to embellish their social standing through the public display of designer clothing and jewelry, luxury cars and homes. An individual might be able to write equally well with a Bic pen as with a Mont Blanc, but only the latter confers social status.

Individuals can earn social status on the basis of their own efforts (athletic ability) or personal attributes (physical attractiveness, intelligence), but there is also a powerful structural dimension to social status—occupations, social classes, racial and ethnic groups, and the sexes are typically ranked relative to one another. For example, at various times and in various places, women and men have formed clearly demarcated status groups. In the United States it was common for males to be openly rated as superior to females by both men and women well into the 1950s and 1960s (McKee & Sherriffs, 1957). Occupational prestige rankings are probably the status hierarchies with which most people are familiar. Occupations around the world are typically arranged on a strict hierarchy of prestige, usually with physicians, lawyers, and scientists at the top and garbage collectors and janitors near the bottom.

The significance of social ranking extends beyond questions of social approval and ego gratification. Status considerations can dictate the form of social interaction between people at different levels. People are likely to show courtesy to those ranked above them, but they tend to expect deference from those ranked below them. Social considerations also lead to practices designed to limit social contacts with people defined as inferior, which shows up in residential segregation and other forms of exclusionary behavior.

Power and Authority

There is a third salient, more complex form of inequality, dealing with the unequal distribution of power and authority in society. Although there is a lack of consensus on precise definitions of such terms, there is general agreement that the essence of **power** is the ability to control events or to determine the behavior of others in the face of resistance, and to resist attempts at control by others. **Authority** refers to a specific form of control where the right to command is considered as appropriate and legitimate. Authority may be based on tradition, or it may reside in organizational position (as with generals' right to direct the behavior of lieutenants or supervisors' ability to sanction workers) or in expert knowledge (lawyers' capacity to prescribe the actions of clients).

　　Discrepancies in power are difficult to document, but it is clear that enormous power is concentrated in the hands of the people who head the large organizations that dominate the business, governmental, military, and social landscape. Sociologist C. Wright Mills (1956) was among the first to point out that the growth of major organizations during the twentieth century consolidated unusual amounts of power in the government (the president and congress), the military (the Joint Chiefs of Staff), corporate executives, labor union leaders, church officials, and university presidents. In contrast, a majority of Americans feel quite powerless politically, believing they have little or no influence over the activities of the government. Four out of five believe the government is run by special interests (Apple, 1995).

Life Chances

Economic, social, and political inequalities are direct and have readily observable consequences, but there are also subtle and less obvious forms of inequality. Max Weber (1946) introduced the concept of **life chances** to identify the role of social class in enhancing or weakening the probability of enjoying experiences that enhance the quality of life or facing barriers that diminish it. It is appropriate in contemporary analysis to extend the term *life chances* to include the implications of race, ethnicity, and gender as well as class. Life chances include the odds of a newborn surviving infancy; the chances of going to college; the risk of suffering mental illness, loneliness, or obesity; and the probability of being a victim of violent crime such as robbery, assault, or rape.

　　The idea of life chances is highlighted by considering the problem of domestic violence or what is now called "intimate partner violence." About 1 million cases of violent crimes are committed by current or former spouses, boyfriends, or girlfriends each year. Murder, rape, sexual assault, robbery, and aggravated and simple assault are included as violent crimes, and 85 percent of the victims are women. The chances of falling victim to violence are not evenly distributed across the stratification system, as shown in Exhibit 1.1. Women in the poorest households are almost seven times as likely to be harmed as those in the top income group. Race also makes a difference, with African-American women victimized more fre-

EXHIBIT 1.1   Intimate Partner Violence by Household Income, Race, Ethnicity, and Gender

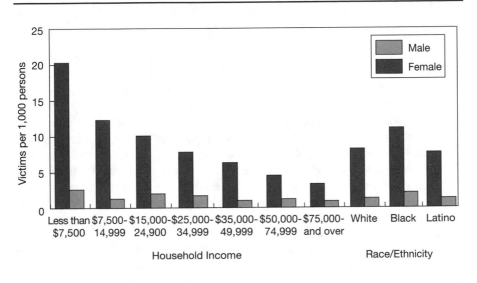

Note: Victims per 1,000 females or males.

Source: Callie Marie Rennison and Susan Welchans. Intimate Partner Violence. U.S. Department of Justice, Bureau of Justice Statistics. Washington, DC: U.S. Government Printing Office, 2000.

quently than in any other group. These numbers can only hint at the scope and significance of social stratification.

THE SOURCES OF INEQUALITY: CLASS, RACE, AND GENDER

Many of the rewards, advantages, and benefits of life in the modern world are shaped by peoples' location in the social structure of society, and there are three that are among the most consequential.[1] Industrial societies are divided into social classes based on position in an economic system of production and distribution, racial and ethnic group membership, and gender. Class, race, and gender are sometimes approached as distinct and separate sources of inequality in contemporary society. Some social scientists go so far as to argue that one of these three factors is more salient than the others. However, they are best understood as overlapping or intersecting bases of inequality and stratification. None can be fully understood or explained without analyzing the interrelationships among them. For example, the

---

[1]Obviously, considerations of factors such as age and sexual orientation are also powerfully important.

experiences and opportunities of middle-class African-American women or work-ing-class white men must be approached as the convergence of class, race, and gender. Therefore, each of the concepts requires clarification.

Social Class

A **social class** is a group of individuals or families who occupy a similar position in the economic system of production, distribution, and consumption of goods and services in industrial societies. For the overwhelming majority of people, social class position is defined by occupation.[2] Social class position is actually much more complex than a job description, but work is the most useful starting point. People's work sets effective limits on financial rewards and social status, influences the stability of employment and the chances for social mobility, locates people in systems of work-place authority and power having consequences that extend beyond the work place, defines some features of social relations on and off the job, contributes to the way people think about themselves and others, and has enduring implications for their children.

Many of the problems of the poorest members of society can be traced to their tenuous link to the economic system. The unemployed and the working poor form a large pool of people lacking a secure position in the work place. They are handicapped by a lack of experience, weak educational credentials, a lack of job opportunities, discrimination, or personal habits. Whatever the combination of reasons that explains the plight of specific individuals, their collective impoverishment has its origins in an economic system that is unable to provide jobs at decent wages for all who seek them.

One of the issues that divides sociologists is the problem of distinguishing the number and form of classes in contemporary industrial societies.[3] Despite some areas of ambiguity and the lack of clear boundaries between class levels, American society can conveniently be divided into five broad social classes.[4] At the top of the stratification system is a small elite class that wields unusual economic, political, and social influence. The elite includes an institutional elite made up of the women and men who direct the dominant national organizations and institutions (government, business and industry, the media, education, and religion) and a capitalist elite of individuals and families whose power derives from wealth and property rather than structural position. One segment of the capitalist elite amassed fortunes through efforts and abilities during their own lives, as is the case of Oprah Winfrey, Pete Sampras, and Bill Gates.

---

[2]Sociologists frequently disagree on the definition and measurement of social class. A good discussion of the issues is found in Grusky & Sorensen, 1998.

[3]There is one school of thought that argues that discrete classes have been eroded by the social and economic forces of postmodern society, a situation of "capitalism without classes" according to one author (Block, 1992: 88). The case for the persistence of classes is given by Hout, Brooks, & Manza (1993).

[4]The composition of classes is discussed in more detail in Chapter 3.

This group is called the *new* capitalist elite to distinguish them from the *old* capitalist elite, where wealth has been passed down through several generations in families such as Mars (the candy family) and Heinz (the food family).

The next level, the upper middle class, combines occupations based on expert knowledge (professional people such as physicians, computer programmers, and scientific personnel) and administrators and managers below the executive level. The lower middle class includes technicians, lower-level administrators, and most clerical and sales personnel. In the United States the term *working class* means manual work, also called blue-collar work, and describes those who do the physical labor in the factories, mills, and mines. Some are engaged in highly skilled work (auto mechanics) while others perform more routine tasks on assembly lines. Skill differentials are an important consideration in understanding how manual workers perceive themselves. At the bottom of the hierarchy are the poor, who live on the very margins of the productive system. Numbered in this class are both the "working poor" who fill the least skilled jobs in the economy and those caught up in unstable and poorly paid jobs (the unemployed, the under-employed, and those discouraged because they believe they cannot find work).

Developing an accurate picture of the class structure of American society is a complex and controversial task, but one model is suggested by Exhibit 1.2. The elite is a small group, comprising no more than 1 or 2 percent of the population. About 30 percent can be defined as upper middle class on the basis of administrative, managerial, and professional occupations. About one worker in three holds a lower middle-class job in clerical, sales, or administrative support positions, and another one in three fills the manual occupations of the working class. Perhaps one in six Americans may be counted among the poor, holding marginal jobs or facing unemployment. This model must be viewed as merely a starting point since considerations of wealth, social status, political power, and life chances will reveal significant patterns of inequality.

Social Stratification

The phrase **social stratification** is a general term used to refer to the hierarchy of layers or strata of individuals and families where position is a major source of rewards. Social stratification has taken many forms in different places and at different points in history, but the three most familiar forms are slave, caste, and class systems. Each form arises under different historical conditions, singles out distinctive social categories of people, generates alternative kinds of hierarchies, and differs in the scope and magnitude of inequalities.

Slave systems divide people into two fundamental groups, the free and the unfree. Slave systems are coercive, with one group imposing its will upon vulnerable groups. Despite a great deal of progress in the area of global human rights, slavery survives in a number of places around the globe such as Mauritania (Masland, et al., 1992). There is also a largely hidden worldwide system of slavery that penetrates even into the United States. As many as 700,000 women and children are forced into

EXHIBIT 1.2   A Simplified Model of Social Classes

Social Class	Percent of the Population	Number Employed
Elite	1–2%	
Upper middle class		
Professionals	28–30%	20,883,000
Managerial		19,584,000
Lower middle class		
Sales workers		16,118,000
Technicians	27–29%	4,355,000
Clerical		18,448,000
Working class		
Craft workers		14,593,000
Operatives		7,386,000
Transportation workers		5,516,000
Protective services	27–29%	2,440,000
Farm workers		3,426,000
Service workers		6,164,000
The poor		
Food and cleaning services		8,480,000
Domestic workers		831,000
Unskilled workers	14–16%	5,265,000
Unemployed		6,008,000
Totals		139,496,000

Source: "Employed Persons by Detailed Occupation," *Employment and Earnings* 47 (January, 2000), Table 11, pages 177–183, and "Unemployed Persons by Reason for Unemployment," *Monthly Labor Review* 123 (June, 2000), Table 8, page 59.

bondage each year according to a C.I.A. report (Brinkley, 2000). Victims from Asian and African countries are enticed by promises of legitimate jobs in industrial nations but upon reaching their destination are forced to work as prostitutes, domestics, or common laborers. It is estimated that 100,000 of this group were transported to America during 1998 and 1999.

Caste systems organize people into fixed hereditary groups in which there is little or no chance for children to escape the caste of their parents. Caste systems have existed at various times in Rwanda (East Africa), Japan, Tibet, Korea, and India and Pakistan. The most well known, the Hindu caste system, was in place as early as the ninth century and prevailed until the nineteenth century. Members of different castes were allocated to specific occupations, and social contacts between castes were regulated by elaborate rituals. The British began to formally dismantle the system in the nineteenth century, but vestiges remain in many rural areas (Beteille, 1992). The dilemmas of the caste system are aggravated by the devaluation of females. Scarce resources are allocated to males while infant girls and women are often malnourished (Cooper, 1997).

Class systems are the product of industrialization where major social and economic rewards are determined by position in the economic system of production, distribution, and consumption. Inequalities do not exist in isolation. Social and cultural ideas explain and legitimize these social divisions and the distribution of rewards associated with them. Powerful nations, for example, enslave subdued groups as a source of cheap labor, then rationalize their actions on the grounds that the victims are inferior people. Women have been commonly and systematically excluded from positions of authority on the grounds that they lacked the necessary psychological attributes to lead and make decisions.

Racial and Ethnic Minorities

Members of racial and ethnic groups are, to quote a widely used phrase, clusters of people who, "because of physical or cultural characteristics, are singled out from others in the society in which they live for differential and unequal treatment" (Wirth, 1945: 347). Several different collective terms are used to describe these groups in a society. Sociologists originally introduced the term **minorities** as a way of emphasizing power differentials, not numerical disparities, since it is typically superior power that allows one group to discriminate against another. Consequently, many contemporary analysts favor terms such as *dominant groups* and *subordinate groups* because these terms more clearly highlight unequal power. In the United States, where major racial groups are differentiated socially by skin pigmentation, the phrase **people of color** gained currency during the 1990s and is used interchangeably with the term *minorities*.

As Wirth emphasized, groups of people can be identified by either physical or cultural traits or a combination of the two. **Races** are groups identified by visible physical characteristics such as skin color, stature, and facial features. It is evident that there is infinite variation within the human race and thus determining the boundaries among groups is a social construction. **Ethnicity** is determined by cultural (or national) origins, which may be manifest in language, religion, values, beliefs, or customs and practices.

The bringing together of peoples of diverse physical or cultural origins does not inevitably produce social, economic, or political subordination. A case in point are the Cossacks and Tungas of Manchuria, groups who coexisted for centuries within a context of political independence and mutual respect (Lindgren, 1938). Another example is Switzerland, which has since 1815 been a nation with three official names and languages, Schweiz (German), Suisse (French), and Svizzera (Italian), where members of these three groups peacefully coexist. Unfortunately, conflict or some form of economic or social exploitation is the more common outcome of the meeting of groups than is peaceful coexistence. Recent events in central Europe (Serbians versus Kosovars), and Africa (Hutus versus Tutsis), are a tragic reminder of the human cost of ethnic hostilities.

New groups enter societies by different paths, and each route has important implications for subsequent intergroup relations. Immigration is the flow of peoples in search of religious or political freedom or economic opportunities. The immigration of non-English ethnic groups to the United States began on a large scale in the 1840s and continues today as waves of newcomers pour into America. In Europe, the 1990s witnessed a massive movement of people in response to the dissolution of the communist bloc and civil wars, producing unrest and the tightening of immigration policies in some western European nations. Sometimes members of ethnic groups are explicitly recruited to provide specific kinds of labor (contract labor). For example, laborers from China were recruited to help build the railroad system in America during the 1850s.

Immigration and contract labor tends to be a more or less voluntary process, but there are also involuntary contacts. Peoples are sometimes forcibly incorporated into a new nation as a result of territorial expansion. More powerful groups pursuing military, economic, or political goals encroach upon previously independent populations, as was the experience with Europeans encountering Native Americans, and relegate them to the lower levels of the economic system. In the most extreme cases subjugated groups are enslaved to fill the need for cheap labor. Slaves may also be imported for the express purpose of providing cheap labor or other duties.

Major Racial and Ethnic Groups in the United States

American society is a mosaic of peoples of diverse racial and ethnic origins. Natives (or their descendants) of at least 150 different countries and 557 American Indian tribes reside within the borders of the United States. Typically, they are consolidated into five broad racial and ethnic groups: African American, Asian American, Hispanic or Latino, Native American, and non-Hispanic white, despite the fact that such designations mask significant diversity within each group. Moreover, these broad categories exclude many other smaller groups such as Arab Americans. Each group has an extended history in America, and the language used to identify each group hints at the social and political realities of their histories. There are internal disagreements within groups about the most appropriate form of self-identification.[5] Exhibit 1.3 illustrates the racial and ethnic identification preferences of a sample of Americans.

African American or Black.[6]   Blacks or African Americans are one of the two largest minority groups in the United States with a population of over 30 million, thus comprising approximately 12 percent of the population. Most families

---

[5]Census Bureau enumeration of membership in racial and ethnic categories is based on self-identification by respondents. The 2000 census was the first time that residents had the opportunity to register their multiracial or multiethnic history. The issue of multiracial identification is considered in more detail in Chapter 6.

[6]The terms *black* and *African American* are used interchangeably in this edition.

EXHIBIT 1.3   How People Prefer to Be Identified

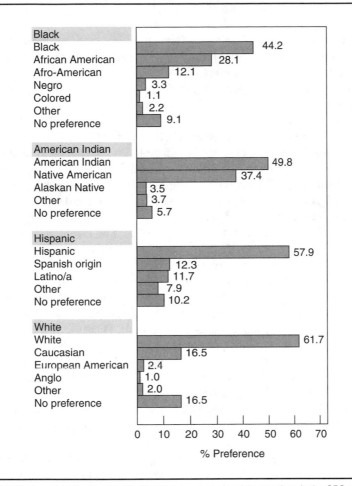

Source: Clyde Tucker and Brian Kojetin, "Testing racial and ethnic origin questions in the CPS supplement," *Monthly Labor Review* 119 (September, 1996): 3–7.

trace their ancestry to African slaves. The institution of slavery was firmly established by the end of the seventeenth century, and some slaves apparently initially
favored the term "African" over the more insulting and derogatory terms used by
others, at least until white supremacist groups mounted campaigns to deport freed
slaves in the post-Civil War era. "Negro" subsequently dominated social discourse
until the 1960s when the former racial slur "black" was adopted by some as a statement of group solidarity and identity. Late in the 1980s some leaders began to champion "African American" to encourage people to identify themselves by their history
and culture rather than their skin color. Surveys show that "black" tends to be the

most favored form of self-identification, although African American is favored by the younger and better-educated.

Hispanic American or Latino.[7]   Thirty million Americans have Spanish language roots, and the 2000 census showed that Hispanic Americans had become the nation's largest minority. They come from at least 22 different countries. The largest group traces its origins to Mexico (roughly 63 percent), geographically concentrated in the Southwest. Puerto Ricans (12 percent) have tended to settle in the Northeast, and Cubans (8 percent) in Florida. The remainder are from Central and South America (12 percent), the Caribbean, or Spain (Pollard & O'Hare, 1999).

The term *Hispanic* has no clear linguistic link to the people it describes. The word has Latin roots, referring to the Iberian peninsula, but it is largely a bureaucratic convenience. The Census Bureau originally referred to members of this group of people as Spanish-speaking, but adopted Hispanic in the 1970s in response to political pressure and in recognition of the fact that many Spanish surnamed people did not use the Spanish language (Gonzalez, 1992). More recently, the terms *Latino* (male construction) or *Latina* (female) have found favor. The male construction Latino has become the preferred collective term.

Some Americans feel that terms such as Hispanic and Latino are like the word *Negro*, labels imposed on a minority group by an English-speaking government. It appears that most members of this group prefer to identify themselves by their native land, but when asked to choose one collective term, Hispanic is the most favored alternative although it is clearly a secondary form of self-identification (Garcia, 1997). Actually, there are many different forms of self-identification. For example, Mexican Americans tend to describe themselves as Chicano, but Texans with Mexican ancestry are likely to call themselves Tejanos.

The sheer number of Hispanics means that they will have an increasing impact on American society and culture. It is already being felt in sports such as baseball and boxing, film, cuisine, and music. Still unclear is their political impact. Hispanics have traditionally had very low turnout at the polls, but in the 1990s voter registration drives arose, and the potential numbers of voters are significant. Large numbers of Latinos are concentrated in 11 key states such as Florida, Texas, New York, and California, which together have over 200 ballots in the electoral college, and only 270 votes are needed to win the presidency.

Asian American.   The Asian American population stands at more than 10 million and is growing at an unprecedented rate. Their numbers more than doubled between 1980 and 1990 and are expected to double again by 2010 (Lee, 1998). Their growth has been fueled by immigration, with Asians representing more than one-third of all legal immigrants admitted to the United States in recent years. They are

---

[7]The terms *Hispanic* and *Latino* are used interchangeably in this edition. Studies done prior to the 1990s usually included all Spanish language people regardless of race.

a diverse group, but nine of ten trace their origins to six nations: China, the Philippines, Asian India, Vietnam, Korea, and Japan. Asian Americans were not surveyed for Exhibit 1.2, but other research suggests that most people in this category prefer to identify with their native land rather than with any single collective category (Goldberg, 1996).

Native American or American Indian. The original inhabitants of the North American continent were a dissimilar group of cultures including the Eskimos of what is now Alaska, the Pueblos of the Southwest, the Iroquois of the Northeast, and the hunters of the Great Plains. They are grouped together because they predated European contact. There are currently over 2 million American Indians and four out of ten are members of the four largest tribes, Cherokee, Navajo, Chippewa, and Sioux. As is well known these people were erroneously named Indians on the assumption that Europeans had reached Asian India. About one half favor the label American Indian, but Native American is the favored form of identification of a sizable proportion of residents, with natives of Alaska and the Aleutian Islands (Aleuts) typically choosing that designation.

White. The white segment of the American population is also a heterogeneous category, composed of 195 million people who trace their origins to countries such as England, Ireland, Italy, Germany, Sweden, Russia, Poland, and scores of others. People have been making distinctions among human beings based on skin color and physical appearance for centuries. Swedish taxonomist Linnaeus was the first, dividing humans into red, yellow, white, and black in the eighteenth century. Terms such as *Caucasian* emerged later as scientists unsuccessfully attempted to translate skin tone into physiological or biological criteria. The phrase *white race* seems to have gained popularity at the beginning of the nineteenth century as a way of maintaining social distance from American Indians and African Americans (Allen, 1994). Most white Americans prefer that term today. It is becoming more common to separate European whites from Spanish-speaking whites by using the phrase *non-Hispanic whites.*

Gender

Gender refers to the social characteristics that distinguish the sexes.[8] The social construction of gender is a subtle and complex process that includes tangible presentations of people (clothing and grooming), a sexual division of labor between women's and men's work, and subtle behavioral and attitudinal expectations. Gen-

---

8 Social scientists originally reserved the word *sex* for the physiological and biological differences that distinguish males and females, and *gender* for socially defined and acquired behaviors and expectations for males and females in a particular culture at a historical point in time. Contemporary usage in the public media tends to use gender for either meaning.

EXHIBIT 1.4   Time Devoted to Paid and Unpaid Work in Industrial Nations

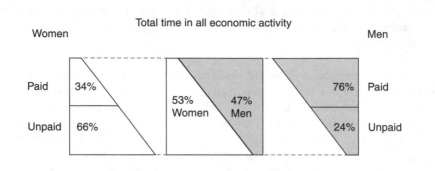

Source: United Nations Development Program, *Human Development Report,* New York: Oxford University Press, 1995, Figure 4.2, page 89.

der is embedded in the social and cultural heritage of a group, and individuals are introduced to it as they encounter differential expectations and are exposed to dissimilar treatment that tends to emphasize differences at the expense of similarities.

One of the most significant obstacles that women everywhere confront is the failure to place fair economic value on their productive efforts. Women worldwide work more hours than men and perform more than one-half of all the economic activities in societies, both industrial and developing, but their work is divided differently (UNDP, 1995: 87–91). Only about one-third of women's work is in a paid labor market compared to about three-fourths of men's work (Exhibit 1.4). The bulk of time devoted to unpaid work in industrial countries involves housework and child care. Social class has an effect on hours worked in the home because members of more affluent families can afford to purchase some of the services that others must perform themselves—laundry, cleaning, meal preparation, lawn and yard care. Women in developing nations typically bear an even heavier burden since they must also do things such as collect water and firewood, and are involved in planting and harvesting. Unpaid work is essential to the survival of families, but it is labor market work that is valued in the sense that it is recognized as "productive work," pays tangible monetary rewards, and earns social status in the society. Thus, men derive greater benefits from their labor than women.

THE INSTITUTIONALIZATION OF INEQUALITY

Inequalities are embedded in the very fabric of society. The phrase the institutionalization of inequality calls attention to the configuration of social arrangements that combine to generate, sustain, and perpetuate social inequalities and social stratification. Included among the most salient aspects of institutionalization are social values, beliefs in the form of stereotypes and myths, laws, institutions, and ideologies that reinforce and legitimize the unequal distribution of rewards and limit people's ability to redistribute rewards.

Values.   **Values** are standards of desirability, collective expressions of what is precious or worthless, respected or disdained, commendable or deplorable. Values are intangible, but are powerful motivaters, encouraging certain courses of action and discouraging others, rewarding some accomplishments and penalizing others. Values place a premium on things such as tangible objects (cars, watches), ideals (democracy, equal opportunity), behaviors (diligence, honesty), or symbols (grades, diplomas) and serve as a guide and a justification for the conduct of individual affairs.

At the most basic level it is important to remember that the very desirability of wealth and status that is so prevalent in the United States is a cultural value. The American value system emphasizes displays of wealth, consumption, and invidious distinctions based on personal possessions. The pursuit of such goals does not extend to all segments of American society. For example, displays of wealth through clothing, jewelry, homes, or other possessions are an activity discouraged by the old-order Amish because its members are devoted to a lifestyle that deliberately rejects the materialism of modern industrial systems in favor of a stable, homogeneous, and devout religious value system (Kephart, 1994).

Widely shared values often underlie the distribution of status. The dignity and worth of human life is a powerful dimension of the social and religious heritage of Western civilization, with the result that occupations that contribute to the preservation of life (physician) tend to enjoy higher social status than work that makes no apparent and direct contribution to the quality of life. A conspicuous example of the cultural value—social status linkage was embodied in the Hindu concept of an "untouchable" caste. Hindus considered it wrong to harm any form of life, which meant that butchers, hunters, fishers, and even shepherds raising animals for human consumption were in occupations that "defiled" or "polluted" them. They were assembled in one caste and excluded from common forms of social discourse.

Beliefs.   **Beliefs** are ideas or assumptions about the nature of social and physical reality. Beliefs define the way people and events are perceived and experienced, and shape responses to them. Beliefs need not be supported by objective evidence. Early in the twentieth century sociologist W. I. Thomas summarized the implications of beliefs by noting that, "If men define situations as real, they are real in their consequences" (Thomas, 1928). It is a reminder that beliefs have repercussions because people act on their beliefs, regardless of their validity. Knowledge based on scientific research is a belief in this context, but so too are stereotypes, myths, urban legends, and religious revelations. They all qualify because they serve to explain the social and physical world and interpret the causes of events even if they cannot be validated by modern science.

Beliefs about the nature of individuals and groups are interwoven with the distribution of rewards. It is, for example, common to discover beliefs that suggest that members of racial or ethnic minorities have social, cultural, or biological deficiencies that explain and justify discriminatory treatment toward them. The waves of Polish and Italian immigrants to the United States in the nineteenth century were often relegated to dead-end, unskilled jobs on the grounds that these groups were lazy or morally dishonest.

Laws.   Inequality is frequently formalized in the legal system of a society. The legitimacy of excluding women from high-status occupations such as law was actually upheld by the United States Supreme Court in the nineteenth century (*Bradwell v. Illinois*, 1873). Moreover, the Court subsequently upheld so-called "protective legislation" that excluded women from a whole range of jobs then defined as too strenuous or dangerous for them (*Muller v. Oregon*, 1908). Protective legislation was legitimized on the grounds that women needed protection because they were not as strong as men, were dependent upon men, and were the mothers of future generations (Hill, 1979). It is no coincidence that such jobs paid more and carried greater probability of promotion.

Social Institutions.   Social institutions such as religion, education, and the family also play a role in the perpetuation of inequalities. For example, the church has sometimes provided overt sacred support for secular inequality. Medieval feudal estates were imbued with a religious-moral purpose by Christian philosophers who maintained that the feudal system was the only possible way of defending the Church against its pagan enemies (Nottingham, 1954). A more subtle link between religion and inequality was proposed by Karl Marx in his criticism of organized religion. He claimed the attraction of other worldly salvation distracted the attention of the poor away from their present suffering and reduced the chances that they would openly challenge it.

Formal educational systems often perpetuate existing patterns of inequality and help to guarantee new generations will inherit the same social position as that of their parents. For example, there is a network of elite preparatory schools and colleges that prepare upper-class children in America to assume the reins of power held by their parents (Kingston & Lewis, 1990). In some high schools tracking systems benefit the children of upper-middle-class parents, while the children of the poor and the working class are more likely to be channeled into unrewarding, dead-end careers in blue-collar or service work (Oakes, 1985).

Ideologies.   The values, beliefs, and laws that explain and justify prevailing patterns of inequality tend to form loose systems of ideas called **ideologies.** Many different ideologies flourish to bolster inequality—"sexism," "racism," "patriarchy," and "meritocracy"—although there is usually a discrepancy between conventional usage, which is notably vague, and the precise meanings employed in social science literature. Economic inequalities in the United States, for example, are grounded in a competitive, individualistic ideology that we think of as the American Dream and which teaches that rewards are earned and deserved on the basis of talent and hard work in an open and fair system (Kleugel & Smith, 1986). This labels the less fortunate as not enterprising or industrious or prudent enough to succeed. The ideology thus simultaneously justifies both the impoverishment of the poor and homeless and the affluence of the wealthy.

Ideologies may be elaborate and coherent systems of ideas deliberately promulgated by a dominant group, or they may be loose collections of ideas that emerge in the process of everyday social relations among groups. In the first category are explicit ideologies developed and advanced by dominant groups to justify their advantaged position. For example, medieval European aristocrats espoused the position that they were the descendants of the Teutons (later called Aryans) who had defeated the Romans, while commoners were descendants of the Romans and other inferior cultures (Shibutani & Kwan, 1965). Members of the aristocratic class were thus members of the line responsible for the flowering of western civilization and hence destined to rule. Not all ideologies are deliberately created. Rather, they may be understood as emerging in a more unsystematic way when isolated ideas are selected out and embraced simply because they can be interpreted to justify inequality. The teachings of white supremacists are usually in this category.

Broad patterns of inequality are deeply set in the structure of society and are constantly enacted and reinforced on a daily basis in social relations. At the most obvious level, class, racial, and gender incidents show up in countless small but maddening instances of disdain, humiliation, hostility, and discrimination. More consequential episodes appear in settings such as job interviews, loan applications, and racial profiling.

CONCLUSION: THE INTERSECTION OF CLASS, RACE, AND GENDER

It is possible to identify class, race and ethnicity, and gender as separate social constructions, but they are impossible to separate in practice because they are lived simultaneously at the personal level (Andersen & Collins, 1992). Therefore, it is essential to remember that they combine and interact to facilitate or frustrate access to rewards, amplifying the impact of any one individually.

The interaction among them is highlighted by focusing on earnings in the United States. The median income for men in 1999 was $37, 574, while women earned $27,370 (U.S. Bureau of the Census, 2000). Significant racial and ethnic differences exist within each group. Non-Hispanic white males earn $41,406 compared to $30,297 for blacks and only $23,342 for Hispanics. Non-Hispanic white females earn $29,369 compared to $25,142 for black women and only $20,052 for Hispanic women.

Differences in earnings are the end result of a combination of factors (West & Fenstermaker, 1995a and 1995b). The most obvious is that women and racial and ethnic minorities doing the same work are often paid less. But a number of underlying factors are also at work. Women and minorities typically have different educational experiences, are underrepresented in better paying occupations, and are more likely to confront barriers to progress over the course of their careers. Each of these factors is considered in subsequent sections.

KEY CONCEPTS

authority	life chances	race
beliefs	minorities	values
ethnicity	people of color	
gender	power	
ideology	social class	
institutionalization of	social status	
inequality	social stratification	

SUGGESTED READING

MARGARET L. ANDERSEN. *Thinking About Women: Sociological Perspectives on Sex and Gender*. (4th ed.) Needham Heights, MA: Allyn & Bacon, 1997. A thorough and comprehensive overview of feminist social science scholarship.

MARIO BARRERA. 1979. *Race and Class in the Southwest*. Notre Dame, IN: University of Notre Dame Press, 1979. An examination of the exploitation of men and women Mexican immigrants as urban and agricultural laborers.

JOE R. FEAGIN and CLAIRECE BOOHER FEAGIN. *Racial and Ethnic Relations.* Upper Saddle River, NJ: Prentice Hall, 1996. This book, now in its fifth edition, provides a comprehensive overview of the history and contemporary status of racial and ethnic minorities in the United States.

DAVID B. GRUSKY, ed. *Social Stratification: Class, Race and Gender*. Boulder, CO: Westview Press, 1994. A useful collection of articles suitable for advanced students.

JUDITH LORBER. *Paradoxes of Gender*. New Haven, CT: Yale University Press, 1994. The author explores the social construction of gender and the implications for women in contemporary society.

KEVIN PHILLIPS. *The Politics of Rich and Poor: Wealth and the American Electorate in the Reagan Aftermath*. New York: Random House, 1990. An overview of the sources of the widening gap between rich and poor in the United States.

HUGH B. PRICE, ed. *The State of Black America, 1999.* Washington, DC: National Urban League, 2000. This latest volume in an annual series provides an insightful analysis of contemporary race relations in the United States.

H. EDWARD RANSFORD. *Race and Class in American Society: Black, Latino, Anglo*. Rochester, VT: Schenkman, 1994. A broad review of the intersection of class, race, and gender inequalities.

RICHARD SENNETT and JONATHAN COBB. *The Hidden Injuries of Class*. New York: Vintage, 1973. A classic analysis of the subtle and invidious consequences of social class.

USEFUL WEB SITES

The University of Amsterdam maintains Sociosite (**www.pscw.uva.nl/sociosite/**) with links to a broad range of sociological concepts. Review *inequality, stratification, class*, and *poverty* for a discussion of these basic concepts.

The Center for Research on Women at the University of Memphis (**www.people.memphis .edu/~intprogs/crow/**) is dedicated to promoting research on southern women and women of color. This web site includes studies of women's health, poverty, and employment.

The United Nations sponsors a major program on the status of women around the world (**www.un.org/womenwatch/**). The web site contains a wealth of useful information.

The National Urban League (**www.nul.org**) publishes an annual appraisal of the state of black America offering a wealth of analysis and information.

Latino.com is a commercial site (**www.latino.com**) that highlights a wide range of news and features on issues of interest to the Hispanic population as well as useful links to other resources.

CHAPTER TWO

Theoretical Approaches
to Social Stratification

THREE THEORETICAL TRADITIONS

Inequality and stratification have captured the attention of social philosophers, moral-ists, intellectuals, and social theorists since the origins of recorded history. Plato may have been the first Western theorist to attempt a systematic examination of the nature and consequences of inequality. A central goal of his utopian *Republic* was to con-struct a society in which inequalities corresponded to the inherent differences among people. But, because of his belief that extremes of wealth and poverty generated undesirable behavior, he also proposed placing limits on the economic assets people could accumulate. The theorists most relevant to contemporary analysis date from the mid-nineteenth century when industrialization was reshaping the fundamental struc-ture of Western societies. Three major theoretic traditions tend to dominate in American sociology.

The work of Karl Marx and Friedrich Engels is the starting point in any con-sideration of stratification theory for they were among the first to perceive the inter-nal dynamics of the emerging industrial order. They asserted primacy to control of the physical means of industrial production and emphasized that certain forms of social relations are inherent in different forms of production as well as the role of this factor in shaping society and in the dynamics of social change. After the death of Marx, Engels developed a systematic analysis of gender stratification.

Max Weber was one of a number of people who carried on a dialogue with the "ghost of Marx." On several occasions he is quoted as defining part of his work as "positive criticism of materialistic conceptions of history" (Bendix, 1962: 591). This should not imply a single-minded attempt to discredit Marx and Engels; rather Weber challenged some interpretations, admitted some insights, and attempted to elaborate on still others. It is more accurate to recognize that Weber objected to the idea that any single factor such as class relationships could provide a universal explanation of social phenomena, hence he developed a multidimensional model of stratification based on economics, status and life styles, and power.

American interest in social stratification intensified during the 1930s and 1940s and tended to emphasize social status and patterns of social interaction. W. Lloyd Warner and his associates studied small communities identified with quaint names such as "Yankee City" and "Jonesville" to disguise their identity. Their original formulation emphasized economic considerations, but eventually came to argue that subjective measures of "status" and reputation superseded economic considerations (Warner and Lunt, 1941). It was Warner who popularized stratification terms such as "upper upper class" and "lower middle class" that have become a permanent part of the American vocabulary.

Harvard sociologist Talcott Parsons' theoretical formulations, and those of some of his students, were particularly influential during this period. Probably the most controversial single contribution was a brief paper by Kingsley Davis and Wilbert Moore (1945) that purported to explain why stratification was both universal and necessary. These developments contributed to the emergence of "functional" theories focusing on prestige and an accompanying decline in interest in conflict and political and economic inequalities. Functionalism eventually dominated American sociology for several decades.

The twenty-first century is a period of multiple models and multiple perspectives on inequality and stratification. Theory and research in the classic traditions initiated by Marx and Weber continue by attempting to reconcile twentieth century developments with models formulated in earlier stages of industrialization. Two major challenges face contemporary theorists. One is the need to come to grips with changes in the nature of capitalism in advanced societies that include the collapse of communism, the globalization of the world economy, the digital revolution, and the accompanying transformation of the occupational structure. This era is variously referred to as the "new economy," or the "post-industrial" or "information age." The other major development is refined analysis of the interrelationship among social class, race and ethnicity, and gender.

THE MARXIAN TRADITION

Karl Marx (1818–1883) and Friedrich Engels (1820-1895) lived and wrote during a period of rapid and disruptive social change stimulated by the upheavals produced by industrialization, urbanization, and democratization. The publication of the *Communist Manifesto* in 1848 coincided with worker revolts all across Europe. In light of their environment, it is not surprising that they were forcefully concerned with the consequences of fledgling capitalist production. Perhaps their most fundamental insight was that capitalism is not simply a way of producing goods and services but an economic, social, and political system. Marx was dismayed by the abuses, misery, and oppression of the urban industrial factory, but could not help being impressed by the more positive aspects of the emerging economic system. In the *Communist Manifesto* there is praise for the capitalist class which, "during its rule of scarce one hundred years, has created more massive and colossal productive forces than have all preceding generations together" (Marx & Engels, 1959: 8). The development of science, the command over nature, the rise of cities, and the breakdown of rule by the feudal nobility could all be attributed to this group. They saw that the progress of science and transportation would lead to the collapse of "old local and national seclusion and self-sufficiency" and produce "universal interdependence of nations," a process we now call globalization (Foster, 2000). However, ultimately they anticipated the revolutionary overthrow of capitalism.

Social Stratification

Marx's collaborator, Friedrich Engels, has provided a frequently quoted passage that provides a succinct summary of their conception of history and social stratification:

> The materialist conception of history starts with the proposition that the production of the means to support human life—and next to production, the exchange of things produced—is the basis of all social structure; that in every society that has appeared in history, the manner in which wealth is distributed and the society is divided into classes or orders is dependent on what is produced, and how it is exchanged. From this point of view the final causes of all social changes and political revolutions are to be sought . . . in changes in the modes of production and exchange (Marx & Engels, 1959: 90)

Thus, the key to understanding the flow of human history, as well as the distribution of inequality and stratification, is found in the organization of the productive forces of the society.

They viewed the whole of human history as divided into a number of major phases that they called primitive communism, slavery, feudalism, and capitalism. Each period was dominated by a pair of social classes defined by their relationship to the means of production and to each other—masters and slaves, or landowners and serfs. Central to Marxian analysis of capitalism was the belief that the idea of private property created a basic cleavage between those who owned economic resources and those who did not, or to use their terms, **bourgeoisie** (who owned capital) and the **proletariat** (nonowners who had only their own labor to sell). Inequalities of wealth in capitalist societies was directly based on ownership of land, buildings, machinery, factories—the means of production. Propertyless workers had nothing but their labor to sell and owners exploited workers by paying them wages that were less than the market value of the products they created. Thus, capitalists' wealth was accumulated by taking control of their resources and expropriating the surplus wealth created by workers. Moreover, as a result of loss of control of the things they built and the loss of most of the wealth they created workers became alienated from their work. Work lost its joy, its meaning, and its rewards.

Interestingly enough, despite the central importance of classes in his vision of society, Marx did not define class in any systematic way. However, it is clear that he visualized class in two separate ways (Wright, 1985). First, structurally, defined by ownership (or the lack) of productive capacity—capital and land—and second, relationally; that is, classes exist in relation to one another. Moreover, they are antagonistic in the sense of having opposing interests and exploitative in that the advantages of one class are gained at the expense of the other. Capitalist wealth is also translated into power in the political sector by control of the apparatus of government and by using government to maintain their wealth and advantaged position. Marx and Engels argued that the potential for domination of society was not simply economic and political, but also social and cultural in that a "ruling class" will be able to shape the laws, values, art, beliefs, and institutions of society—the **ideological superstructure**—to their advantage. The ideas of the ruling class are in every epoch the ruling ideas; i.e., the class ruling the material forces of society is at the same time the ruling intellectual force. The class which has the means of material production at its disposal has control at the same time over the means of mental production (Marx & Engels, 1959: 78). Their ideas are disseminated through the press, the church, the schools, and the various political institutions and are calculated to legitimize their advantaged position.

Class Consciousness and Class Conflict

Marx believed that capitalism was destined to be supplanted by socialism and eventually communism. The concepts of class and social change intersect with the idea of class conflict, for the disadvantaged classes spawned by the economic system are to be the instruments of social change. Therefore,

> The history of all hitherto existing society is the history of class struggles. Free man and slave, patrician and plebeian, lord and serf, guild-master and journeyman, in a word, oppressor and oppressed, stood in constant opposition to one another, carried on an uninterrupted, now hidden, now open fight, a fight that each time ended, either in a revolutionary reconstitution of society at large, or in the common ruin of the contending classes (Marx & Engels, 1964: 78).

Since ruling classes never voluntarily relinquish their position, conflict is inevitable. In this context, Marx introduced and explored the critical link between economic position and subjective class awareness. Both bourgeois and proletariat form nominal groups as a result of their relative location in the economic system. He called such groups **klasse an sich** (class of itself), with class position defined by structural position. Members of the opposing classes have shared interests by virtue of their position. These common interests are most clearly perceived by the bourgeois, for it is more readily evident that their advantaged position is based on private property. Yet, members of disadvantaged classes need not be aware of their common interests. Their interests may be fragmented by differing religious beliefs, ethnic loyalties, and prestige distinctions, or obscured by rhetoric. Therefore, Marx raised the question of conditions which could transform a heterogeneous aggregate into a cohesive, organized group, a **klasse fur sich** (a class for itself) aware of its interests and acting to realize its own interests.

Marx anticipated that a combination of several social and economic forces would combine to stimulate self-conscious action on the part of workers. A major factor would be economic deprivation. He expected that the discrepancy between wealth of the bourgeois and proletariat would widen for two reasons. Increases in productivity would produce ever greater profits, and ever more wealth would be concentrated in the hands of an ever smaller number of capitalists as they competed among themselves for a larger share of the wealth. Another factor in awakening class consciousness would be the homogenization of the proletariat. Divergent interests would be become less meaningful as members of the working class became more similar. For example, mechanization would reduce all workers to unskilled laborers, thus reducing rivalries among different crafts. Finally, continued confrontation with owners (e.g., boycotts and strikes) would display and solidify their common interests.

The sources of revolution were not explained in any detail, nor did they spell out the nature of the societies that would follow the downfall of capitalism (Grabb, 1997). It appears that capitalism will first be replaced by a temporary period of "socialism." Marx sometimes referred to this period as the "dictatorship of the proletariat" in which control of the economic system would be centralized in the hands of the government that would represent the interests of all segments of society, not just the special interests of the bourgeois. The state will make the changes necessary to alleviate the worst abuses of capitalism, such as abolishing child labor, taking ownership of some industries, and instituting a graduated income tax, all of which were radical ideas at the time. Taxes were to be used for education, health care, and social service. Workers would be rewarded fairly but not equally, on the basis of individual effort. Each "receives back from society . . . exactly what he gives to it."

Socialism was seen as a transitional historical phase in the progression toward communism. The centralized state will be replaced by a system of decentralized administration, and the distribution of goods will be guided by Marx's famous declaration, "From each according to his ability, to each according to his needs." Communist society is only vaguely defined and is obviously utopian. This is because Marx had profound faith in the innate decency of people and believed that the greed and self-interest spawned by capitalism would disappear once capitalism was abolished.

It must be noted that the works of Marx and Engels are often embroiled in controversy because the words "socialism" and "communism" became entangled with a variety of totalitarian political regimes around the world in the twentieth century, making it easy to discredit their ideas because of things done in their names. Actually, the 150th anniversary of the first publication of the the the *Communist Manifest* in 1998 was greeted with optimism by academics, union organizers, and other adherents (Marcus, 1998). They pointed out that those oppressive regimes bore little resemblance to the socialist ideals visualized by Marx. As one put it, "We are celebrating the legacy of the struggle for social, racial and gender equality that was started by the young Marx and Engels in 1848" (Sachs, 1998). Therefore, it is important to focus on their ideas rather than the ways these ideas have sometimes been utilized in the pursuit of political objectives.

Engels and Gender Stratification

Engels is often credited with the first sociological theory of gender stratification (Collins & Makowsky, 1984: 49–54). His approach is a continuation and extension of the basic Marxian perspective. In fact, he links the origins of gender stratification to the first decisive step in the process that eventually produced capitalism—the transition from communal to private property. "The first class opposition that appears in history coincides with the development of antagonism between man and woman in monogamous marriage, and the first class oppression coincides with that of the female sex by the male" (Engels, 1972: 129).

Based on the anthropological research of his time, Engels concluded that both hunting and agricultural societies were characterized by matrilineal descent and gender equality. (More recent anthropological research does not support the thesis that all hunting societies are or were equalitarian.) Because they fully participated in the production of food women enjoyed equal social status. However, as advanced agricultural methods created the potential for an agricultural surplus, males wanted to be able to pass their accumulated property on to their children. Patrilineal descent and monogamous marriages were created to foster this, and women became excluded from economic production and relegated to household tasks. As a consequence of not producing for the market women become economically subordinate to their spouses.

Thus, Engels effectively links gender subordination to the dynamics of industrial production systems. More recent thinking in the Marxian tradition has elaborated on that perspective, suggesting that women have been forced into playing a vital, but largely invisible role in perpetuating the economic system. They reproduce the working class by bearing and socializing children to become the next generation of workers.

The Legacy of Marxism

In retrospect it is easy to emphasize that Marx and Engels were so wedded to the idea of dichotomous classes that they failed to fully anticipate the future of capitalism in the West, especially the implications of an emerging middle class. Perhaps they were too much products of their time, led to overgeneralize from what was occurring in nineteenth-century England. From that historical vantage point, it was tempting to visualize industrialization and urbanization producing a small class of industrial capitalists ranged against an expanding mass of propertyless and impoverished urban laborers. It was a period of some of the worst industrial abuses— crowded tenements, hazardous factories, subsistence wages, child labor, and minimal standards of public health. It was also the era of unrest and ferment in the fledgling labor movement; trade unions and socialist political parties were active and industrial conflict common. However, it must be remembered that both men were political reformers as well as social analysts, and it has been argued that "prophets have always been dualists," seeing history as a conflict between the forces of good and evil, lightness and darkness (Feuer, 1959: xviii). The fact remains that the writings of Marx and Engels have stimulated extensive analysis of industrial society and isolated some of the key issues that continue to form the basis of current thinking about inequality and stratification.

Classes.   The concept of classes based on position in a specific productive system in which some groups are in a position to exploit others remains a powerful tool for understanding the distribution of wealth, power, and privilege in industrial societies. Some sociologists would replace social class with occupation, but that is merely replacing a broad conception of structural position with a narrow one.

The Middle Class.   Their tendency to view the world in dichotomous categories led Marx and Engels to minimize the role of the emerging middle class of office workers, professionals, and managers who occupy an intermediate position between proletariat and bourgeois. Marx clearly recognized a growing middle class "who stand between the workman on the one hand and the capitalist and landlord on the other," but he did not work out the long-term implications of this development (Burris, 1986). For example, at one point he merely suggested that intermediate groups such as small business persons, farmers, shopkeepers, and craft workers would "sink down into the proletariat," although he was not clear about precisely how that might happen.

The proliferation of a broad middle class creates a dilemma for that part of Marxian theory that emphasizes the polarization of society into two opposing groups. Some feel that the evolution of capitalism has created a new middle class that falls outside the traditional bourgeois–proletariat division. One way of handling this issue has been to expand the basis of exploitation by showing that the evolution of industrialization has created additional forms of exploitation (Case Study). Others insist that the basic owner versus nonowner dichotomy continues to be the most fundamental cleavage in society since it focuses on the fact that a tiny minority are in a position to control the work of the vast majority (Sorensen, 2000).

Class Consciousness.   The question of defining the conditions that facilitate or hinder the emergence of class consciousness and collective action is the subject of continuing interest and research. It is clear that most Americans are aware of class divisions in society and willing to identify with a particular class (Jackman & Jackman, 1983). Consciousness of class is important since it contributes to understanding lifestyles and helps to explain voting patterns.

Power Structures.   The idea that a small elite may form a dominant class in industrial society has stimulated a great deal of analysis. Contemporary sociologists have explored the interrelationship between the industrial and political sectors, with

CASE STUDY:
A Contemporary Marxist Approach to Social Class

University of Wisconsin sociologist Erik Olin Wright is among the most prominent contemporary social scientists pursuing a Marxist model of class in modern capitalist societies. He notes that there are quantitative divisions within the class of owners of capital assets. This category encompasses independent self-employed persons (petty bourgeoisie) and includes a range of employers from those employing only one or two people (small employers) to the managers of giant industrial corporations (capitalists) employing hundreds of thousands. This is the basic Marxian idea of control of productive resources or "assets" (Exhibit 2.1.).

All others are employees, but there are new kinds of resources or assets that shape the social relations of work. There are what are called "organizational assets," the authority to make policy decisions (managers) or direct the work of others (supervisors), and "skill assets," employees whose job requires unusual educational credentials (experts). The class location of managers, supervisors, and experts remains a quandary because they are simultaneously proletariat in the sense that they work for others *and* bourgeois in the sense that they control productive resources or supervise the working of others. Hence, they occupy a contradictory class position. By far the largest category of employees (workers) possess no productive assets. They do not exert control over the production process or other workers, or even their own effort. The working class in the United States defined by these criteria would include approximately one-half of all employed persons (Wright & Martin, 1987).

EXHIBIT 2.1   A Contemporary Marxian Model of Class Structure in Capitalist Societies

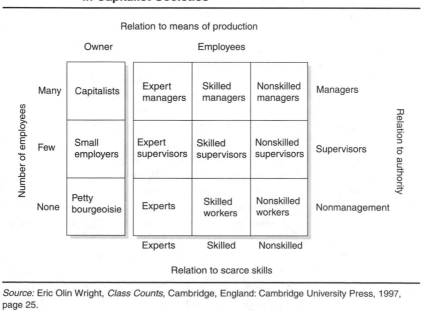

Source: Eric Olin Wright, *Class Counts,* Cambridge, England: Cambridge University Press, 1997, page 25.

some suggesting that business and other special interest groups exert unusual influence on the conduct of the state. Other social scientists are pursuing the concept of ideological domination by exploring the ways that cultural ideas and beliefs support systems of inequality.

Class, Race and Gender.　Marx and Engels were clearly aware of the disadvantaged position of women and minorities within the stratification system, and contemporary analysis increasingly focuses on the intersection of class, race, and gender in understanding the dynamics of inequality.

THE WEBERIAN TRADITION

Max Weber's (1864–1920) approach to analysis of social stratification is a more multidimensional approach to stratification than that of Marx. Weber recognizes the central importance of position in the social organization of industrial production, but he emphasizes the existence of three forms of inequality in society—economic, status, and power. His words are direct,

> Whereas the genuine place of "classes" is within the economic order, the place of "status groups" is within the social order, that is, within the distribution of "honor," . . .(and) "parties" live in the house of "power." Their action is oriented toward the acquisition of social "power," that is to say, toward influencing communal action no matter what the content may be (Weber, 1946: 194).

In short, capitalism generates three kinds of groups.

Class

The first groups are economic, based on "market situation," which does not differ in principle from the Marxian division of propertied and propertyless. However, Weber distinguished three different types of market situation. There is the labor market, which divides society into employers and employees; the money market, which separates creditors from debtors; and the commodity market, which differentiates between buyers and sellers (landlords and tenants). Accordingly, those who participate in all three markets could be members of three distinct economic classes. In addition, Weber noted that the propertyless have different levels of skill (ranging from the unskilled to the professional worker), a point that Wright uses to refine Marxist conceptions of class. Weber's observations about skill differentials among those who are without significant capital resources marks his attempt to deal with the question of the emerging middle class.

Weber noted that classes are groups of people who share a common market situation, and, in turn, class position strongly influences their rewards and their opportunities. (This is where he introduced the concept of "life chances.") Common economic position does not imply or even guarantee a sense of common identity. An awareness of common interests and collective action might emerge under the right conditions. For example, class action by workers is fostered by the presence of a clear and unambiguous opponent, physical concentration of workers in a single place which facilitates interaction and communication, and clear goals articulated by political leaders (Weber, 1946: 180–184). Thus, he does not differ substantially from Marx on the question of class consciousness.

On the matter of gender stratification, he displayed a strong interest in Engels' analysis of the family and feminist theory of his day (Collins, 1986). He challenged Engels' notion of the evolution of sexual domination but accepted his perspective as making a valuable contribution to understanding the situation. His own ideas on the family define it as a set of sexual and economic relationships regulated by political power.

Status and Status Groups

Weber termed his second form of inequality *status honor* (or what is today referred to as social status or prestige), grounded in the prevailing values, beliefs, and ideals of the society. Economic resources and status form separate hierarchies, but Weber admitted that those with the most economic resources also tend to have the highest status. Taking this a step further led him to visualize society as a hierarchy of "status groups" having unequal prestige. Status groups are, in Weber's thinking, communities of people having some degree of awareness of commonality. These communities may be based on property, income, ethnicity, ancestry, education, or occupation, but consumption patterns and styles of life are primary.

The way in which status groups develop is one of Weber's most influential and enduring contributions. Because members of prominent status groups are aware of their shared interests, they are likely to attempt to develop mechanisms for maintaining and protecting their position and that of their children. A set of formal and informal exclusionary rules will be established, and members of higher status groups will selectively interact only with others whom they consider to be their social equals—socialize with them, join the same organizations, and send their children to the same schools. Outsiders viewed as social inferiors will simultaneously be deliberately excluded from such contacts. It follows that marriage partners will also be among social equals, for restricted patterns of interaction will limit the pool of potential partners to members of the same status group. It is in this way that privilege is maintained through generations.

Weber believed that in the most extreme cases, status groups evolve into what he called "castes," where distinctions of social status are maintained by rigid social conventions, or even laws that prohibit marriage outside the group. Moreover, even physical contacts with lower caste members can be considered degrading, as though physically encountering lower caste members might contaminate them. He felt that exclusionary practices were usually associated with class position, but other bases of exclusion were race, language, and religion, and he cited the Jews as the most persistent historical example, along with other cases that can be assumed to include the "untouchables" of Hindu India.

Parties

Finally, Weber focused on the question of power and identifies **parties**, groups or associations deliberately organized for the pursuit of power. His term *parties* would encompass the contemporary idea of political parties but is broader, more inclusive, including any group whose "action is oriented toward a goal which is striven for in a planned manner" (Weber, 1946: 180–184). Thus, parties encompass professional associations such as the American Medical Association, special interest groups such as the Chamber of Commerce or the National Organization for Women. Although vague on the nature of parties and how they coalesce, he did point out that economic or status interests are very important. However, other motives besides class interests and status may be operative. He would thus include environmental groups such as the Sierra Club or consumer groups as parties. The ways in which they may gain power can range from naked violence to persuasion, subterfuge, or hoax.

The Weberian Legacy

Max Weber actually devoted only one relatively short essay directly to the topic of social stratification, yet he is widely quoted. His importance derives from his multi-dimensional model of social phenomena, which is more consistent with social science reasoning that emphasizes the complexity of society and social behavior. Consequently, Weber's legacy has often been more generalized than specific.

Multiple Forms of Inequality.   Many theorists feel that Weber's most enduring contribution to the study of social stratification is his recognition of the many forms of social inequality. Thus, while not disputing the Marxian concept of economic classes, Weber did postulate a more complex picture of inequality and stratification. His scheme encompasses a broader view of economic classes and also includes status groups and parties, thus allowing individuals and families to be located on at least three hierarchies of inequality. He asserts that inequalities of lifestyles, prestige, and power can be independent of one another but concedes the primacy of the economic factor in most situations. "Property as such," he notes, "is not always recognized as a (prestige) qualification, but in the long run it is, with extraordinary regularity" (Weber, 1946: 185).

Bureaucracy.   Although not explicitly linked to his work on stratification, Weber did extensively explore the implications of the role of emerging bureaucratic structures and correctly predicted that they were destined to be the dominant form of social organization in industrial society. Most individuals are subject to some form of bureaucratic control, whether industrial, political, educational, or religious. Thus, while Marx and Engels emphasized the alienation of people from their work, Weber worried about the implications of bureaucracy that threatened to rob individuals of their individuality and their initiative. Obviously, there is also the question of the concentration of power since leadership in these bureaucracies is the source of unusual power and influence over individuals and society, a point developed later by other theorists.

Religion and Capitalism.   One of Weber's most well-known works, *The Protestant Ethic and the Spirit of Capitalism*, develops the thesis that Protestant beliefs set the stage for the emergence of capitalism in the West. His theory earned quick fame because it challenged the Marxian premise that gives primacy to economic relations in shaping social institutions and offered a new connection between religion and economic development. As Weber saw it, the unique combination of religious ideas developed by Luther and Calvin fostered certain kinds of secular behavior—disciplined effort, self-denial, devotion to work, emphasis on material success, and individual responsibility—values that encouraged and fostered the emergence of capitalist economic organization. His theory has generated considerable controversy, but does command attention to an alternative interpretation of interrelationships between social institutions and the stratification system.

Patriarchy.   Weber explored gender inequality as a form of male domination that had its origins in the sheer physical strength of men (Collins, 1986; Grabb, 1997). Eventually actual physical domination was replaced by "patriarchy," a system of social values and beliefs that legitimize the subordination of women in the family and other institutions and the economic system. One consequence is that gender can become the basis of the formation of status groups that result in the exclusion of women from male-dominated groups.

THE FUNCTIONALISM TRADITION

Functionalism has diverse theoretical and empirical roots, traceable to the work of Emile Durkheim and British social anthropologists A. R. Radcliffe-Brown and Bronislaw Malinowski. The most influential work in this tradition in the United States was produced in the 1940s and 1950s by Talcott Parsons (1940; 1953) and two of his students, Kingsley Davis and Wilbert Moore (1945). Functionalists approach society as an organic system of interrelated institutions and structures and attempt to explain the function of these arrangements for the workings of society (Grabb, 1997). Some functionalists argue that societies have "needs" that must be fulfilled if society is to survive, while others define functions more broadly as simply the results or consequences of structures for the operation of the whole system.

Occupational Status

Parsons focused on the social status (prestige) dimension of inequality, not ignoring differences in wealth and power, but assigning them secondary importance. His emphasis on prestige follows logically from his broader perspective on society, which was aimed at the analysis of some fundamental questions, How is social order

possible? What integrates and what holds society together? His perspective emphasizes that one of the most important integrative structures of a society is a common
value and belief system that serves to weld members of society together. That value
system is also the basis of inequality since rewards are distributed on the basis of the
importance of people's roles in society.

In his first article on the subject of stratification, the focus is clear, "the differential evaluation (of members of society) in the moral sense" (Parsons, 1940).
Within any society, Parsons argues, its members are evaluated and ranked by other
members of the society on the basis of conformity to a shared value system. The link
between societal values and social prestige was made earlier by Weber. Parsons further suggests that some institutions are more important than others and that consequently higher value will be attributed to those who make the most important
contribution to society. In industrial societies that will be the economic system; in
other societies at other times, religious or cultural institutions might have higher priority. This leads him in the direction of assuming that prestige will be allocated primarily on the basis of the type of work that people perform.

Is Stratification Universal and Necessary?

Parsons suggests that a hierarchy of prestige will emerge in every society, and his
students Davis and Moore addressed the question of why it is apparently universal.
They take the position that the universality of inequality means that it must serve
some vital social function since they claim that the social institutions and social patterns that survive in a society must play some fundamental role in the continuation
of that society. Their view is that every society is confronted with the need to motivate people to fill the most essential positions and perform their roles effectively and
diligently. Phrased differently, it is the question of how society can ensure that
enough people will want to become physicians (or judges or computer scientists). It
is a crucial issue because such jobs require lengthy and costly training, depend on
finding people with scarce talents, and are more important to the survival of society
than other occupations such as janitors.

Their answer is direct: Those positions must be handsomely rewarded materi-
ally and symbolically in the form of things that contribute to sustenance and com-
fort, humor and diversion, self-respect and ego expansion. "Social inequality is thus
an unconsciously evolved device by which societies ensure that the most important
positions are conscientiously filled by the most qualified persons" (Davis & Moore,
1945: 249). Medicine is an apt example; training is costly, arduous, and long, and
people would not be inclined to become physicians without the lure of societal
rewards. The Davis-Moore functional theory of stratification can thus be reduced to
a series of propositions (Case Study).

Inequality thus has its origins in consensus and ensures that the most competent and well-trained persons will conscientiously fill the most important positions
in a society. The rewards are both economic and the subjective approval of others.
Since it is a general framework, it does not claim to explain either the relative

---

CASE STUDY
A Functional Theory of Social Stratification

Some positions in society are more functionally more important than others for the survival of the society. The continuation of society requires that these positions be filled by qualified people.

The number of people with the talent to fill these roles is limited.

Translating this natural talent into useful skills requires a period of prolonged training.

People must be induced to make the sacrifices of time, effort, and cost to undertake the training.

Therefore, society allocates proportionately greater rewards to those positions that are more important and require unusual or scare talents.

Inequality is thus a socially evolved mechanism for enhancing the potential survival of society.

Inequality and stratification are both indispensable and positively functional for society.

Sources: Adapted from Kingsley Davis and Wilbert E. Moore, "Some principles of stratification," *American Sociological Review* 10:(1945) 242–249, and Kingsley Davis, "Reply to Tumin," *American Sociological Review* 18 (1953), 394–397.

---

degree of inequality or the form of stratification in a particular society, for that will depend upon social values, external conditions, level of development, and historical circumstances.

Functionalism is the subject of wide-ranging debate. One group of critics points out that the theory has a strong ideological bias, asserting that it serves as a rationalization for the existing unequal distribution of rewards as both just and moral. Moreover, it fails to take account of constraints on individuals' opportunities (poverty, discrimination, unequal education). A second problem is conceptual and methodological. The idea of "functional importance" is, at best, a vague idea, meaning that there are no objective criteria for establishing the relative importance of social institutions or positions. There have been a number of attempts to test this theory, but they fail to provide consistent support. Finally, it is often asserted that functional theory depends upon some obscure anthropomorphic reference to the role of "society" in allocating rewards that ignores the dynamics of power.

The Legacy of Functionalism

Despite its more narrow focus, it must be noted that functional theory did have a powerful influence on theory and research in sociology during its ascendance. The last two decades of the twentieth century also witnessed the emergence of attempts to restructure and advance Parsons' work in light of developments in social theory such as symbolic interaction (Alexander, 1998).

Occupational Prestige. Probably the most important single consequence of functionalism was to direct attention to the distribution of occupational prestige. It is clear that there is broad consensus within societies on the ranking of occupational prestige. Sociologists continue to debate the sources of social prestige and have accumulated a large body of research on prestige rankings in societies across the world.

A Classless Hierarchy. A focus on occupational prestige suggests a continuous distribution of social status rather than classes as distinct social groups with common interests, as suggested by other theorists. Classes are thus translated into groups of people with similar occupational prestige. This is more consistent with ideas of individualism, open opportunity, and democracy that typify American society. Therefore, this theory provides legitimization for the existing distribution of inequality.

Pluralism. The functional view that society is composed of a system of different institutions that contribute to the overall working of society is consistent with the pluralism of Weber and other theorists. Each institution—religious, governmental, educational—is a separate source of rewards that increases the number of opportunities for mobility and access to rewards (Parsons, 1953; Alexander, 1990).

Structural Constraints. It is also possible to suggest that functional theory has stimulated theory and research that is a reaction to it, rather than an elaboration of it. For example, one weakness of the theory, recognized by the authors themselves, is that there is no guarantee that the most qualified persons will actually be able to gain access to the highly rewarded positions. At a minimum, wealthy and advantaged parents will be able to provide their children with access to the education and other advantages that are prerequisites to more desirable rungs on the ladder of prestige. These are advantages not available to the poor. And obviously, race and gender matter. Moreover, as Weber pointed out, members of groups that enjoy privileged positions can actively close off access to others. Consequently, there is the need to analyze the ways in which social classes act self-consciously to protect their position.

CONCLUSION: THE CENTRAL ISSUES

These disparate theoretical traditions continue to offer valuable insights into the dynamics of inequality and stratification, and contemporary sociologists continue to pursue answers to the issues raised by earlier theorists, although there are currently many different strands of thought within each.

All stratification theory is ultimately stimulated by the question of inequality, and analysis is directed at understanding the forms it takes, the sources of the uneven distribution of societies' valuable resources, and the ramifications of these disparities. Some see the stratification process as essentially benign, an articulation of the fundamental values of society and eventually benefiting society. At the other extreme is the Marxian tradition, which emphasizes the role of power and subterfuge.

Once stratification systems are in place they tend to remain in place until circumstances change. This is in part because the advantaged groups are loath to surrender their privileges. Some systems are maintained by sheer force. Industrial systems tend to be viewed as legitimate even if large numbers of people at the bottom of the hierarchy may lack luxuries, health insurance, or even homes. The opportunity for success in America is sustained by the "American Dream" that celebrates the role of industriousness and effort over the handicap of modest social class background. There is, over time, enough upward social mobility to confirm the ideal, although most people remain in the class they are born into.

Weber used the term *life chances* to stress the broad implications of class for the quality of people's lives, and there is a broad body of social science research to document the ways in which class penetrates people's lives. There are significant class-based disparities in the distribution of wealth, prestige, and political power. Gender, race, and ethnicity have the potential to exaggerate these patterns of inequality. Differences in homes and cars are apparent, but there are more invidious implications. The "hidden injuries of class"[1] include the quality of health, access to quality education, access to the internet, psychological functioning and self-esteem, exposure to violence, and exposure to toxic chemicals.

KEY CONCEPTS

bourgeois	*klasse an sich*	proletariat
functionalism	*klasse fur sich*	
ideological superstructure	parties	

SUGGESTED READING

JEFFREY C. ALEXANDER. *Neo-functionalism and After.* Oxford: Blackwell, 1998. Contemporary functional thinking by a leading proponent of the approach.

RANDALL COLLINS. *Weberian Sociological Theory.* New York: Cambridge University Press, 1986. A comprehensive review of the work of Weber and his successors.

RANDALL COLLINS. *Four Sociological Traditions.* New York: Oxford University Press, 1994. A useful history of sociological theory including stratification theory.

---

[1]This phrase comes from the title of Sennett and Cobb's 1973 analysis of the disadvantaged in America.

Ralf Dahrendorf. *Class and Class Conflict in Industrial Society.* Stanford, CA: Stanford University Press, 1959. A pioneering attempt to elaborate Marx's incomplete theory of classes and class consciousness.

Edward G. Grabb. *Theories of Social Inequality: Classical and Contemporary Perspectives,* 3rd ed. New York: Harcourt Brace, 1997. This readable volume provides a comprehensive overview of historical and modern stratification theory.

Rhonda F. Levine, ed. *Social Class and Stratification: Classic Statements and Theoretical Debates.* New York: Rowman and Littlefield, 1998. The author combines sixteen original readings with useful analytic introductions and contextual commentary.

John F. Sitton. *Recent Marxian Theory.* Albany: State University of New York Press, 1996. A discussion of the many different strands of contemporary Marxian theory for advanced students.

Erik Olin Wright. *Class Counts.* Cambridge, England: Cambridge University Press, 1997. A current Marxian analysis of the implications of social class by a leading scholar in the field.

USEFUL WEB SITES

The Red Feather Institute (**www.tryoung.com**) is a student-friendly organization dedicated to liberal causes including civil rights, feminism, and contemporary Marxism.

The Dead Sociologists Society includes Marx and Weber among its biographies (**www.rave.jmu.edu/~ridenelr/dss/index.htlm**).

PART TWO

Stratification
in Industrial Societies

Social classes in industrial societies are the product of the intersection of economic, political, and social developments that began in the eighteenth century and supplanted stratification systems based on agriculture and land ownership. The early stages of this transformation involved a combination of technological innovations (such as steel making), mechanization, the utilization of new power sources (steam, internal combustion engines), and social changes (the factory system) that contributed to the creation of five basic social classes. The world economy is currently in the midst of the latest phase of this process—a digital revolution fueled by technological advances, computers, and the internet. Economic and technological change was accompanied by beliefs and ideologies that provided the rationale for the unequal distribution of rewards. Chapter 3 discusses the key elements shaping the basic five-class model common to most industrial nations. Chapter 4 traces the evolution of the ideology of individualism that supports the distribution of inequality and related values and beliefs that define the place of minorities and women in the stratification system.

CHAPTER THREE

Industrial Class Systems

THE TRANSFORMATION OF SOCIETY: FROM AGRICULTURE TO E-COMMERCE

Prior to the eighteenth century societies were largely rural and agricultural, with most people devoting their lives to some form of farming. Cities were small by today's standards, and most products were handcrafted. Most wealth was based on trade or land ownership. The industrial revolution began to reshape Europe at that point and displaced stratification systems based on land ownership and agriculture with systems based on position in the emerging industrial order. The transformation took shape in Europe and North America over the course of the nineteenth and the first half of the twentieth centuries. Other nations experienced the process at different times and at different rates, and much of the world is still in the early stages of the process.

The middle of the twentieth century witnessed the first stirrings of the digital revolution with developments in computers, the internet, and the creation of a true global economy. It has produced changes such as the migration of jobs from industrialized nations, a widening of the earnings gap in some areas, the changing nature of the relationship between workers and their employers, and the new emphasis placed on the importance of formal education. These developments have altered the distribution of inequality, but do not appear to have distorted the basic outlines of the class system.

THE INDUSTRIAL REVOLUTION

There is a tendency to measure the industrial revolution solely on the basis of inventions that facilitated the mechanization of the productive process—the cotton gin or the steam engine—but it is more appropriately understood as a complex and interrelated set of social, economic, demographic, and organizational changes that transformed work and restructured entire societies. Key developments in the process were technological innovation, the evolution of the factory system, slavery and immigration in North America, the consolidation of businesses, and the expansion of central governments. The internal politics of industrializing nations took them in different directions with respect to the role of government in the production and distribution of resources. The industrial transformation in the West was typically driven by capitalism, private ownership of productive property, and the distribution of goods and services through a market system. In contrast, China, the Soviet Union, and some other nations followed a socialist model that minimized private property and centralized control of the economy in the hands of the government. Dramatic differences in politics must not obscure the fact that industrialization also produces some common structural arrangements and major similarities in class structures.

Technological Innovation

A key development in the industrial transformation was the introduction of power-driven machinery and inventions that magnified the productive capacity of workers. The earliest innovations showed up in the British textile industry, where the cotton gin mechanized the separation of cotton fiber and steam power (later replaced by electricity and the internal combustion engine) made it possible for machines to take over the spinning and weaving of cloth. Mechanization spelled the demise of a system of production where people performed those tasks by hand in their homes and small shops. Independent weavers, hatters, shoemakers, and others became factory workers. New machinery was not always welcomed by workers, and there were many instances of workers sabotaging equipment. In 1769, the British Parliament was actually forced to make the destruction of some kinds of machinery a crime punishable by death. The cost of the new machinery and the demands of production stimulated the demand for urban workers and led to the centralization of manufacturing in factories and mills.

The Factory System and the Creation of an Urban Working Class

Mechanization displaced the independent individuals who crafted products manually and created an ever-increasing demand for laborers and factory workers as well as iron and coal miners to provide the raw materials for industry. The situation of the emerging urban working class was often bleak in the early stages of industrialization. It was the desperate condition of the working class that caught the attention of Karl Marx and Friedrich Engels. Wages were low, hours long, working conditions dangerous, and tenements overcrowded and dirty. Women, men, and children as young as age 10 sometimes worked ten to fourteen hours a day. It is a situation that prevails today on a large scale in countries that are in the early stages of industrialization, and it also occurs in clandestine sweatshops scattered around the cities of the United States and other advanced societies. The working hours in factories were not necessarily much longer than those in farming or domestic production, but the pace of the machines was unremitting and working conditions hazardous. In many places workers rioted to protest low wages and intolerable working conditions.

Slowly, over the course of the nineteenth century and into the early decades of the twentieth century, conditions in the factories improved. Legislation outlawed the worst abuses and imposed minimum safety and health standards. Labor unions struggled to win benefits for their workers. As a result, wages and working conditions improved, and jobs in industries such as autos and steel came to offer stable and secure employment for a large portion of American workers. However, businesses also employ a large number of unskilled labor in the form of construction laborers, seasonal agricultural workers, stock handlers, and janitorial people. The work is strenuous; pay remains low and working conditions poor. Unskilled jobs are always filled by those with the fewest options—the young, the uneducated and inexperienced, immigrants, and the unfree.

Slavery

Many nations relied on slaves to perform the arduous work in the early stages of industrialization. The use of slaves is an ancient system of forced labor, existing in Mesopotamia, Egypt, Greece, and Rome, and the final, formal worldwide abolition of **slavery** did not occur until a United Nations Convention in 1956. Although the pact was subsequently ratified by virtually all nations, many human rights groups claim that it still exists in several places scattered around the globe. The nation most frequently accused of allowing chattel slavery to flourish is Mauritania in western Africa where anti-slavery organizations assert that 100,000 men, women, and children are subject to being bought and sold (Montefiore, 1996). Public slave auctions were held there until 1994, but they are now conducted in secret. Slave owners are likely to be Moors and slaves the descendants of the original black inhabitants—the Bafours, or conquered peoples. The slaves haul water, tend the herds, and pick dates, and the women bear the next generation of human property (Burkett, 1997).

The key feature of all slave systems is the division of society into two basic categories—free and unfree. Slaves are typically denied political and civil rights granted other segments of the society. For example, slavery in both ancient Rome and nineteenth century United States included stipulations that slaves could not own property, enter into contracts of any kind (including marriage), make a will (or inherit anything), and were excluded from participation in most legal proceedings. Thus, those relegated to slavery can be denied their freedom, endure personal indignities, be deprived of the rights and privileges others enjoy, and suffer severe economic and social deprivation. Perhaps the most important consequence is that it strips people of their basic humanity, relegating them to the status of property.

Although involuntary servitude is a common feature of all slave systems, it is important to note that colonial American slavery included a racial dimension not found everywhere. Slaves and masters came from different racial and cultural backgrounds—African and European. In addition, Europeans who had immigrated voluntarily tended to think of America as their home and see displaced Africans as outsiders, meaning that even second- and third-generation slaves, although born in the United States, were still considered aliens. Consequently, slavery became intermingled with claims of racial inferiority. The result was that involuntary servitude, race, and social definitions of inferiority became inextricably linked; race meant inferiority and race was the basis for slave status (Kolchin, 1988; Russell, 1994). This is not always the case in compulsory labor systems. Slavery in Greece, Rome, and Russian serfdom made no such link; slaves were not inferior persons, merely legally *unfree* persons. Once an ideology of innate differences among the races becomes institutionalized there are enduring consequences. Among the most important is that although the formal abolition of slavery can grant legal rights to former slaves, it cannot guarantee them social rights. Emancipation does not necessarily bring about the demise of the ideological underpinnings which exist to legitimize and justify enslavement.

Migration and Immigration

Migrants from rural areas provided one source of a new labor force and accelerated the process of urbanization. To illustrate, nearly 75 percent of all Americans lived on farms in 1820, compared to less than 3 percent in the twenty-first century. Many present-day farmers supplement their incomes with paid jobs in the urban work force. In the United States, waves of immigrants, first from western Europe and later from eastern Europe, swelled the ranks of the urban working class. There was also a flow of internal migration of black Americans from rural to urban areas and from the South to the North after the Civil War.

The United States is often described as a "nation of immigrants," and the first large group of immigrants came from the British Isles. Their language, institutions, and culture dominated the nation during the colonial period and contributed more to shaping the core American culture than any other single group. Unhappily, the indigenous American Indian population was decimated in the process. It is estimated that there was a pre-Columbian North American population of 5 to 7 million people, but a combination of disease, famine, and military casualties reduced that number to merely 250,000 by the end of the nineteenth century (Snipp, 1996). Once on the verge of extinction, the Native American population staged a remarkable comeback, standing at approximately two million at the beginning of the twenty-first century.

The language and customs of the immigrant groups that followed the British enriched American society, but individual immigrants tended to fill lower-level blue-collar and service jobs. Several major waves of immigration to America occurred during the nineteenth century, some groups fleeing desperate economic or political conditions in their native lands, or being openly recruited for agricultural or industrial labor. Famine and political conflicts with the English between the 1830s and 1860s attracted over a million Irish Catholics, and many found work

EXHIBIT 3.1 Percentage of Foreign-Born Population, by Region of Birth, 1850–1997

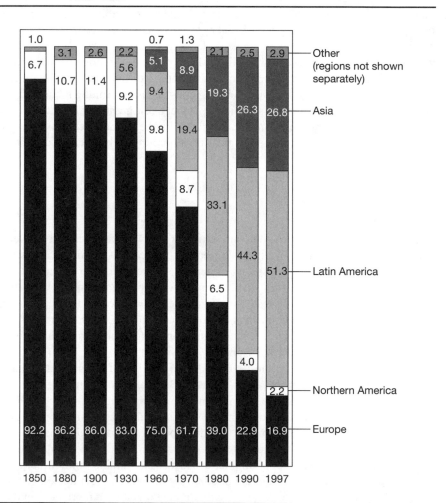

Source: U.S. Bureau of the Census, *Profile of the Foreign-Born Population*, Current Population Report P 23–195. Washington, DC: U.S. Government Printing Office, 1999. Figure 2–2.

in the mining industry. About the same time four million Germans fled poor economic conditions. Soon a large number of Scandinavians moved to America in search of farmland and settled in the mid-West. During the 1850s and 1870s Chinese workers were recruited to build the railroads and fill service jobs. Japanese were recruited in the 1880s as agricultural workers on Hawaiian fruit plantations and later moved to California as unskilled and domestic workers.

The period between the 1880s and the 1920s was the peak period of immigration in terms of sheer numbers and was dominated by Southern and Eastern European groups. Italians came in large numbers and many found work in factories or the construction industry. Four million Austrians, Czechs, Hungarians, and Slovaks fled poverty and filled the factories and the foundries. Jews—many from Russia—sought to escape religious persecution.

Levels of immigration then declined until the 1960s when immigration began to increase, with Latin American and Asian groups making up the bulk of the influx (Martin & Midgley, 1999). Poverty, political unrest, and repression has brought large numbers of immigrants from Mexico, Central America (Honduras, El Salvador), and the Caribbean (Dominicans, Haitians, Puerto Ricans, Cubans, and Jamaicans). Latin Americans account for about one-half of all current immigration. Asians account for about another 30 percent. They come in large numbers from the Philippines, China, India, Vietnam, and Pakistan. Contemporary immigrants are entering a changing economy with manufacturing being replaced by services and high-tech firms. Thus, those handicapped by limited education and poor facility with the language are relegated to the lowest-level jobs in agriculture, industry, and commerce. Exhibit 3.1 shows the native lands of the foreign-born population in the United States between 1850 and 1997.

It is a pattern being repeated today in Western Europe, which is experiencing similar forms of political and economic change. The creation of the European Union has eliminated internal borders, easing the movement of workers. Middle-class people in Germany, France, and Britain rely on foreigners to clean their homes, mind their children, lay their bricks, deliver their pizzas, and harvest their crops (*The Economist*, 2000a). For example, Moroccans pick tomatoes in Spain, Poles work the fields in Germany, Indian Sikhs collect fruit in Belgium, and Russians harvest Irish crops.

CASE STUDY
The Dilemmas of Immigration

Immigration is a worldwide phenomenon, with an estimated 100 million people (2 percent of the population) living outside their homelands. Individuals migrate for many family, social, political, and economic reasons, but the hope of a better life for themselves and their children is a powerful factor in most cases. Most nations impose some restrictions, with the result that not everyone who wants to enter is able to do so legally. Legal and illegal immigration creates dilemmas for the individuals who move and for the nations they seek to enter.

Industrial nations depend on immigrants in different ways. Highly skilled workers are welcome because they compensate for shortages created by declining birth rates and domestic educational systems unable to provide enough trained workers. High-tech workers are in short supply in the United States and Germany and some other industrial nations. They also depend on unskilled workers to do undesirable and low-paying work, to work the fields,and to do heavy labor. However, nationals also limit the number who may immigrate and exclude certain categories of people. The U.S. Congress first excluded criminals and prostitutes in 1875. In 1882 Congress added paupers and mental defectives and used national origin for the first time by excluding Chinese people, a law in effect until 1943 (Martin & Midgley, 1999). Chinese workers had been recruited to build the transcontinental railroad, but after its completion anti-Chinese groups and urban unions who feared they would drive down wages persuaded Congress to ban further immigration. Farmers who depended on their labor unsuccessfully fought the legislation. In the 1920s quotas designed to maintain the existing racial and ethnic make-up of the nation were enacted to favor people of northern and western European origin. In the 1960s these restrictions were lifted and priority given to immigrants join-ing families already here and people with special vocational skills, especially scientists. Since 1980 different categories of refugees seeking asylum from political, religious, or racial persecution have been admitted. It is thus easy to see that nations face a number of opposing pressures—protectionism and racial antagonism versus humanitarianism and the need for workers—that present difficult dilemmas as they seek to set realistic immigration policies.

About one million immigrants enter the United States each year, most (80 percent) legally. They are fleeing poverty, lured by the offer of jobs, escaping religious or ethnic persecution, or hoping to reunite with family. Whatever the lure of the new nation each faces the dilemma of leaving other family and friends behind in order to move to a strange and sometimes hostile new envi-ronment. Surveys suggest that 2 out of 3 citizens feel that immigrants take jobs away from Americans and increase their taxes (Page, 1997). Consequently, immigrants often encounter discrimination in housing and hiring and often con-front open antagonism. About one third have less than a high school education and are relegated to low-level jobs. The well-educated have more occupational opportunities but start out earning only about half that of native-born Ameri-cans in comparable work, although they do reach 90 percent after a decade.

Quotas limit the number of people who may lawfully immigrate with the result that there are also some illegal immigrants. The best estimates suggest that there are 5 million illegal immigrants in the United States, and that num-ber increases by 250,000 each year. Surprisingly, a large proportion originally entered legally as students, tourists, or temporary workers and stayed after their visa expired. The rest are people who are willing to take great risks in try-ing to steal across unguarded borders. It is estimated that in one four-year period 1,185 people died of exposure, drowned, or were hit by cars while attempting to cross the U.S.–Mexican border (Verhovek, 1997). A wide range of predators victimize illegal immigrants. Smugglers charge between $15,000 and $50,000 to transport Chinese to industrial nations (Dickey & Bartholet, 2000). In June of 2000, fifty-eight Chinese suffocated while being herded into Britain when the air vents on the truck transporting them were obstructed. Illegals have been robbed, raped, or abandoned after paying, and others have been forced into sweatshops to pay off the cost of the trip. Once here their illegal status makes them vulnerable to exploitation by unscrupulous employers.

But still they come, willing to endure the hardships. They do not dwell on the problems they encountered but rather compare their lives to what they left behind, and they know that their lives have improved significantly. A political refugee explains, "In (my country) they hate Christians there. They kill Christian people" (Moss, 1993).

The Growth and Concentration of Industry

In the first stages of capitalism relatively large numbers of small companies compete with one another, but over time there is a tendency for larger firms to eclipse smaller ones. The auto industry is a good example. In 1904 there were scores of car makers in the fledgling auto industry around the world, thirty-five separate firms were manufacturing cars in the United States alone. Competition in the form of takeovers, buyouts, mergers, and failures continuously narrowed that number. By the beginning of the twenty-first century just six major auto makers—General Motors, Ford, Daimler Chrysler, Volkswagen, Toyota, and Honda—accounted for about three-quarters of the 30 million vehicles produced world-wide (*The Economist*, 2000b). The six had revenues of $640 billion and $100 billion in cash reserves in 1999 (Naughton, 1999). This process concentrates great wealth and power in the hands of a small number of businesses and their owners and managers. Americans clearly feel uneasy about the power and reach of corporations, with three out of four saying that business has too much power over too many aspects of life (Bernstein, 2000).

The concentration of industry contributes to the emergence of an elite class, composed of current executives of the corporations and inherited wealth in the hands of the families of earlier business leaders. Business history has witnessed several different phases of industrial growth, each fueled by different kinds of enterprises. Early in the nineteenth century industrial expansion was centered in iron making, railroads, and textiles, and the owners amassed vast fortunes that are the basis of the contemporary wealth of families such as Stanford and Vanderbilt. The second half of the nineteenth century saw expansion in oil and steel, banking and meat packing, creating fortunes for families such as Rockefeller, Mellon, J. P. Morgan, and Swift. Other segments of the economy flourished over the course of the first half of the twentieth century, cars (Ford) and newspapers (Hearst) among them. These families amassed great wealth, which has been passed down through many generations so that the descendants of these industrialists and business leaders form part of a contemporary elite class with tremendous economic power and influence.

Governmental Expansion and White Collar Work

Industrialization and urbanization, population increase, and shifting attitudes about the role of government stimulated tremendous growth in the size and influence of governments. Governments almost always assume responsibility for basic public services (education, law and order), national defense, and infrastructure expenditures (roads and sewers). Nations vary significantly on the range of activities undertaken by government beyond these fundamental functions. For example, the communist socialist governments of the former Soviet Union and Eastern Europe owned virtually all of their nation's productive capacity at one time. The United States is at the other end of the continuum with government ownership generally limited to railroads and some major utilities. Democratic-socialist nations of Western Europe have often controlled a broad range of basic industries including airlines, banks, telecommunications, and health care, although there is a current movement toward privatization. The size of government can be measured by state spending as a proportion of total domestic spending (Exhibit 3.2).

The governments of major industrial nations account for nearly one-half of the domestic national product of these societies. The United States is at the low end at about 33 percent, and Sweden is highest at 64 percent. By these criteria it can be seen that the role of government in all industrialized nations has expanded during the twentieth century, with a notable acceleration occurring after World War I and a more dramatic expansion since the 1960s. The role of governments in industrial nations began to increase in the 1920s and 1930s as the scope of state activity increased. For example, public services such as education were expanded to ever-broader segments of the population. The worldwide depression of the 1930s stimulated governmental intervention in the economy, public works, and the expansion of the sheer number of public employees. Military budgets became a major factor from the 1940s onward. Since the 1960s, social welfare payments in the form of health care, pensions, and income support to the unemployed and poor have consumed a major share of total government spending (Crook, 1997).

Governments are thus both major employers and major consumers. In addition, governments influence the distribution and redistribution of wealth through social welfare programs and tax policy. Moreover, regardless of the political system, all industrial governments centralize unusual political and economic and social power in the hands of top governmental officials in legislatures, courts, and executives. Members of the central government such as presidents, prime ministers, and cabinet officers must therefore be counted as members of the elite.

Between them, governments and large businesses create the need for many levels of white-collar workers who form the core of a lower middle class. First line supervisors direct and monitor the performance of production workers. Clerical workers handle the flow of information in modern organizations. They collect, record, analyze, file, and transform data. Administrative support personnel assist managers, perform secretarial tasks, and do staff work for executives.

EXHIBIT 3.2   Government Spending in Industrial Nations, 1870 to 1996

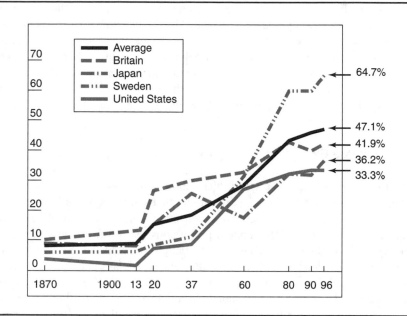

Note: Government spending as a proportion of Gross Domestic Product. The average base includes seventeen industrial nations in Europe and North America as well as Japan.

Source: Clive Crook, "The future of the state." *The Economist* 344 (September 20, 1997), Chart 1, page 7S. © 1997 The Economist Newspaper Group, Inc. Reprinted with permission. Further reproduction prohibited. www.economist.com

Scientific Management and the Organization of Work

Early in the industrialization process factory owners and managers were confronted with complex organizational problems as they sought to coordinate the labor of the emerging urban working class. Their goal was to maximize productivity and profits, but many workers were foreign immigrants or rural migrants lacking the skills and attitudes necessary to function effectively in the new factories. In other cases, skilled craft workers such as printers and steel makers were reluctant to surrender control of the work process to factory owners. For example, the making of steel was in the hands of skilled steel makers—not factory owners—well into the 1920s (Braverman, 1974).

The social organization of industrial firms became dominated by the thinking of Frederick W. Taylor and a management philosophy called **scientific management**. One of the central principles of scientific management is specialization, which, combined with the invention of the assembly line, shaped the way jobs were performed. Complex jobs are minutely subdivided into numerous separate operations that can be assigned to workers without experience or skills. Using this approach the meat packing industry replaced skilled butchers with a series of simple operations that semiskilled and unskilled workers performed on animal carcasses as they moved past them on moving conveyor belts. The work involved continuous repetition of one task that could be closely monitored. The result was that countless blue-collar jobs became narrow, routine, repetitive tasks. Narrow specialization of tasks reduced workers' bargaining power and income because they could easily be replaced by other workers.

The Knowledge Explosion

The first scientific journal appeared in the middle of the seventeenth century when new knowledge began to accumulate so rapidly that scientists needed some mechanism for sharing their discoveries with each other. The expansion of knowledge prompted the emergence of the modern professions that form the bulk of the contemporary upper middle class. They are occupations devoted to the creation (biologists, chemists, physicists), application (engineers, physicians and nurses, computer programmers), and dissemination (accountants, lawyers, educators) of information. Their expertise places these professionals at an advantage over other white-collar workers in the competition for wages and helps to elevate their position in the class system.

THE DIGITAL REVOLUTION

The middle of the twentieth century witnessed the opening of the **digital revolution** with the creation of primitive first-generation primitive computers. By the beginning of the twenty-first century the combination of digital technology, powerful computers capable of performing amazingly complex tasks, the internet, e-mail, and the proliferation of personal computers unlocked public access to these electronic tools. The full consequences of this revolution are only beginning to take shape, but it has already reshaped communications, medicine, genetics, robotics, and countless other aspects of society. There are also significant developments having implications for inequality and stratification.

A number of economic and social changes are accompanying the digital revolution, although not all can be directly linked to it. These changes are so dramatic that some refer to these developments as the "second industrial revolution." The nations of the world are being tied together in a single global economy, and digital technology is contributing to the reshaping of the workforce in industrial nations, with occupations expanding or shrinking in response to the emergence of digital technology. There are also developments in the basic relationship between employers and workers. And, the rapid rate of change is putting new emphasis on the value of formal education.

Global Capitalism

Nations have always been linked by trade, but improvements in communications and transportation is creating a single global economy. **Global capitalism** offers developing nations imports, allowing access to consumer products they are unable to produce, which means extended exports and jobs for advanced economies in the United States, Canada, Japan, and Europe. On the other hand it simultaneously becomes easier to move factories and less skilled jobs to nations with lower labor costs, thus threatening the loss of jobs in advanced industrial nations. Textiles provide one of the most dramatic examples of this process. Over the last three decades the United States, Russia, and Japan have been losing jobs in textile production to places such as China, India, Pakistan, and Indonesia where labor costs are more competitive (Carson, 1998). Industries such as textiles, steel, and autos provided stable jobs during most of the twentieth century, and the loss of jobs is helping to shrink the working class. This has long-term implications because it means fewer opportunities for workers with only a high school education or less.

Deindustrialization

The early phases of industrialization generate the need for a large force of blue-collar workers—skilled craft workers to build the infrastructure, machine operators to run the factories and mills, and unskilled laborers to dig canals, lay railroad tracks, and haul materials. At the dawn of the twentieth century one worker in four in the urban labor force in America was a blue-collar worker. As economies mature the proportion of jobs in manufacturing begin to decline, a process that has been noted in advanced industrial nations since the 1960s. The loss of manufacturing jobs is referred to as **deindustrialization**.

Deindustrialization is in part prompted by improvements in productivity and by technological changes that mechanize or automate physical and manual labor, as when earth-moving machines eliminate the need for construction laborers or when automation displaces auto and steel workers. To illustrate, the United States permanently lost 300,000 manufacturing jobs between 1997 and 1999 (Martel & Kelter, 2000). The loss of blue-collar work has important implications. Unskilled work offers jobs to those with limited educational credentials or lacking work experience. It provides a point of entry into the labor force where individuals can acquire job skills, demonstrate ability, and, for some, hope subsequently to move on to better jobs. It was also the starting point for generations of successive waves of immigrants to America.

The Information Age and Education Credentials

The explosion of information that began in the nineteenth century continues apace in all areas but is accelerating at an unprecedented rate in fields such as electronics, physics, biology, chemistry, and medicine. There are several significant implications for the class system. One is the proliferation of new occupations organized around specialized areas of expertise. Consider health care where literally scores of new subspecialties have emerged over the course of the twentieth century—physicians' assistants, neonatal surgeons, surgical technicians, physical therapists, dietitians, nuclear medicine technologists, occupational therapists, clinical pharmacists, and geneticists among them.

The second implication is the potential to segregate the labor force into higher and lower skill and pay occupations. At one extreme are low-skill occupations with low pay and limited chances of advancement, notably in the lower middle class, the working class, and the poor. At the other end are high-paying upper-middle-class jobs that demand digital skills and advanced education. Projections of job growth in this century plainly display the outlines of this division. All but a few of the increases are concentrated in occupations at the top or the bottom of the range of earnings (Exhibit 3.3). The occupations with the largest anticipated growth are clearly divided between low-skill, low-paying jobs (cashiers, janitors and cleaners, retail salespersons, wait staff) and jobs requiring a minimum of a college education and paying above average wages (nurses, system analysts, and teachers). The earnings gap between the university educated and the less educated rose sharply in industrial nations during the 1990s. This development has the potential to foster a growing disparity between the top and bottom of the stratification system.

Nontraditional Work

Many people once worked for a single company their entire working lives. However, rapid technological change, an increasingly competitive global economy, and the need for firms to quickly respond to a dynamic environment is altering the traditional relationship between workers and employers. Downsizing in the form of mass layoffs to reduce operating costs has weakened the link between employer and employee. At the same time, employees have become more willing to move among firms in search of better pay, promotions, or working conditions.

One corporate response has been to depend upon part-time workers. At least 4 million people involuntarily work part-time schedules, and research suggests that they earn less than comparable full-timers and are less likely to have heath benefits (Raeburn, 2000). Managers earning $800 per week on a full-time schedule are reduced to as little as $200 to $300 for a twenty-hour week. Moreover, working part time is seen as an "automatic career breaker" in many organizations that exact a heavy commitment of time from their people.

Part-time work in the United States and around the industrialized world is dominated by women. Typically, seven out of ten part-timers are women. Many women are limited to reduced schedules because of child care or elder care obligations, and some choose it because of the flexibility that it offers, but the result is that a large number of women earn less and have fewer benefits than full-time workers in the labor force.

EXHIBIT 3.3   Occupations with the Largest Projected Growth, United States, 1998–2008

Occupation	Projected Employment	Numerical Change	Percentage Change	Salary Rank
Systems analysts	1,194,000	577,000	94	1
Retail sales	4,620,000	563,000	14	4
Cashiers	3,754,000	556,000	17	4
Managers	3,913,000	551,000	16	1
Truck drivers	3,463,000	493,000	17	2
Office clerks	3,484,000	463,000	15	3
Registered nurses	2,530,000	451,000	22	1
Computer support	869,000	439,000	102	1
Personal care	1,179,000	433,000	58	4
Teacher assistants	1,567,000	375,000	31	4
Janitors, cleaners	3,549,000	365,000	11	4
Nursing aides, orderlies	1,692,000	325,000	24	4
Computer engineers	622,000	323,000	108	1
Teachers, secondary	1,749,000	322,000	23	1
Office supervisors	1,924,000	313,000	19	2
Receptionists	1,599,000	305,000	24	3
Wait staff	2,322,000	303,000	15	4
Guards	1,321,000	294,000	29	4

Note: Rankings are based on earnings quartiles using one-fourth of total employment to define each quartile.

Source: Douglas Braddock, "Occupational employment projections." *Monthly Labor Review* 122 (November, 1999), Table 4, page 73.

Another result is the growth of the discontinuous work situation called **contingent employment**. Contingent workers are, by definition, people who do not expect their jobs to last. There are different kinds of contingent workers—temps, independent contractors and consultants, and somewhere between 2.5 and 5.5 million workers face this situation (U. S. Bureau of Labor Statistics, 1999). Contingent employment has long been a part of industrial economies, with agricultural day laborers migrating to harvest crops, sales workers employed to cope with the holiday crush of shoppers, bookkeepers added as tax deadlines approach, and seasonal lifeguards hired in beach towns. What is different about the current situation is the increasing proportion of the workforce that fits in this category. Temporary employment, once generally limited to female clerical help filling in during vacations and peak business periods, has spread to virtually every kind of work imaginable. It is not only possible to hire a secretary, security guard, janitor, factory worker, or telemarketer, but also a temporary executive or professional—a lawyer, registered nurse, or physician.

Several different factors have combined to produce the expansion of contingent work. Some individuals voluntarily choose contingent arrangements because it grants them the flexibility to determine their days and hours. Other contingent workers are forced to accept this arrangement because of demands of other obligations such as child care. Cost containment and flexibility seem to be the major advantages for employers. The flexibility of being able to bring together workers as needed is obvious, but also many contingent workers are less costly since training costs and record keeping are reduced, and workers are not paid during slack periods.

For employees, a key disadvantage of contingent work is insecurity. There is no guarantee of a job and thus no guarantee of a reliable paycheck. Moreover, they earn lower pay than comparable full-time workers and have fewer fringe benefits such as health care and pensions (Hipple & Stewart, 1996). These drawbacks create a cadre of workers who suffer a significant financial disadvantage, and who face the uncertainty of unstable employment.

Overall Occupational Trends

The impact of these developments is reflected in the changing occupational structure of the United States during the twentieth century (Exhibit 3.4). The professions based on expert knowledge have grown dramatically, as have the numbers of technicians, and these are expected to continue to expand. The growth of large business, industrial, and government organizations generated a significant expansion of managers and clerical workers over the century, although the current emphasis on corporate efficiency and productivity are producing a contraction in these occupations. Jobs in sales are experiencing a period of rapid growth. Blue-collar jobs employed one-third of the work force at the turn of the century, but the demand for operatives and unskilled laborers is in the midst of a long-term contraction due to deindustrialization. The fastest growing sector of the economy by most estimates is the service sector that includes food preparation, cleaning services, health care, and personal service work. Less than 3 percent of the population earns their living from agriculture, compared to more than three workers in ten at the beginning of the twentieth century.

A FIVE-CLASS MODEL

It is possible to identify five broad social classes in contemporary American society. Classes reflect a combination of economic, social, and political factors, and occupation is the best single consideration in locating people in the system despite having some obvious limitations. Not every occupation can be neatly classified in a particular class. For example, school teachers occupy an ambivalent position in the stratification system, certainly having professional credentials but not enjoying the financial rewards of other professionals such as physicians or architects. Moreover,

EXHIBIT 3.4   The Changing Shape of the Workforce, United States, 1900–2008

Occupation	Percentage of Paid Workers					
	1900	1920	1940	1960	1980	2008
Professional	4.3%	5.4%	7.5%	11.4%	16.0%	15.6%
Technicians	–	–	–	–	–	3.8
Managerial	5.8	6.6	7.3	10.7	11.2	10.7
Clerical	3.0	8.0	9.6	14.8	18.6	16.6
Sales	4.5	4.9	6.7	6.4	6.3	11.0
Crafts	10.5	13.0	12.0	13.0	12.9	10.5
Operatives	12.8	15.6	18.4	18.2	14.2	9.1
Laborers	12.5	11.6	9.4	5.4	4.6	3.6
Service	3.6	4.5	7.1	8.9	12.6	16.4
Private household	5.4	3.3	4.7	2.7	1.2	.7
Farm workers	37.5	27.0	17.4	7.9	2.8	2.8
Labor Force (millions)	29.0	42.2	51.7	65.7	99.3	160.8

Note: Labor force data are not strictly comparable over time due to changes in methods of enumeration.

Sources: U.S. Bureau of the Census. *Historical Statistics of the United States.* Washington, DC: U.S. Government Printing Office, 1975; U.S. Department of Labor. *Handbook of Labor Statistics,* Washington, DC: Government Printing Office, 1985; Douglas Braddock, "Occupational employment projections to 2008," *Monthly Labor Review* 122 (November, 1999), Table 1, page 52.

there is often a great deal of variation within a single occupation with respect to working conditions and earnings. Law illustrates this situation, with public defenders and state prosecutors working for as little as $35,000 while partners at large urban firms can earn $500,000. Nevertheless, occupations remains the best single indicator of position in the stratification system.

The Elite

The apex of the American stratification system is occupied by a small group of individuals and families that command unusual wealth, power, and social status. Membership in this class is based on inherited wealth or institutional position, or some combination of the two. Although they follow different paths into the elite, members of the two segments of the elite often do travel in the same social circles.

Capitalist Elite.   One segment of the elite is comprised of individuals and families that possess extensive economic resources in the form of land, businesses, property, and stocks and bonds. In short, wealth derived from ownership of productive resources and are therefore referred to as the **capitalist elite**. There are some families where wealth has passed through many generations. They often have familiar names—Ford, Mars (the candy people), Rockefeller (oil), Heinz (foods), and duPont (chemicals) and are sometimes referred to as "old money" or the old capitalist elite to underscore a long tradition of wealth. Others, typically referred to as the "new rich," or the new capitalist class have amassed their fortunes more recently, people such as the Walton family whose father Sam Walton founded the Wal-Mart retail chain or Wayne Huizenga who pioneered Blockbuster movie rentals. They control great wealth and the power and influence that accompanies riches.

Institutional Elite.   The other segment of the elite is positional, based on leadership of the major organizations and institutions of society. The sheer size of the federal government (and some large states), the military, immense global businesses, universities, and other institutions concentrates unusual power in the hands of the people that direct these enterprises. Consider, for example, Daimler-Chrysler does $150 billion worth of business and employs 500,000 people worldwide. Sociologist C. Wright Mills identified this group as the "power elite" in the '50s (Mills, 1956), but this segment of the elite is now defined by the term **institutional elite** to focus attention on structural position.

There is no standard way to define membership in this group, but one widely used approach focuses on leadership positions in the corporate, public interest, and governmental sectors (Dye, 1995). The value of this approach lies in isolating the most powerful institutional spheres in industrial societies. Professor Dye defines the institutional elite in the corporate sector as the top executives in organizations that control more than half the nation's total corporate assets. This produces a list of 4,325 executives of industrial corporations, banks, insurance companies, and investment firms. In the public sector are the administration of the major media (the fifteen major newspaper chains that account for one half of the nation's daily circulation, the news magazines, and television networks), the 25 largest private colleges and universities, the 50 largest foundations that control about half of all endowments, the senior partners in the 25 largest law firms, and various civic and cultural organizations (Red Cross, Kennedy Center for the Performing Arts). There are 2,705 such positions. The governmental sector is made up of 284 legislative, executive, judicial, and military positions, including the president, vice-president, cabinet officers, chairs of major congressional committees such as Finance and Armed Services, members of the Federal Reserve Board, the nine Supreme Court justices, the Joint Chiefs of Staff, and all generals and admirals.

It is clear that this relatively tiny group of individuals has tremendous potential to influence others and shape society. The choices of media executives determine what people read and see on television. Factories employ hundreds of thousands of workers, and executive strategies determine the future of their jobs. Decisions about where to locate industrial plants can affect the economy of cities. Legislation on controversial matters such as gun control and capital punishment strike at the core values of citizens.

There are, of course, more than a few cases of a convergence of economic and institutional elites in specific individuals or families. The Ford family is a prime example within the corporate world, both owning and controlling the auto company that bears their name. Moreover, the current practice of supplementing executive pay with substantial stock options means that dozens of top managers are multi-millionaires.

Upper Middle Class

Expertise and organizational position define the **upper middle class**. The expansion of knowledge during the industrial transformation and digital revolution created a group of knowledge-based occupations in science, computer specialties, law, and medicine. These fields require at least a college education and many involve advanced degrees. The proliferation of public and private organizations created the need for many levels of managers to coordinate and direct the operations of these organizations and supervise employees. Thus, there is now an upper middle class made up of higher level managers, administrators, and professionals. Most members of this class occupy mid-level positions in large public and private organizations. They are stock brokers, accountants, biochemists, systems analysts, university faculty, engineers, and the plethora of organizational middle managers with ambiguous titles such as associate director. At the upper levels are plant managers, directors of human resources, deans, research scientists, chiefs of surgery, and undersecretaries of cabinet departments in the federal government. At the lower levels of this class are clergy, teachers, and social workers.

Lower Middle Class

The **lower middle class** occupies the lower levels of organizational hierarchies in clerical and administrative positions. Members of this class collect, code, transcribe, file, record, and transmit data. Among the specific jobs are bank tellers, data entry keyers, file clerks, postal clerks, receptionists, and secretaries. There are, in addition, a large number of sales workers who act as representatives of a company to its customers, telemarketers, and retail sales personnel. There is also a large group of workers—approximately four million men and women—holding first-line supervisory jobs at the lowest levels of organizational authority with job titles such as foreman or team leader. Members of the lower middle class generally work directly for members of the upper middle class. The scope of their authority is typically narrowly circumscribed, seldom extending to decisions about job structures or rates of production; these decisions are made at higher levels.

Working Class

The **working class** or blue-collar class labors in the factories and fields, garages and repair shops, mills and mines, largely isolated from the white-collar world of offices, laboratories, law courts, and classrooms. The world of the blue-collar worker is manual labor organized around the production, distribution, and repair of products. Blue-collar workers build houses and skyscrapers, assemble cars, pack boxes, construct furniture, operate sewing machines, repair telephones and Xerox machines, drive trucks, and harvest crops. There is great diversity within this group, with some workers earning high wages and enjoying stable well-paying employment while others face harsh working conditions and an uncertain future. Skill differentials within the working class are an important consideration, producing an internal division between the skilled crafts and the less skilled work of machine operators, assembly line workers, truck drivers, and unskilled laborers.

Craft Workers. All craft occupations involve a combination of manual dexterity; mastery of a broad knowledge of tools, materials, and processes; and expertise gained from long experience. Included in this segment of the working class are people in the construction trades (electricians, carpenters, plumbers), automotive technicians, metal workers, and printers. Preparation for craft work combines both formal and experiential knowledge. Formal knowledge is taught in apprenticeship programs that emphasize both class work and experiential knowledge that is acquired, refined, and sharpened by prolonged on-the-job training. Their high level of skill results in these workers sometimes being described as the "aristocracy of labor" (MacKenzie, 1973).

Operators and Fabricators. The other major block of blue-collar workers are referred to as operatives and fabricators to emphasize their connection to the machinery of modern manufacturing. Much of their work involves operating, adjusting, feeding, tending, or maintaining machines of one sort of another. This occupational category only makes sense if we recognize that "machines" includes the whole range of tools and equipment from the simplest to the largest and most complex: hand-operated power tools, trucks and planes, textile machines, and steel furnaces. It also includes tasks in which the worker does not really control the machinery, such as assembly line work, but rather attends a mechanized, machine-paced process. Scientific management defined operative's jobs in many American plants as narrowly specialized and repetitive, with workers denied much discretion in the control of the work. This was the dominant pattern until the 1980s when worker dissatisfaction, rapid turnover, absenteeism, and declining quality made it clear that high wages and job security were not, in and of themselves, sufficient to overcome boring, repetitive, unchallenging work. At one G.M. plant, for example, turnover was 8 percent per month, and an average of 10 percent of the assemblers failed to show up on any given Friday or Monday (Braverman, 1974). Such problems, combined with strong foreign competition is encouraging many firms to reorganize work to empower blue-collar workers to some extent.

The Poor

Economic systems are not always able to create work to provide stable employment at reasonable wages for all members of society. People in this position form the bottom layer of the stratification system. Many factors account for their situation. The quest for profits sometimes stimulates employers to keep pay as low as possible, especially if there is a glut of workers. Some people lack the experience, skills, or motivation to excel. Others are handicapped by physical or mental illness, and still others have family responsibilities that preclude employment. The **poor** as a social class thus includes those working on a regular basis for low wages—the working poor, people having intermittent employment, and the chronically unemployed.

The Working Poor.   The **working poor** fill the most marginal jobs in the economic system, those who do routine physical and mental labor, usually in unpleasant conditions with rigid and often harsh supervision, and who face the threat of periodic joblessness. This would include urban occupations such as stock handlers, machine feeders, construction laborers, gas station attendants, dishwashers, janitors in offices and hotels, and some food service people. To this must be added paid agricultural workers who do routine physical farm labor—cleaning, clearing, and harvesting. The defining feature of the work is low pay, pay that is sometimes insufficient to raise workers above the poverty level even if they work year-round on a full-time basis. Approximately 40 percent of Americans living below the official poverty threshold worked for at least some part of the previous year, and 10 percent had full-time, year-round jobs (U.S. Bureau of the Census, 1997).

Intermittently Unemployed.   The poor also encompasses people who face bouts of unemployment. The fact is that virtually all workers face the threat of unemployment at some point in their careers, but the risk of joblessness is greatest among those in specific kinds of work. There are seasonal workers—migrant farm workers who follow harvesting seasons, construction workers whose work is determined by weather and the availability of jobs, and blue-collar workers who are displaced in response to the ebb and flow of business cycles. In addition, globalization often means that plants close or move, leaving workers stranded.

Even during the prosperity of the 1990s unemployment rates never fell below 4 percent of the labor force, and it must be remembered that 4 percent of a labor force of 140 million translates into between 5 and 6 million people without work. The average worker seeks work for over thirteen weeks before finding a new job, and 10 percent spend at least twenty-seven weeks without work. Ultimately, about three-quarters of the displaced find work within two years (Hipple, 1997). Most people are covered by unemployment insurance that buffers the early stages of unemployment, but those who face prolonged failure exhaust their benefits. The result is that only one unemployed worker in four is currently receiving benefits (Hipple, 1997). Social welfare programs also help to protect the most vulnerable.

The Poorest of the Poor: An Enduring Underclass? At the bottom of the stratification system is a group of people tenuously linked to the economic system. Most have little formal education and face prolonged periods of joblessness and poverty. It is a group often referred to as the **underclass**.[1] Although there is no consensus on the definition or measurement of this segment of the poor, William J. Wilson's definition (1987: 8) is a useful introduction:

> that heterogeneous grouping of families and individuals that are outside the mainstream of the American occupational system. Included in this group are individuals who lack training and skills and either experience long-term unemployment or are not members of the labor force, individuals who are engaged in street crime and other forms of aberrant behavior, and families that experience long-term spells of poverty and/or welfare dependency.

The underclass is, in short, a group of people at risk of being trapped in a cycle of persistent poverty and lacking the resources to break free. It is difficult to identify the size of the underclass, but research on displaced workers suggests it may number in the millions. There are about 1.5 million jobless men and women who are discouraged because they believe there is no work available or that there is none for which they qualify and therefore search only sporadically or not at all (Martel & Kelter, 2000). It is a bleak prospect for both the society and the individuals involved.

There is deep disagreement over the origins and future of the underclass between behaviorists and structuralists. The behavioral interpretation focuses on individual pathology as the root cause, manifest in a lack of commitment to jobs or the future causing people to behave in ways (e.g., dropping out of school, substance abuse) that facilitates a descent into the cycle of poverty. The structural interpretation traces the creation of an underclass to the convergence of broad economic, political, and demographic sources (Wilson, 1996). Among them are racial discrimination, declining need for low-skill entry-level jobs, unresponsive and underfunded schools, the flight of jobs and the middle classes from center cities, and the lure of a lucrative underground economy. Depressed levels of effort are thus born of frustration and disappointment but could be revived by redress of the structural causes of disillusionment.

There is a tendency to stigmatize the very poor as "morally inferior" because

---

[1] The term *underclass* was first used by Swedish sociologist Gunnar Myrdal (1944). The concept of an underclass is sometimes linked to Karl Marx's idea of a "lumpen proletariat," but the idea of a permanent group of impoverished people different than mainstream Americans can more accurately be traced to Oscar Lewis's "culture of poverty" (1966) and Edward Banfield's "lower class" (1970). The structural analysis of the underclass originated with the work of William J. Wilson (1987).

of their situation. For example, in Britain, media coverage of a highly publicized murder case clearly created the impression that sexual violence was a crime almost exclusively of the unemployed and other economically marginalized men (Grover & Soothill, 1996). There is also a tendency to equate race and persistent poverty. The major media (newsmagazines and television) consistently exaggerate the number of African Americans among the underclass, and underreport the number of blacks among the working poor. One study revealed that between 53 percent to 66 percent of the poor are portrayed as black, more than twice their actual representation among the poor (Fitzgerald, 1997). This is not necessarily an intentional bias, but it does perpetuate a myth. The consequence of this is to set this group apart, to suggest some form of moral inferiority that would render useless any attempt to rehabilitate the long-term poor.

CONCLUSION: THE IMPACT OF E-COMMERCE

The internet, which had its origins as an esoteric medium for the exchange of information among academics, is changing the conduct of business at both the retail and wholesale levels. The conduct of business on the internet has been labeled **e-commerce**, which requires a vast array of hardware and software for maintaining and supporting it—silicon chips, computers, servers, operating systems, portals and search engines, web page designs, and many more. E-commerce is thus opening unprecedented new opportunities that have an impact on the occupational structure and the distribution of wealth.

E-commerce has produced unusual opportunities for entrepreneurs, venture capitalists, and new businesses. Among the most famous success stories are internet booksellers such as amazon.com, auction sites such as ebay.com, and on-line brokers such as etrade.com. At the same time, older retailers such as Gap and Structure have added on-line sales options. The future of e-commerce is uncertain, but it has already had an impact on the distribution of inequalities. E-commerce stock soared in value during the 1990s before declining rapidly beginning in 2000. In the process literally hundreds of new multimillionaires were created. In fact, Microsoft's Bill Gates became the wealthiest person in America during the 1990s. Some of these entrepreneurs have retired in their thirties and now devote themselves to philanthropy or other endeavors. In addition, generous stock options for rank-and-file employees have elevated countless other people into the ranks of the upper middle class. It is easy to enumerate spectacular corporate successes in e-commerce, but obviously internet-based businesses also fail, as was the case of firms such as eToys.com, and most analysts predict a series of bankruptcies and takeovers as the industry matures. Fortunes will be lost in the process.

E-commerce has also been especially helpful in attracting enterprising immigrants with expertise in digital technology. A study of the 4,063 high-tech start-ups in California's Silicon Valley between 1995 and 1998 shows that 20 percent were Chinese Americans and 9 percent Indian Americans (Lardner, 2000). These people are drawn to the United States by the lure of an open and flourishing economy. The American advantage is expected to erode as it becomes increasingly practical to physically generate e-commerce from anywhere in the world.

The demand for workers in industries supporting e-commerce continues to grow. It is obvious that well-paying occupations such as programmers and system analysts will continue to be in demand, but there are also less rewarding jobs. For instance, on-line sales has created the need for people to staff customer service centers and high-tech help lines. One estimate puts employment at these posts at 5 million (McDonald, 2000). Not only is the pay low ($6 to $10 an hour), but the hours irregular and the work repetitious.

The competitiveness and breakneck rate of change in the world of e-commerce has also opened corporate hierarchies to the young and talented who succeed the founders. In contrast to older manufacturing firms where people seldom reached top executive positions before age 50 or even 60, people can now rise rapidly in managerial careers, reaching top corporate positions while still relatively young. For example, Carley Fiorina (Hewlett-Packard) and Mike Capellas (Compaq Computers) were only 44 when they became CEOs of their firms.

KEY CONCEPTS

capitalist elite	global capitalism	the poor
contingent employment	institutional elite	underclass
deindustrialization	lower middle class	upper middle class
digital revolution	scientific management	working class
e-commerce	slavery	working poor

SUGGESTED READING

Tom Bottomore and Robert J. Brym, eds. *The Capitalist Class*. New York: New York University Press, 1989. A collection of essays on the capitalist class in industrial nations, debating their power and influence.

Harry Braverman. *Labor and Monopoly Capitalism*. New York: Monthly Review Press, 1974. This original analysis of the emergence of monopoly capitalism retains its salience for the twenty-first century.

Eliot Friedson. *Professional Powers: A Study of the Institutionalization of Formal Knowledge*. Chicago, IL: University of Chicago Press, 1986. A lucid sociological analysis of the evolution of the professions in industrial society.

Kevin Henson. *The Temp*. Philadelphia, PA: Temple University Press, 1996. An exploration of the implications of a contingent labor force.

Joan Moore and Raquel Pinderhughes, eds. *In the Barrios: Latinos and the Underclass Debate*. New York: Russell Sage Foundation. This collection explores the ways in which the economic structure of urban centers fosters the development of poverty among Latinos.

STEPHEN P. WARING. *Taylorism Transformed: Scientific Management Since 1945*. Chapel Hill, NC: University of North Carolina Press, 1991. A critical examination of scientific management that suggests its goal is worker control rather than industrial efficiency.

ERIC OLIN WRIGHT. *The Debate on Classes*. London, Verso, 1989. A discussion of the class structure in industrial societies using a Marxist perspective.

USEFUL WEB SITES

The American Staffing Association (**www.natss.com**) is a trade association representing companies that handle about 70 percent of contingent staffing in the United States. This site provides information on the advantages of contingent employment.

Temps 24-7 (**www.temps24-7.com**) is maintained by and for temporary workers and offers a forum for displeased temporary workers to discuss their problems and air their grievances.

The Population Reference Bureau (**www.prb.org**) sponsors research on a broad range of demographic subjects including migration and immigration.

CHAPTER FOUR

Institutionalizing
and Legitimizing Stratification

THE ORIGINS AND MAINTENANCE OF STRATIFICATION SYSTEMS

Social classes are the product of the industrial transformation that began late in the 1700s. The explosion in productivity that accompanied industrialization created great wealth for merchants and factory owners and fostered the emergence of a comfortable upper middle class of business and professional families. The expansion of organizations opened the way for the emergence of a lower middle class of white-collar workers. Most factory workers did not at first prosper, but eventually they won better wages and working conditions and raised the standard of living of broad segments of the population. The poor did not disappear, for there are many low-paying jobs, and even in the best of economic times some 4 to 5 percent of the population is unemployed. Industrialization generated stratification systems with the potential for both great wealth and deplorable poverty.

Shifting our focus from the structure of the economic system that shaped the class system to the social arrangements and beliefs that foster and maintain the class system reveals that there are two analytically distinct sociological processes at work. The first, the institutionalization of stratification, refers to the social arrangements that enhance or inhibit access to higher social class positions. These arrangements include overt things such as forcible slavery or things as subtle as the systematic exclusion of whole categories of people from the advanced formal education that would open opportunities for well-paying jobs. In contrast, the rationale or justifications that sustain the distribution of rewards is a different process, a process that sociologists call legitimation. An example would be the idea that certain people are incapable of benefiting from formal education and it is thus appropriate to exclude them. The two processes overlap and interact and cannot be understood independently of one another.

The Institutionalization of Inequality

The **institutionalization of inequality** refers to the structural dimension: the collection of laws, customs, and social practices that combine to create and sustain the unequal distribution of rewards based on class, minority status, and gender. Openly discriminatory laws and codes have often played a role in this process. Early in the twentieth century contractors openly advertised to pay "whites" $1.50 per day but only $1.15 to "Italians" (Feagin, 1984: 123). In addition, women and racial and ethnic minorities were long formally excluded from professional schools (law and medicine), apprenticeships and craft unions, and other opportunities that could lead to well-paying jobs. Such practices often survived informally long after they were prohibited by law.

The institutionalization of inequality often operates in more subtle and invidious ways. Schools and school systems, for example, sometimes offer unequal educational opportunities for students. Money is an obvious factor, because richer school districts are able to devote more resources to education than poorer districts. Moreover, even in integrated school districts upper middle class students are more likely to be found on "college prep" tracks that feed into higher education, while minority students and poor and working-class children are more likely to be on tracks that lead to more modest educational and occupational attainments (Oakes, 1985).

The institutionalization of inequality is, in extreme cases, maintained by physical force, intimidation, or even terrorism. The period between the Civil War and World War II in the south witnessed the exercise of both private (the Klan) and public (law enforcement) violence and intimidation. As late as the 1940s, city police departments were implicated in forcibly providing workers for the cotton plantations (James, 1988). In the contemporary world women from poor nations are lured to industrial nations with the promise of legitimate jobs but are actually forced into sweatshops or even prostitution (Drummond & Kennedy, 2000). Exclusionary practices are seldom maintained exclusively by naked force but are usually sustained by social ideas that make such actions appear proper.

The Legitimation of Inequality

Legitimation refers to the social psychological dimension: the social definitions, beliefs, and values that serve to support, rationalize, and justify patterns of inequality by making them seem valid or right or moral. There are three key forms of legitimation, stereotypes, myths, and ideologies.

Stereotypes are generalizations and simplifications applied to all members of a group. Stereotypes show up when people begin a sentence about a group of people with "all," as in "All _____ are lazy, dirty, emotional, or undependable." All of the following groups—Catholics, Protestants, Muslims, Jews, Asians, blacks, whites, Latinos, women, men, and others—have been the victims of stereotyping. Stereotypes seem to emerge when people single out a trait of a few individuals and apply it to all others. Once created, stereotypes are then transmitted from one generation to the next.

People hold ideas about the nature of the social and physical world. Some beliefs are based on scientific evidence, while others are contradicted by science but persist because of misunderstandings, misperceptions, or simply naiveté. The term **myth** is used here to characterize mistaken, unfounded beliefs. Public perceptions about the poor are, for example, dominated by certain myths (O'Hare, 1992). One such myth is that most of the poor are poor because they do not want to work. The fact is that about half are either too old or too young to work, and about one-third actually do work but fail to earn enough to lift themselves out of poverty.

The most complex forms of legitimation are ideologies. An **ideology** is a loosely organized system of myths and ideas that support discrimination against socially defined groups. For example, in the pre-British Hindu caste system members of lower level castes were seen as ritually impure and limited to the most odious occupations such as cleaners and shepherds. Nineteenth-century racism was buttressed by an ideology that combined "science" and "biology" to guarantee the relegation of African Americans to the lower ends of the stratification system. The doctrine that slaves were members of an inherently inferior group is a perfect justification for enslaving them. It is important to emphasize that ideologies need not be logically consistent, nor based on an accurate picture of the situation.

The elements of an ideology may be consciously recognized and accepted by dominant members of society or may operate below the conscious level. Long-standing ideologies often enjoy the force of tradition. Patterns are learned and passed on to subsequent generations through the socialization process, and they often seem to have no other justification than their antiquity. This kind of ideology is often evident in social stereotypes that are grounded in unrecognized beliefs and assumptions about categories of people.

Institutionalization and legitimation are thus interlocking features of stratification systems. The analytic distinction between two processes is important in understanding the persistence of inequality through time. Institutionalized discrimination may be discredited and outlawed, but the underlying stereotypes and myths can persist long after formal barriers to opportunity have crumbled. There are any number of contemporary examples which can be understood in this way. To illustrate, white-collar workers continue to enjoy higher social status than blue-collar workers, despite the fact that the original basis of the distinction has been eroded by economic and technological change. And racial stereotypes still plague African-American workers in job applications although formal occupational barriers are illegal.

THE AMERICAN DREAM AND THE IDEOLOGY OF INDIVIDUALISM

Contemporary American perceptions of the legitimacy of the distribution of wealth, social status, and political power are deeply rooted in an ideology celebrated as the "American Dream." It emphasizes a direct link between individual effort and success in an open, merit-based system. The American dream has lured countless immigrants, both legal and illegal, to America and rural migrants to the cities. Social scientists are more apt to refer to this belief system as the **ideology of individualism**, and it may formally be phrased as follows (Huber & Form, 1973; Feagin, 1972; Klugel & Smith, 1986; Lipset, 1990; J. Hochschild, 1995).

> *There are abundant economic opportunities.*
> *Individuals must be industrious and competitive.*
> *Rewards in the form of education, jobs, income, and status are, and should be, the result of individual talent and effort.*
> *Therefore, the distribution of rewards is generally fair and equitable.*

Although there may be a weakening of the power of this ideology, especially since World War II, it continues to have relevance for significant segments of the population and provides legitimation for location in the stratification system in America. Individuals must bear responsibility for a lack of success because there is virtually unlimited opportunity, and those who flourish deserve personal credit for their success. The origins of the ideology of individualism can be traced to Europe and the Protestant Reformation of the sixteenth century.

The Puritan Ethic

A key element in this religious philosophy was an emphasis on individual responsibility for one's own fate (both spiritual and secular). Puritans brought this individualistic spirit with them to America, and it came to form the centerpiece of the colonial cultural value system. The importance of independence and self-reliance was solidified and elaborated by the unique circumstances of a frontier society and later by industrialization and the celebration of emerging capitalism.

Protestantism in the sixteenth century must be understood as a rejection of the elaborate bureaucracy of the Catholic church and its doctrine that a Christian was only able to achieve salvation through the auspices of the church. Reformers such as Martin Luther and John Calvin emphasized individuals' personal responsibility for their own actions and their own fate. They also made work a key feature of an individual's social and moral obligations. Prior to the Reformation, all work except religious endeavors was perceived as a burden to be endured as a means of survival. Martin Luther elevated the value of every occupation by arguing that all forms of work played an integral part in God's worldly plans. Influential ministers demanded relentless industriousness in pursuit of a person's occupation, no matter how menial. Hard work offered countless rewards; it was intrinsically worthwhile but also was a way of serving God and a protection against the temptations of the secular world. More than one Calvinist theologian defined lack of employment as a crime or a sin. The unemployed were, in several colonies, actually subject to imprisonment or whipping (Feagin, 1975: 25).

Puritanism also gave religious sanction to social inequality, because economic success, or the lack of it, came to be associated with personal character. Calvinists proclaimed that wealth was a worldly sign of God's grace, for God would certainly not allow the immoral to prosper. He rewarded only the virtuous. Hence, individual failure was an indication of some personal flaw, not a consequence of family background or structural limits on opportunity. Some groups such as the Quakers spoke out against this view, but without much impact, and the powerful emphasis on individual responsibility for financial success or decline spread beyond the confines of Calvinists.

Benjamin Franklin was one of the chief advocates of the Puritan ethic. Writing in 1726 he resolved, "To apply myself industriously to whatever business I take in hand, and not divert my mind from my business by any foolish project of growing suddenly rich; for industry and patience are the surest means to plenty" (Franklin, 1961: 183). It was this link between industriousness and wealth that attracted the attention of Max Weber, who argued that Protestantism was a major factor in fostering the spirit of capitalism.

The Frontier and the Land of Opportunity

The American ideology of individualism was encouraged and reinforced by an abundance of open land on the western frontier. The frontier was much more than a distant geographic boundary, it was a symbol of unlimited opportunity (Turner, 1920). The image of plentiful land on the western frontier nourished a convenient mythology for the nation. There was no reason for anyone to fail for there was always the vast untapped land to the west, with prosperity in forestry, farming, or fishing awaiting the strong and talented willing to seize the opportunity. This image was furthered in the mid-nineteenth century with discovery of gold in California, and in 1862 by passage of the Homestead Act that offered cheap land to virtually everyone. The inherent risks—uncharted land, an indigenous population seeking to protect its lands, and lack of law and order—merely accentuated the rewards awaiting the adventurous and self-reliant. This led to the celebration of the rugged individualist, symbolized even today by the cowboy.

It was an ideology that could flourish in a largely agrarian economy with a broad expanse of open land and lacking traditional class barriers to success (with the notable exception of slaves). The flourishing of industrialization in the nineteenth century presented a different kind of opportunity—paid work in the factories, mills, and mines. There was also the opportunity for wealth through personal ingenuity, and early capitalism created millionaires out of those who invented or perfected production techniques—people such as Henry Ford and Thomas Edison. As the nation and individuals prospered it became viewed as the "land of opportunity." The image of a nation of apparently limitless economic opportunity attracted waves of immigrants fleeing poverty, famine, or oppression in their native lands. Most non-English immigrants met with discrimination and open hostility and were typically relegated to the least rewarding work in the factories. Yet their economic status was often much better than it would have been in the lands they abandoned, and there were opportunities for those from humble origins to prosper and support the belief system. The success of individual immigrants fueled the myth. Andrew Carnegie, for example, came to America from Scotland as a poor boy of 13 and eventually amassed a fortune in the iron and steel business. Those who did not themselves prosper were sustained by the notion that their children would enjoy the benefits of a better life.

Social Darwinism

People like Carnegie and J. P. Morgan amassed great wealth in the nineteenth century, and toward the end of the century a new variation of the dominant ideology emerged, one that created a link between science and affluence. Charles Darwin published *On the Origin of the Species* in 1859, and it soon became the basis for a social and economic theory of inequality. Themes such as the "struggle for survival" and "survival of the fittest" were appropriated from a biological theory of evolution and grafted onto economics to explain and justify inequalities in wealth and power. John D. Rockefeller, speaking to a church school explained,

> The growth of a large business is merely a survival of the fittest. . . . This is not an evil tendency in business. It is merely the working out of a law of nature and a law of God (Feagin, 1975: 35).

Soon thereafter sociologist William Graham Sumner lent academic legitimacy to Social Darwinism with his view of the rich,

> millionaires are a product of natural selection, acting on the whole body of men to pick out those who can meet the requirement of certain work to be done. . . . They may fairly be regarded as the naturally selected agents of society. . . . There is the intensest [sic]) competition for their place and occupation [and] this assures us that all who are competent for this function will be employed in it (Sumner, 1914: 90).

Therefore, he concluded, that there should be no attempt to redistribute wealth or interfere with the evolutionary process. He believed that hard work could triumph over the most humble circumstances; hence, he had these words of advice for impoverished urban workers,

> Let every man be sober, industrious, prudent and wise, and bring up his children to be so likewise, and poverty will be abolished in a few generations (Sumner, 1914: 57)

The Great Depression

The themes of individualism, self-reliance, and boundless opportunity became difficult to sustain during the Great Depression of the 1930s. More than 6 million workers were thrown out of work between 1929 and 1930 alone, and a record 14 million were displaced in the mid-1930s. It is commonly estimated that one in four workers was jobless at the peak of the depression. It became evident that no amount of individual effort could protect even the most diligent worker from joblessness as businesses failed and factories closed. The economic chaos of the period stimulated two major changes in public policy. There was, first, a dramatic increase in governmental intervention in the functioning of the economic system. Government spending practices were used to stimulate the economy. Massive public works projects were undertaken to expand the infrastructure and create jobs. Regulatory agencies such as the Securities Exchange Commission were created to monitor the stock market. At the same time, the government began to fashion a "safety net" to assist individual victims of unbridled capitalism. For example, the Social Security Act of 1935 provided payments to the unemployed and established retirement benefits, and minimum wage legislation (1938) created a floor under wages for some workers. Such mechanisms were an open acknowledgment that capitalism was not benign and that individuals at the mercy of the system deserved some protection and aid from their government.

Further challenges to the emphasis on individual achievement surfaced during the turmoil of the 1960s. The civil rights and women's movements and the rediscovery of persistent structural poverty left little doubt that discrimination and structural barriers placed artificial limits on opportunities for significant segments of American society. Social scientists marshaled evidence that located at least some of the blame for poverty on the failings of institutions such as the schools and industries that failed to pay the wages necessary to support families. These developments challenged exclusive reliance upon individual success or failure, and focused on social, political, and economic factors beyond the direct control of individuals, however highly motivated they might be.

E-Business

The digital revolution begun at the end of the twentieth century changed the way people communicate and the way business is conducted. E-commerce revitalized the validity of the American Dream. The success of people in computers, software, or retailing who started with little more than an innovative idea and became fabulously wealthy in a few years is widely celebrated. Individuals such as Jeff Bezos, Bill Gates, and Steve Jobs confirm the American Dream of success flowing to those who work hard, and suggest that unlimited opportunities await others with ambition and drive. Obviously, not everyone in such businesses flourishes, but successes are more visible than failures.

Contemporary Class Ideology

The ideology of opportunity and individualism that shaped American society and culture for much of its history survives. The majority of white Americans still generally see America as a "land of opportunity" (Kluegel & Smith, 1986), and two out of three people insist that "hard work" is the key to economic success (Mitchell, 1996). An overwhelming 93 percent of recent English-speaking immigrants feel that anyone who works hard can get ahead in America (Puente, 1995). Contemporary perceptions of individual chances for success have been vindicated by a decade of prosperity despite the loss of jobs to foreign competitors and corporate restructuring that is displacing countless workers.

The causal link between individual effort and economic success remains strong, although Americans are sensitive to the prevailing structural barriers to access, especially for minorities, women, and the poor. Although ideologies are complex social phenomena, they can sometimes be highlighted by a single issue, a single topic, or a single question. Many social scientists believe that inviting people to explain the causes of success is such a focal issue because it demands that people distill their feelings and attitudes into a single response.

When confronted with the question of the basis of success, about seven out of ten Americans attribute it to hard work rather than luck or sponsorship (Exhibit 4.1). It is striking that the ideology of individualism flourishes among all groups, women and men, young and old, black and white, and even among those with limited education that relegates them to the bottom of the stratification system.

Other analysis of individualist responses reveal the survival of the traditional values of Ben Franklin. The major causes of poverty are identified as the absence of some positive personal trait such as lack of thrift or proper money management, lack of effort, lack of ability and talent, or loose morals and drunkenness (Kluegel & Smith, 1986: 79). In contrast, when asked to explain the sources of great wealth, a majority favors factors such as personal drive, risk-taking, hard work, and initiative, although it is conceded that inherited wealth is some advantage. Those who emphasize social structure see the sources of wealth or poverty, success or failure originating with social barriers or in the circumstances that individuals confront in their own lives. They assign the greatest weight to factors such as discrimination, exploitative wages, or weakness in the schools.

The ideology of individualism is also visible in the decades-old tendency of Americans to make a distinction between the "deserving" poor and the "undeserving" or "unworthy" poor. The worthy poor are seen as those who are hard-working but are the victims of circumstances and hence deserving of compassion and aid, while the unworthy poor are responsible for their own problems and do not deserve respect or help. The American aversion to the use of the term "social class" also has roots in the ideology of individualism because recognition of social classes admits that society is divided into groups whose opportunities and rewards are enhanced or limited by the workings of the economic system (DeMott, 1990). The convergence

EXHIBIT 4.1   Perceptions of the Source of Success

	Hard Work	Luck, or Help of Others	Both Equally Important
Overall	69%	11%	19%
Gender			
Female	70	9	20
Male	68	12	19
Racial Group			
White	69	11	19
Black	66	12	22
Education			
Graduate degree	61	6	32
Bachelor's	66	11	22
High school	71	10	18
Less than high school	70	12	16
Age			
18 to 29	73	8	18
50 to 59	70	9	22
60 to 69	63	12	25

Note: Percents may not add to 100 because "don't know" or no answer are excluded. The question was worded as follows: "Some people say that people get ahead by their own hard work; others say that lucky breaks or help from other people are most important. Which do you think is most important?"

Source: Susan Mitchell, "Hard work or luck?" *The Official Guide to American Attitudes.* Ithaca, NY: New Strategist Publications, 1996, p. 222. Reprinted with permission.

of these various elements forms an ideology of individualism that stresses individual responsibility for the rewards that people enjoy and their place in the stratification system.

RACE, ETHNICITY, AND STRATIFICATION

Members of racial and ethnic groups are often concentrated at the lower levels of stratification systems. Mexican-American men illustrate this situation. Seventy-seven percent are in service or blue collar work, compared to 49 percent of white men (del Pinal & Singer, 1997: 38). Consequently, 15 percent of Mexican families earn less than $10,000 a year, compared to 5 percent of white families. There are several different approaches to understanding the concentration of minorities at the lower levels of society, and they can conveniently be divided into three basic theories (Feagin & Feagin, 1996). One approach focuses on competition among groups for scarce resources; a second emphasizes deliberate systematic coercive exploitation of minorities; and assimilation theorists emphasize the sociocultural characteristics of minority group members that place them at a disadvantage in a system dominated by members of a different culture.

Competition Theory

Competition theory focuses on the clashes that occur when groups contend for scarce resources. The resources can be tangible assets such as wealth, housing, or land or social capital in the form of jobs, education, or social status. The history of relations between Native Americans and Europeans must certainly be seen in this context as a struggle for land, minerals, and natural resources. Europeans usually visualized the land as an economic resource, while the land also had deep religious and lifestyle implications for Native Americans.

Jobs and the rewards that accompany them are among the most frequently contested resources in urban societies. Members of occupations often seek to keep their numbers small in order to keep their bargaining power, wages, and prestige. The most extreme manifestation of this showed up in the nineteenth century when some skilled crafts sought to limit access to the sons of current members (Foner, 1964). Women and racial and ethnic minorities are often the target of exclusionary practices. For example, the legal profession during the 1920s and 1930s erected barriers to limit the number of African-American and Eastern European immigrants (Auerbach, 1976). White-controlled unions systematically excluded blacks from membership and apprenticeship programs and prohibited their members from working with nonunion members, thus pressuring employers to exclude blacks (Foner, 1964). Such practices were part of some union constitutions between the 1880s and the 1940s.

Groups also contest intangibles such as values and beliefs. Groups are often separated by **ethnocentrism**, the tendency of a group to view its own values and ideas as superior to all others. Religion is often at the root of ethnocentrism because most religious belief systems define their creed as "the one true faith," thus establishing an unequivocal basis for judgments of inferiority. Ethnocentrism thus emphasizes social differences among groups and exacerbates the potential for conflict as groups seek to impose their values on others. Competition, in turn, can intensify antagonism. The reasoning is that competition and the presence of disparate groups encourages a sense of solidarity on both sides, and that, in turn, leads to mobilization and open conflict (Olzak, 1996; Nagel, 1995).

Competition among racial or ethnic groups is all-too-frequently settled by violence—either actual or threatened. European expansion at the expense of Native Americans was eventually decided by the superiority of weaponry and military personnel. White supremacist groups flourished in the aftermath of the Civil War to intimidate the newly freed black population and still survive in the twenty-first century in smaller groups such as National Alliance, World Church of the Creator, and the Klu Klux Klan in the United States and neo-Nazis in Germany. The Internet has become the preferred channel for the dissemination of their message of hate (Kaplan & Kim, 2000; Wolf, 2000). One estimate suggests there are at least 3,000 web sites promoting hate groups. Lawmakers face a difficult dilemma in attempting to hinder the spread of hate and bigotry without violating First Amendment guarantees of free speech.

EXHIBIT 4.2   Known Hate Crimes in the U. S., 1991-1998

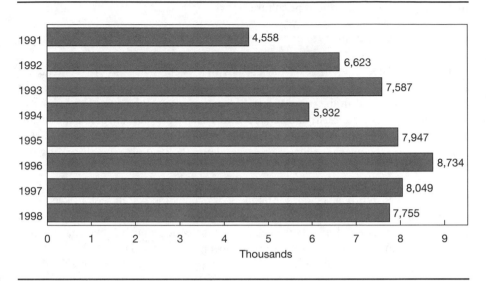

Thousands

Source: Federal Bureau of Investigation, *Uniform Crime Reports, 1999.* Washington, DC: U.S. Government Printing Office.

Speech may be protected, but physical violence and intimidation is not. The term **hate crime** was coined in 1985 to describe acts of racial, religious, and anti-immigrant violence (Grattet, 2000). Since then the definition has come to include violence based on gender, sexual orientation, or disability. Incidents reported to the FBI during the 1990s show that it is not uncommon for 8,000 such incidents to occur in one year (Exhibit 4.2). Moreover, these numbers are clearly an undercount because not all attacks are reported to authorities, and because not all states cooperate in the collection of data.

The validity of competition theories is supported by historical analysis showing that antagonism tends to increase when immigration expands and puts pressure on competition for jobs and during economic downturns when there are fewer jobs (Nagel, 1995). Although the focus of competition centers on the exclusion from jobs, it is not limited to the occupational sphere alone. It takes place within the larger context of exclusionary practices designed to keep minorities poor, uneducated, and powerless, thus discouraging competition and ensuring another generation of workers.

Internal Colonialism

Political scientists use the term *colonialism* to describe the political control and economic use of weaker nations and groups at the hands of more powerful nations. Similar processes can occur within the borders of nations, and hence social scientists use the term **internal colonialism** to identify the political domination and economic exploitation of racial and ethnic groups by more powerful groups (Blauner, 1972). The thesis is embedded in economic imperatives, and it is argued that vulnerable (usually non-native) groups are explicitly exploited as a pool of low-wage workers to generate profits for agricultural land owners or industrial employers. This approach illuminates the American experience of certain non-white groups, starting with the forced importation of blacks as slaves beginning in the seventeenth century, continuing in the mid-nineteenth century with the importation of poor Chinese laborers to work the mines and build the railroads, continuing in the twentieth century with the influx of Mexicans to do field work and harvest the crops in the southwest. Today, internal colonialism is likely to be found in urban sweatshops (Case Study).

Not all exploited racial and ethnic minorities labor in sweatshops. Many are migrant farm workers toiling in the fields. It is estimated that there are 2.2 million paid farm workers and that 85 percent are foreign-born, and nearly one-half (46 percent) live below the poverty level (Potok, 1996). Most are legal and illegal immigrants attracted by wages much higher than can be earned in their native lands. Some remain in the United States, migrating around the country as work becomes available, while others are "shuttle" migrants who work in one area during harvesting and then return home for the rest of the year.

Assimilation Theory

Assimilation theory is strongly influenced by the American experience. During the nineteenth century the United States was populated by succeeding waves of European immigrants. It began with the Irish and later included Germans, Chinese, Scandinavians, Poles, Austrians, Czechs, Hungarians, Slovaks, and Italians. Most were driven from their homes by economic and social conditions—poverty, political unrest, and overpopulation. Each succeeding wave of immigrants tended to be concentrated at the lowest levels of the stratification system due to a combination of hostility by members of the dominant group and individual characteristics (lack of marketable job skills, absence of educational credentials, language barriers, and different cultural and religious traditions) that handicapped them in the competition for jobs and promotions. However, succeeding generations were usually able to improve their position by adopting the social and cultural attributes of the host society, a process called assimilation. The assimilation perspective emphasizes the erosion of the salience of racial and ethnic differences as the basis of inequality over time as immigrant groups surrender their cultural background and adopt the attributes and perspectives of the dominant culture.

Assimilation theory is an optimistic approach, suggesting that as succeeding generations of immigrant groups embrace the dominant culture (language, values, customs) they are able to compete educationally and economically, leading to a weakening of prejudice and discrimination. Assimilation occurs because the racial and ethnic differences that originally set them apart and disadvantaged them are blurred. The experience of German, Scandinavian, and Irish immigrant groups confirm the operation of the process. However, acceptance is gained at a price called Anglo-conformity, rejection of their identity and acceptance of the values and perspectives of the prevailing English and Protestant culture. Ultimately, assimilation has not worked equally well for all groups, especially African Americans and Native Americans.

CASE STUDY
Sweatshops: Historic and Contemporary

Sweatshops are firms that employ workers for long hours at low wages in poor and dangerous working conditions. Sweatshops flourished in urban areas of the United States in the nineteenth century. The apparel industry generated many of the worst examples during the Civil War. Large clothing retailers subcontracted the manufacture of uniforms to small independent firms. Subcontractors' profits were the difference between what they earned and what it cost to produce the garments. They subdivided the various stages of the process into simple, relatively unskilled tasks such as cutting, stitching, and sewing that could be mastered by children and unskilled adults. Money devoted to higher wages or better working conditions reduced profits, hence the margin was "sweated" from workers by paying them as little as possible for long hours in the most unsanitary and unsafe conditions. Sweatshops were located in tenements, over saloons or stables, in basements, attics, and lofts, wherever cheap rent could be found. There were no restrictions on hours, and workdays stretching from 5 A.M. to 9 P.M. were common. It is estimated that there were at least 20,000 sweatshops in New York City tenements at the beginning of the twentieth century (Adams & Sumner, 1985). "The workers, all immigrants lived and worked together in large numbers, in a few small, foul smelling rooms without ventilation, water or nearby toilets" (Seidman, 1942: 56). The disreputable conditions were highlighted by a fire in the Triangle Shirtwaist Factory in 1911 when 146 girls and young women died, many because doors were locked to keep workers in and union organizers out. That tragedy helped to prompt legislation regulating hours, wages, and working conditions.

The origin and proliferation of sweatshops in the nineteenth century reflected the convergence of three conditions: industries depending on extensive manual labor (such as apparel, cigar making, and meat processing), the practice of subcontracting work among many small producers, and the availability of a pool of vulnerable and exploitable workers who had few practical options (children, poor women, illegal aliens, refugees, and rural migrants). Unfortunately, sweatshops have not been eliminated. The same conditions continue to exist; the major change is that the Italian, Jewish, and Polish garment workers of the nineteenth century have been replaced by Asians and Latinos.

It is estimated that 2,000 sweatshops operate in New York City alone, and they are also common in other cities where there is a ready pool of immigrant labor such as Los Angeles, Miami, and El Paso, Texas (Hedden, 1993; Finder, 1995). Most are small operations employing twenty to thirty people, mostly young females, that open and close so frequently and so quickly that they easily evade the efforts of understaffed government inspection agencies. Children as young as age 10 spend up to sixty hours a week toiling at sewing machines for less than minimum wages. One undercover investigative reporter in New York City was paid 96 cents an hour for eighty-four hours of work per week (Lii, 1995). Some workers are illegal immigrants, who cannot complain about pay or working conditions, and others owe huge sums to the smugglers who helped them enter the country. There are even instances of immigrants being held against their will. For example, a group of forty-four deaf Mexican men, women, and children were discovered after being smuggled into the United States and forced to sell trinkets on New York City subways (Beals & Springen, 1997). Sweatshops are not just an urban problem. Legal and illegal migrants are lured to meat-packing plants in Nebraska, Iowa, Kansas, and Texas where they work in plants with staggering illness and injury rates (M. Cooper, 1997).

Many sweatshops are concentrated in the garment industry. Although some garment workers enjoy decent wages and working conditions, it is estimated that one- half of all women's garments made in America are produced in whole or in part at factories that flout wage and safety laws (Hedden, 1993). To illustrate, a random check of sixty-nine garment makers in California found 93 percent guilty of health and safety violations, 68 percent refused to pay overtime rates and 51 percent paid less than the minimum wage (Chandler, 1995).

Sweatshops are a global problem, and at least some of the clothing sold by well-known American designers and retailers is alleged to be produced in sweatshop conditions in developing nations such as the Dominican Republic, the Philippines, Malaysia, Thailand, and Vietnam. College students at more than 175 campuses have mobilized into United Students Against Sweatshops to demand that companies that market clothing bearing their college logos work to overhaul exploitative practices (Marklein, 2000a). A number of American firms have adopted codes of conduct for subcontractors that include features such as the prohibition of child labor, minimum work and safety standards, the right to unionize, and guarantees that workers be paid the prevailing minimum wage.

It is often difficult to monitor overseas factories, but some companies make an honest effort to improve working conditions. The core problem is that these are nations in which massive segments of the population—sometimes as much as one-half—live in poverty. Consequently, subsistence wages are common everywhere, and sweatshop wages may actually offer advantages over life on the farms. Industrializing nations also worry that such rules will mean that other nations will take the jobs. The problem of sweatshops will continue as long as the availability of highly vulnerable workers makes it possible for unscrupulous manufacturers to place profits over human dignity.

Ideological Racism: Legitimizing Racial and Ethnic Inequality

Discriminatory and exclusionary practices are supported by values and belief systems that legitimize such practices. Almost all forms of subordination are shaped by some variation of ideological racism.[1] **Ideological racism** is a system of ideas that divides the world population into groups (races) based on physical traits that are, in turn, claimed to be unalterably linked to intellectual and psychological characteristics (Feagin & Feagin, 1996: 7).[2] Not surprisingly, the group controlling the ranking is always at the top of the intellectual hierarchy. The inferiority imputed to subordinates by the dominant group thus justifies disparate treatment and unequal rewards.

The emergence of the European concept of races as groups of people with distinctive physical, attitudinal, and behavioral characteristics is associated with expansion into the western hemisphere beginning in the seventeenth century. Indigenous peoples and imported Africans were enslaved to perform heavy physical labor. For example, by 1700 somewhere between 500,000 to 600,00 African slaves had been brought into Brazil to work on the sugar and tobacco plantations and in the mills and mines (Russell, 1994: 42). African slaves were characterized as an inferior race as a way of justifying their servitude, even by people such as Thomas Jefferson who championed political democracy for whites.

The eighteenth and nineteenth centuries witnessed countless efforts by scientists and others to sort people into groups on the basis of physical characteristics such as skin color, hair, and facial structure, and to assert the inferiority of some groups. Many elaborate pseudo-scientific theories flourished. There was, to illustrate, the theory of "polygenesis," which held that the various human races evolved at different times and that Africans, who were claimed to be the first to evolve, were consequently the most intellectually primitive. Moreover, since culture and civilization were the product of biological capacity, less advanced races could never create cultures comparable to those of higher races. Consequently, it was argued that since Africans were incapable of developing civilization on their own they had to be segregated and concentrated in menial tasks. In an ironic twist of ideological racism, it was argued that their importation and exposure to white culture was actually a privilege.

---

[1]It must be emphasized that ideological racism as used in this context has a specific meaning distinct from the word *racism* as it is commonly employed in popular usage. In the media and elsewhere *racism* is used as a generic term to refer to any negative attitude or hostile act directed toward members of minority groups.

[2]Historically, the term *race* was used to identify groups of people distinguished by any number of observable physical or social characteristics. The basis for such classifications could be religion (e.g., Jewish race), language (Arab race), nationality (Irish race, Mexican race), or physical characteristics (white race). Race is thus ultimately a social construct, not a biological reality.

Racial and Ethnic Stereotypes

Racial and ethnic stereotypes play a key role in legitimizing discriminatory treatment by attributing inadequacies or negative traits to subordinate groups. They buttress inferiority in subtle and invidious ways. The experiences of African Americans and Mexican Americans illustrate the dynamics of the process. In both cases stereotypes center on the failure to conform to the standards of the ideology of individualism that demand talent and industriousness.

Stereotyping Black Americans. The moral ambivalence of Thomas Jefferson toward blacks is well known; he opposed slavery, but was a slave owner, he argued that blacks should be free, but he stereotyped them as mentally inferior, apparently ignoring the fact that slaves were unschooled by law. By the middle of the eighteenth century it was common to stereotype African Americans with terms such as "careless," "lazy," and "childlike." Such stereotypes had dual implications. First, it meant that African Americans did not have the characteristics demanded by the ideology of individualism—dedication, hard work, and thrift. Second, because they lacked those traits it was logical and acceptable to exclude them from positions of authority and responsibility. They were, in short, deserving of relegation to the bottom of the system.

Sexual imagery also played a significant role in the process of stereotyping and subordinating African Americans. Black men were cast as sexual aggressors, thus justifying oppressive measures to protect white women. In contrast, black women were cast as seductive and promiscuous, which offered justification for the sexual exploitation of black women by white slave owners. Some black artists believe that the degraded sexual imagery imposed on African Americans has long limited the ability of black writers and artists to explore black erotica for fear of providing confirmation of the stereotype (Marriott, 1997).

There were, in addition, subcategories for women of color. One was the myth of the aggressive and domineering "strong black woman," having more masculine than feminine traits, which can be twisted to explain racial inequality (hooks, 1984). The reasoning follows this logic: the strengths of black women violate broader social expectations of women and consequently emasculate black men, contributing to the breakup of the family, which in turn causes poverty. The function of the stereotype is thus to locate the causes of the problem within the personality of victims rather than in ideological racism and the structural problems that produce poverty.

Stereotyping Mexican Americans. The characteristics attributed to African Americans are repeated in the relations with Mexican Americans. Alleged laziness, incompetence, and backwardness abound. The origins of stereotypes reflecting ideological racism directed at Mexicans can be traced to the middle of the eighteenth century through selective perception and distorted interpretation of events (Feagin & Feagin, 1996). The defeat of the Mexican army in the struggle for territory in the 1840s became the basis of stereotypes that attributed cowardice to them rather than

CASE STUDY
Sports and Ideological Racism

Sports is sometimes referred to as the great equalizer. Ideological racism may survive in society and even in locker rooms or front offices, but on the playing field race is irrelevant; it is talent that counts. Consequently, African-American athletes achieve fame and fortune in professional sports, earning millions of dollars in salaries and endorsements.

Most Americans see this as a positive development, but there is also another perspective on black athletic success. It can, in subtle and destructive ways, perpetuate stereotypes and hinder the progress of future generations of blacks (Hoberman, 1997). Hoberman argues that supremacy in sports celebrates physical prowess, strength, violence, and ferocity, and these traits resonate with nineteenth-century images of primitive and savage black men. Moreover, success in athletics can easily be interpreted as confirmation that African Americas are incapable of intellectual achievements. In short, it resurrects the slavery-era notion of biological inferiority that took so long to discredit.

In addition, the immense rewards that go to the small number of superstars can undermine the opportunities of future generations of African Americans. Fixation on sports by some black youth encourages them to concentrate on athletics and neglect the academic efforts that can be translated into advanced education and occupational careers.

recognizing defeat at the hands of a superior military force. The period of internal turmoil that accompanied the Mexican struggle for independence was transposed into political incompetence. In the 1850s one observer invoked the usual claim that Mexicans lacked the abilities that Europeans did, describing than as "thoroughly debased and incapable of self-government, and there is no latent quality about them that can ever make them respectable" (Feagin & Feagin, 1996: 297). Media images of Mexican Americans during most of the twentieth century emphasized unclean sombrero-wearing caricatures who were either enjoying a siesta or engaging in criminal behavior.

Stereotypes are a powerful force in American society, shaping the way people think about members of minority groups. Well into the 1960s at least one-third of Californians endorsed the notion that Mexicans were "shiftless and dirty" (Brink & Harris, 1967). Such overt and open manifestations of ideological racism began to dissipate under the pressures of the civil rights movement in the 1960s and 1970s. However, negative stereotypes of Mexican Americans persist. In 1997 a major airline used a manual that warned pilots that Latin American passengers are often unruly and drunk and call in false bomb threats when running late for a plane (Alexander, 1997). A national survey showed that one in five whites believe Latinos lack the ambition and drive needed to succeed (Feagin & Feagin, 1996: 299).

In most public situations it has become inappropriate to use disparaging stereotypes of racial and ethnic groups. This is not true on the internet where openly racist web sites flourish. In fact, some groups have registered offensive domain names so that they cannot be exploited by bigots. For example, nigger.com is owned by the N.A.A.C.P. and kike.com is held by the Anti-Defamation League (Safire, 2000b).

GENDER AND STRATIFICATION

Anthropologists and historians have developed comprehensive analyses of gender and labor that document a sexual division of work as a common feature of human societies, in the sense that at least some tasks are typically reserved for either men or women. This gendered division of labor is central in explaining patterns of inequality. Biological or physiological differences between the sexes ultimately contribute little to the explanation of the division of labor because responsibilities allocated to men in one society may be the province of women in another, or vice versa. For example, in the Philippines, sales work is dominated by women (69 percent female), but an almost exclusively male occupation (99 percent male) in the United Arab Emirates (Jacobs, 1989). There are also countless examples of shifts in the gender composition of occupations in one society over time. Men were the telephone operators and clerks in nineteenth-century offices in the United States and Britain until such jobs became women's work over the course of the twentieth century.

The nature of women's work is central to an understanding of women's place in the stratification system. Women have always been in the *paid* labor force, but the most dramatic increases in labor force participation in the United States dates from the 1940s. The rate of female participation has increased steadily since and now stands at over 60 percent. Female participation rates vary around the world, ranging from about 56 percent in China to less than 25 percent in Peru (Exhibit 4.3). Overall rates of participation mask important demographic differences, with poor women, urban residents, and women of color always likely to be found working for wages. It is conventional to divide the history of the role of gender in the workplace into several broad periods, beginning with the period prior to industrialization.

Varieties of Feminist Theory

The gendered division of labor is best understood as the outcome of the social, economic and political forces that feminist theory seeks to explain. The term **feminism** is generally understood to mean a commitment to equal treatment and equality for women. Feminist theory seeks to explain inequality and barriers to women's social and economic justice. There are three main strands of feminist thought that focus on the social, political, and economic subordination of women: liberal feminism, socialist feminism, and radical feminism (Andersen, 1997).

EXHIBIT 4.3 **Labor Force Participation Rates for Women**

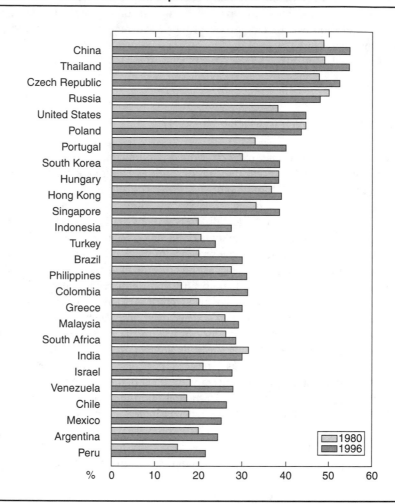

Source: "Women in work," *The Economist*, November 29, 1997, page 110. © The Economist Newspaper Group, Inc. Reprinted with permission. Further reproduction prohibited. www.economist.com

Liberal Feminism. Liberal feminism locates the main sources of inequality in gender socialization and patterns of discrimination that flow from traditional gender roles. Traditional gender roles are social constructions that emphasize differences between the sexes based on stereotypes that attribute intrinsic differences to men and women. To the extent, for example, that women are perceived as more emotional and less rational than men, stereotypes form the justification for channeling females away from careers in science, engineering, and medicine that are defined as demanding traits that men possess. Advocates of this position seek the erosion of social stereotypes that impose artificial limitations on the development of individual potential and the elimination of legal barriers and social customs based on gender stereotypes. The ultimate goal is equality of opportunity.

Radical Feminism. Radical feminism emphasizes that inequality and the allocation of women to the lower ends of the stratification system are facets of a system of institutionalized physical control over women by men. The concentration of power in the hands of men is referred to as **patriarchy**, and is supported ultimately by actual and threatened violence against women. Radical feminists point to verbal harassment, physical threats, intimidation, domestic abuse, sexual aggression, incest, and forcible rape as the most invidious ways of maintaining patriarchy. Obviously, not all men brutalize women, but violence directed against women is all too common in the United States, where it is estimated that one women in three will be physically assaulted by a male intimate during their adult lives. Consequently, the reality of violence can create a climate of intimidation. Patriarchy thus accounts for inequalities based on the control of women through their allocation to inferior jobs, the gender gap in pay, and the glass ceiling, which can only be eliminated by restructuring institutions created by men.

Socialist Feminism. Socialist feminism locates the origins of women's subordination in the nature of capitalist economic systems. The profit motive inherent in capitalism acts as an incentive to exploit the labor of vulnerable groups. Patriarchy also plays a role in socialist thinking because it is one of the factors that intensifies women's exploitation. Historically, women have, for example, often been used to displace male workers or pitted against men to reduce wages. Socialist feminism, which has its origins in the thinking of Marx and Engels, emphasizes the link between capitalism and class relations.

The Division of Labor in Agricultural Society

From colonial times to the beginning of the nineteenth century the individual household was the basic unit of production and consumption for the majority of the free white population. There were, of course, wealthy landowners and urban merchants at one extreme and slaves and sharecroppers at the other extreme. It appears that some labor in family enterprises was generally divided along gender lines, at least on modest family farms, with men having primary responsibility for agricultural production and women responsible for the inner economy—food, clothing, child care (Anderson, 1988). However, members of both sexes easily crossed these lines, with husbands involved in the socialization of children for adult community and religious roles and particularly active in preparing sons to follow agricultural pursuits. Wives participated in production through keeping inventories, caring for livestock, and overall supervision of workers as well as helping with planting, cultivating, and harvesting during peak periods. Households were largely self-sufficient, but cash was needed for the purchase of tools and services (such the milling of grain), and wives often produced the products and services that generated extra cash income, either by weaving, growing food on small plots, or even working as midwives. Some elements of that pattern survive on contemporary family farms.

Industrialization, Gender, and Work

The first stirrings of the industrial transformation and the creation of a large urban working class were seen around the beginning of the nineteenth century with the proliferation of mines, factories, and mills. Displaced rural men, women, and children provided the bulk of the labor force for those early factories. A large share of the first workers were the daughters of rural families who contributed to household income through paid work, but they were soon supplemented by foreign-born immigrants (Kessler-Harris, 1982). The first major wave of immigrants were the Irish Catholics, who first reached this country in large numbers in the 1840s. The men worked the docks and the textile mills, built the railroads, dug the canals, and supplied farm labor. Wives, daughters, and single women were most likely to end up as domestic servants for the wealthier classes. To illustrate, in 1855, 75 percent of all domestic workers in New York City were Irish women (Feagin, 1984: 93).

The most rapid and explosive industrial growth occurred between the Civil War and World War I. One measure of the scale of industrial transformation is that within two decades after the Civil War industrial workers outnumbered farm workers for the first time in American history. The family farm did not disappear, but there was a shift toward commercial production for the market. This was a decisive period in the evolution of gender and work, for it was during this period that a number of forces combined to solidify a separation of men's and women's social and occupational roles. It was an extraordinarily complex period because several different forces were at work.

An obvious difference between agrarian and urban industrial economies was that the workplace became physically separated from the place of residence. That made it more difficult for women with child-rearing obligations to combine domestic responsibilities with full-time paid work. Some continued in various forms of income-producing work at home. The wives of lower-middle- and working-class men were doing laundry at home or taking in boarders as a means of supplementing family income well into the 1920s and 1930s (Kessler-Harris, 1982). Countless others did industrial "home work," jobs such as sewing clothing, making lace or buttons, or even rolling cigars that were decentralized in private homes on a piecework basis. The home work practice was eventually banned in the 1940s because it was used by unscrupulous employers to avoid minimum wage and child labor laws.

Many women were thrust into the paid labor force on a more or less full-time basis during this period, often to supplement family incomes. Rural African-American women did field work, while urban black women, their options severely limited by overt discrimination, were typically relegated to domestic service. Factory work was largely the province of young single white women, usually immigrants or the daughters of immigrants. This was the period of massive Italian immigration. They toiled under some of the worst working conditions in the disgraceful sweatshops, and as result women were active in fighting for improved working conditions, both in the larger trade union effort and in organizing along gender lines with groups such as National Women's Trade Union League (Bose, 1987). In 1881, three thousand African-American women participated in a washerwomen's strike (Hunter, 1997). Although occupational data of the time are unreliable, it appears that at least one in four workers in the paid labor force was a women in 1900.

Some enduring patterns of gender segregation in occupations emerged during this period. The segregation of occupations along gender lines was legitimized and fostered by a configuration of gender beliefs and attitudes that defined the appropriate social and occupational roles of men and women (Deaux & Kite, 1987: 97). These ideas did not emerge during this period, but were thrown into strong relief by the process of industrialization.

Gender Stereotypes.   In some cases women and men were channeled into different jobs on the grounds that physical and mental skills are gender based. A common version of that justification for the division of labor was that women had more skilled and delicate hands and more patience for tedious work. Assembly line work in electrical products and in the auto industry illustrate the process. The assembly of light bulbs and small appliances began as, and tends to continue as, women's work. Eighty percent of light bulb assembly work was female in 1910 when it was still a hand operation (Milkman, 1983). Women were recruited because it was thought that they naturally excelled at the precise operations required in assembling electrical components: speed, dexterity, endurance, and attention to detail.

In contrast, it was argued that women lacked the physical strength to handle the heavy manual labor of building cars. Consequently, auto manufacturing became men's work after initially being open to both sexes. Women were gradually displaced, and by 1929 over 99 percent of Ford Motor Company employees were men and 88 of the 110 auto factory job classifications were exclusively male (Lewchuk, 1993). This pattern prevailed until temporarily disrupted by World War II when large numbers of women were drawn into the plants, but as soon as the war began to wind down, women were again displaced by men.

It is interesting to note that Henry Ford was compelled to redefine the very concept of masculinity in order to convince men to accept the monotonous and repetitive work of the assembly line. "There is one thing that can be said about menial jobs that cannot be said about a great many so-called more responsible jobs," he claimed in his autobiography, "and that is, they are useful, respectable, and they are honest" (Lewchuk, 1993). His goal of replacing a craft model of masculinity emphasizing skill, pride, and autonomy with one based on brawn was nourished by arguing that only the "manly" could handle the strenuous demands of assembly work. This was encouraged by segregating women and creating a men's club atmosphere in the factory. The debate over differences in men's and women's abilities continues into the present, especially in jobs in the military. American women are excluded from ground combat despite the fact that they may serve in that capacity in many nations, including Israel, Canada, and South Africa (Stone, 2000).

CASE STUDY
Gender Stereotypes and Management Careers

Gender stereotypes can contribute important insights into the dynamics of the workplace. One consistent pattern that emerges is the perception that gender involves two distinct clusters of traits. Men tend to be viewed as strong and active, with potent needs for achievement, independence, dominance, autonomy, and aggression. Women are seen as caring, expressive, and sensitive, with powerful needs for affiliation, nurturance, and deference. The following list of adjectives, summarized from a broad body of research, provides an outline of the perceived attributes of women and men (Deaux & Lewis, 1984; Williams & Best, 1990). Attempts to capture the essence of these clusters in a single word or phrase has popularized expressions such as "instrumental," "competency," "task-orientation" or "agency" for men and "expressive," "social orientation," or "communion" for women. Moreover, there is a general consensus (among both men and women) on these configurations of characteristics, and some indication that a number of these traits show up in other cultures.

Male Traits	Female Traits
active	affectionate
aggressive	changeable
confident	emotional
courageous	gentle
daring	helpful
forceful	poised
inventive	sensitive
rational	sophisticated
stable	submissive
unemotional	sympathetic
unexcitable	warm

Such popular beliefs can work to the advantage or disadvantage of men and women in the occupational sphere in more than one way. If persons are persuaded of the salience of stereotypes they can disqualify themselves from the pursuit of specific occupations. It is more likely that they are held back or disqualified as they encounter barriers based on the assumption that they lack the traits necessary to function in certain fields or at certain levels. The link between occupational attainments and stereotypes is highlighted by considering the characteristics, attitudes, and temperaments *believed to be* necessary for success in management careers. It is more common to associate male characteristics (aggressive, self-reliant, stable) than female characteristics (helpful) with success in management (Schein, 1973; Brenner, et al., 1989). This discontinuity between female sex-traits and managerial success means that women are perceived as less likely to have abilities to compete in the high-powered world of administration. The perceived characteristics of successful management may also be stereotypical since they are defined by men who dominate senior management positions, but their existence has the potential to place women at a disadvantage.

Paternalism.   Paternalism has been used in many different ways to limit and constrain occupational and educational opportunities. The ideology of **paternalism** defines women as less capable than men, and in need of protection and guidance (Reskin & Padavic, 1994). Paternalism often has been supported by "scientific" research on sex differences in intelligence and ability. Nineteenth-century craniometrists used the observation of average sex differences in stature to support claims of lower intellectual capacity among women. Social psychologist Gustave LeBon concluded that

> All psychologists who have studied the intelligence of women recognize today that they represent the most inferior forms of human evolution and that they are closer to children and savages than to adult, civilized men (Deaux & Kite, 1987: 93).

This doctrine is highlighted by the rationale used to rebuff women who sought to surmount occupational barriers. When, for example, Myra Bradwell sought a license to practice law in Illinois in the 1870s, she was rejected by state courts and the United States Supreme Court. Her suit was denied on Constitutional grounds, but Justice Bradley located the decision in a broader historical and social context:

> Law, as well as nature herself, has always recognized a wide difference in the respective spheres and destinies of man and woman. Man is, or should be, woman's protector and defender. The natural and proper timidity and delicacy which belongs to the female sex evidently unfits it for many of the occupations of civil life. . . . The paramount destiny and mission of women are to fulfill the noble and benign offices of wife and mother. This is the law of the Creator. And the rules of civil society must be adapted to the general constitution of things. (*Bradwell v. Illinois*, 1873: 141–142).

The male protector and defender ideology also included an economic dimension. It was used to support labor unions' struggle for higher wages for men. Unions fought for a "family wage," on the grounds that it was the responsibility of husbands to provide financial support for their families. Samuel Gompers, speaking in 1905, proclaimed, "In our time, . . . there is no necessity for the wife contributing to the support of the family by working" (Foner, 1964: 224). There is a remnant of this idea in contemporary society among some men at all class levels who resist working wives as coproviders.

Paternalism also contributed to protective legislation that was introduced to protect women from hazards of the workplace. Protective legislation limited women's hours, strenuous activity, and exposure to hazardous substances. In retrospect, it is noted that considerations other than health were at stake, for the protected jobs were usually traditional male jobs and often the highest paid. In 1908 the U.S. Supreme Court ruled in *Muller v. Oregon* that special legislation for women was appropriate because women were not as strong as men, were dependent upon men, and were the mothers of future generations. Perhaps the key feature of that decision was that it placed all women in a separate legal classification because all women were potential mothers. Protective legislation excluding women of child-bearing age from jobs on the grounds of "fetal protection" was not finally eliminated in the

United States until 1991. It is apparent from the perspective of the twenty-first century that the family wage, protective legislation, and occupational segregation benefited some men by excluding women from competition from the more lucrative jobs in the paid labor force.

Competition for Jobs.   There was also an economic dimension to exclusionary practices. Women were sometimes exploited as pawns in the struggle between employers and workers. For example, early working-class solidarity between men and women in the printing industry was eroded over the course of the nineteenth century when unskilled women were used to displace skilled male printers or were employed as strikebreakers (Baron, 1980). Skilled printers worried that the "petticoat invasion" threatened to depress their wages and undermine the skilled traditions of their craft. Consequently, gender cooperation faded in this and other areas, and women came to be perceived as competitors for scarce jobs. It was a pattern repeated in many other craft unions leading to exclusionary practices that made the crafts the province of white males.

Men's and Women's Work in the Twentieth Century

While segregation along gender lines was occurring in the occupational sphere, households were also changing, at least among the upper middle class. Among the most important developments was the shift away from production for the family. The introduction of mass-produced clothing and foods combined with new-found affluence made home work less necessary, creating a "domestic void" for these middle-class women, stripping them of meaningful work in the form of goods and services for the family, and they were caught up in the emergence of a home economics movement that transformed housework into an unpaid occupation (Ehrenreich & English, 1979). The home economics movement itself represented the convergence of several broader trends—wider availability of single-family homes, concern with the breakdown of the traditional, tightly knit family, the rise of scientific child rearing, and medical science's discovery of the germ theory of disease (making wives responsible for cleanliness). Advocates of Frederick Taylor who were seeking to rationalize the workplace also turned their attention to the home, encouraging housewives to carefully study and analyze the best way to perform tasks such as peeling potatoes, maintain household records, and hold to rigorous schedules. Out of this emerged a new social ideal for upper-middle-class women, often called the "cult of domesticity." This ideal demanded dedication to home decoration, cleanliness, nutrition and meal planning, and child rearing. The cult of domesticity served to legitimize certain patterns. One was that it located the male role in the paid labor force (the public sphere) and the female role in the home (the private sphere). It is not at all clear how many women were able to realize this ideal, for many working class wives, immigrants, and women of color continued in the paid labor force.

Trends in occupational segregation that had been set in motion earlier intensified during the period between the two World Wars, along with the intensification of gender stereotyping of work. A whole range of occupations proliferated during this period, and they tended to split along gender lines. The professions—law, medicine, science, engineering—proliferated, but along sex lines. Office work was initially a male domain, but the feminization of clerical work began at the end of the nineteenth century so that women outnumbered men by the 1920s and in the early 2000s hold over 90 percent of jobs such as bank teller, secretary, and typist. It has been suggested that men abandoned clerical work at least in part because it did not enable them to demonstrate masculine traits (Lockwood, 1958), but it may also have been influenced by the lack of mobility opportunities.

The power of gender stereotypes of work was forcefully demonstrated during the decade of the Great Depression (Milkman, 1983). It might be expected that the high rates of unemployment in manufacturing would constrain men to attempt to displace women from jobs, but that did not generally happen. Apparently neither employers nor unemployed men were willing to move into female-typed work such as nursing, teaching, or secretarial jobs, even in the face of joblessness. Thus, for example, although more men moved into schoolteaching, it remained an overwhelmingly female occupation. The flourishing middle-class ideal for housewives took on new meaning and added responsibility during this period. Aided by technological innovations directed toward work in the home (vacuum cleaners and washing machines) and prompted by mass advertising and the proliferation of women's magazines, upper-middle-class wives were expected to attain new heights of cleanliness, neatness, and creative cooking in the home. The more affluent could afford domestic servants, relegating unpleasant physical tasks to a corps of black women (Palmer, 1989). All during the first half of the century and continuing into the 1960s, housewives devoted increasing hours to housework. More importantly, wives' income and social status came to be defined by their husband's occupational attainments, and the expectation was that their personal success and satisfactions should be subordinated to those of spouses and children.

Work and Ideology: 1940–2000

World War II had a profound impact on women's situation. The influx of women into the civilian labor force to replace men in the military set the stage for the eventual blurring of the distinction between the public and private sector. Women filled jobs of all kinds (in both civilian industry and the military), including those that they had presumably lacked the psychological traits to master. As the war wound down, an overwhelming majority expressed a desire to remain in the workforce. Although many were eventually displaced to make room for returning servicemen, the rate of participation of women in the paid labor force began an increase that has become permanent. An expanding economy created hundreds of thousands of new jobs. Older (over age 45) married women with diminished child-rearing responsibilities were the first group to seek work in larger numbers, and since the 1970s it has been younger married women. Today, more than 60 percent of mothers with young children are in the paid labor force.

EXHIBIT 4.4   Gender Segregation in Selected Occupations

Occupation	Percentage Female
Auto mechanics	1.4%
Carpenters	1.2
Welders	5.7
Mechanical engineers	7.1
Clergy	14.2
Sewing machine operators	79.9
Registered nurses	92.9
Teachers, K and Pre-K	98.4
Secretaries	98.6
Dental hygienists	99.1

Source: "Employed persons by detailed occupation, sex, race, and Hispanic origin." *Employment and Earnings* 47 (January, 2000), Table 11, pages 178–183.

Social and legal change weakened many occupational barriers and opened opportunities in the upper middle class. Law schools, once an almost exclusively male domain, now enroll 40 percent women, and women make up more than 70 percent of the enrollments at schools of veterinary medicine. However, the segregation of jobs along gender lines that emerged during earlier phases of industrialization often survive. This is underscored by seeing the proportion of women in some specific occupations (Exhibit 4.4). Virtually all auto mechanics and carpenters are men, while almost all teachers, dental hygienists, and secretaries are women in the United States. The skilled crafts have been slow to welcome women, while traditional women's work in nursing, elementary school teaching, and clerical work continues to be almost exclusively female.

CONCLUSION: AMERICAN DILEMMAS

In the 1940s Swedish sociologist Gunnar Myrdal's study of the situation of black Americans in the United States exposed a moral contradiction that he called an **American dilemma** (Myrdal, 1944). He noted that the United States was a nation founded on democratic and individualist principles and yet simultaneously maintained social and legal barriers that openly discriminated against a sizable proportion of its citizens. In fact, the American dilemma can more accurately be traced much further back in time, to the colonial period. And it was never just African Americans who suffered. Barriers based on class, race and ethnicity, and gender had long been common. It must, for example, be noted that women, American Indians, slaves and former slaves, and the propertyless were all denied the right to vote at some point in American history.

Ideologies legitimize and sustain the dilemmas. Ideologies resolve the apparent contradiction between ideals and reality by offering justifications for unequal treatment. The tenets of individualism, paternalism, or ideological racism legitimize inequality and offer justifications by explaining that members of subordinate groups lack some key attributes or are in some way inferior—biologically, socially, behaviorally.

There has certainly been much progress in the decades since Myrdal's book, but the dilemmas linger. Most of the formal barriers have been reduced or eliminated. There is, then, cause for some optimism because the evidence of progress is everywhere. Medicaid buffers the poor from catastrophic illness, women once denied the right to even vote now hold political offices at all levels, ideological racism is discredited and a solid black middle class has emerged. But undercurrents of hostility persist. Minorities continue to encounter discrimination in competition for jobs (Cross, et. al., 1990). Women in the military and elsewhere continually confront strongly entrenched sexism. The poor are still blamed for their misfortune by some segments of society. Perhaps the most invidious side of the dilemma is the fact that the poor, women, and people of color continue to encounter countless everyday humiliations, indignities, and disrespect that continue the American dilemma. There is no better example than the allegation that some police officers routinely stop drivers based on their race. Investigations begun in the 1990s showed that minorities were often disproportionately targeted for traffic investigation stops. In one state 17 percent of the motorists traveling on Interstate 95 were African American, but they accounted for 70 percent of the police stops—apparently their only "offense" was DWB: driving while black (Bowles, 2000).

KEY CONCEPTS

American dilemma	ideological racism	legitimation
assimilation theory	ideology	myth
competition theory	ideology of individualism	paternalism
ethnocentrism	institutionalization of	patriarchy
feminism	inequality	stereotypes
hate crime	internal colonialism	sweatshops

SUGGESTED READING

Fergus M. Bordewich. *Killing the White Man's Indian*. New York: Doubleday, 1996. A revealing exploration of the problems of contemporary Native Americans as they seek to establish control over their own lives and culture.

Ellis Cose. *The Rage of the Privileged Class*. New York: HarperCollins, 1994. The author describes the everyday humiliations that infuriate members of the black middle class.

Jennifer L. Hochschild. *Facing Up to the American Dream: Race, Class and the Soul of the Nation*. Princeton, NJ: Princeton University Press, 1995 An instructive discussion of the ways in which black and white perceptions of the American Dream converge and diverge.

RICHARD HOFSTADER. *Social Darwinism in American Thought*, Boston, MA: Beacon, 1955. The classic work on the impact of this powerful idea on individuals and societies.

ALICE KESSLER-HARRIS. *Out to Work*, New York: Oxford University Press, 1982. Among the best historical discussions of women in the labor force.

JAMES R. KLUEGEL and ELIOT R. SMITH. *Beliefs About Inequality*. New York: Aldine de Gruyter, 1986. A comprehensive analysis of Americans' perceptions of the class system.

CATHERINE A. MACKINNON. *Only Words*. Cambridge, MA: Harvard University Press, 1993. An outspoken feminist lawyer argues that pornography degrades women and bolsters patriarchy.

BARBARA RESKIN and IRENE PADAVIC. *Women and Men at Work*, Thousand Oaks, CA: Pine Forge Press, 1994. A useful overview of the role of gender in the world of work.

WEISS, RICHARD. *The American Myth of Success: From Horatio Alger to Norman Vincent Peale*. Champaign: University of Illinois Press, 1988. This social and intellectual history of the ideology of individualism focuses on the late nineteenth and twentieth centuries.

JOHN E. WILLIAMS and DEBORAH L. BEST. *Measuring Sex Stereotypes: A Multination Study*, Newbury Park, CA: Sage, 1990. A rich and rewarding investigation of gender stereotypes around the globe.

USEFUL WEB SITES

United Students Against Sweatshops (**www.umich.edu/~sole/usas/**) is a nationwide college student organization dedicated to bringing about changes in the overseas plants that produce logo clothing for their schools.

Sweatshop Watch (**www.sweatshopwatch.org**) is a coalition of organizations and individuals committed to eliminating sweatshop conditions in the garment industry around the world.

The Institute of Labor Research at Cornell University maintains this site (**www.ilr.cornell .edu/trianglefire/navigation.html**)covering the 1911 Triangle Shirtwaist Factory disaster and the events that preceded it.

The Women's Bureau of the United States Department of Labor (**http://gatekeeper .gov.dol./wb**) is the primary source of government data on the employment of women.

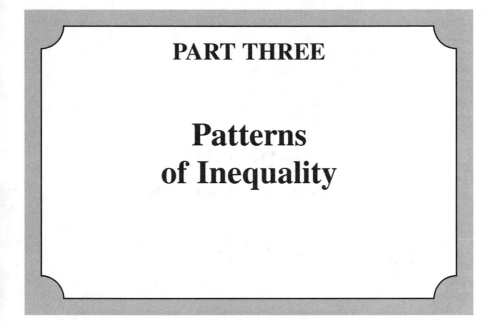

PART THREE

Patterns
of Inequality

Social class position has broad implications for individuals and groups, and economic, social, and political inequalities are among the most profound. Chapter 5 focuses on the distribution of income and wealth in industrial societies and emphasizes the disparities between the extraordinary wealth concentrated in the hands of a small number of people and the millions living in poverty. Chapter 6 explores social evaluations and rankings including occupational prestige and the dynamics of class, race, and gender in interpersonal relationships. Chapter 7 deals with access to positions of power and authority in the political system and the ability of class-oriented groups and organizations to influence the actions of the state.

CHAPTER FIVE

The Dynamics
of Economic Inequality

THE DISTRIBUTION OF INCOME AND WEALTH

Some individuals have done very well financially in recent years. New York state senator Hillary Rodham Clinton earned an $8 million advance for her book. David Pottruck, co-chief executive officer of on-line broker Charles Schwab earned $127 million in 1999 salary and bonuses. Athletes did very well too, with tennis star Venus Williams signing a $40 million endorsement deal with a sportswear company and baseball star Alex Rodriguez agreeing to a $252 million contract with the Texas Rangers. It is estimated that there are about 5 million millionaires in the United States and 267 billionaires (Puente, 2000). Obviously, not everyone enjoyed that level of success. More than 30 million people lived in poverty in every year of the 1990s, and countless others hovered near poverty because of marginal or unstable incomes. For them, financial considerations are a matter of survival, touching upon such fundamental matters as hunger and basic nutrition, medical care, and housing. The most visible segment of the poor are the homeless. Somewhere between 444,000 and 842,000 people are without shelter at any given moment, and about one-third are families with children (Wolf, 2000).

Between these extremes is a broad range of middle-income families, who are able to enjoy a comfortable standard of living that includes home ownership, an array of consumer goods, decent health care, and provision for the education of their children. However, it is not always a safe and secure income. Most people depend upon their jobs for the bulk of their income, and the ongoing restructuring of the workplace results in the continual disappearance of jobs. Consequently, just about one-half of all Americans worry that they or someone in their household will be laid off in the foreseeable future.

There are two different ways of measuring economic inequality in a society. Annual income counts the amount of money a family makes in a year from salaries and investments, and net worth includes the value of all forms of wealth and possessions. Both confirm the existence of a wide gulf between the privileged and the disadvantaged in the United States and other industrial nations.

ANNUAL INCOME

The most basic way of visualizing the scope of financial inequality is to focus on the total **annual income** of families. This measure takes into account wages and salaries, investments in stocks and bonds, and other direct sources of income. Households are the unit of analysis in calculating income to accommodate families with multiple earners and the situation of dependent children. The most common way of highlighting discrepancies among income levels is to divide the population into quintiles (fifths) and compute the share of total income earned by each of the five income groups, as shown in Exhibit 5.1. Using this approach shows that the lowest fifth earns less than 4 percent of the total income while the highest fifth takes in

EXHIBIT 5.1   Share of Annual Income Held by Families in the United States

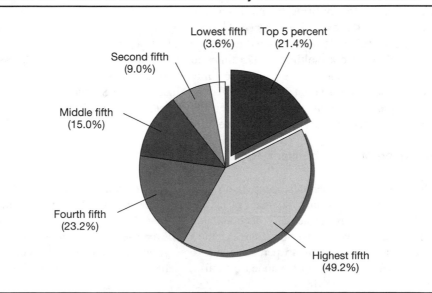

Lowest fifth (3.6%)
Top 5 percent (21.4%)
Second fifth (9.0%)
Middle fifth (15.0%)
Fourth fifth (23.2%)
Highest fifth (49.2%)

Source: U.S. Bureau of the Census. *The Changing Shape of the Nation's Income Distribution, 1947–98.* Current Population Report P60–204. Washington, DC: U.S. Government Printing Office, 2000.

almost 50 percent of the total money income. The top 5 percent of families earns 21 percent of all income. The 60 percent of families in the middle divide the remaining 46 percent of income.

Notable among the people in the top quintile are sports and entertainment figures and corporate executives who form a part of an institutional elite of multimillionaires. Corporate executives are at the core of the economic elite. A recent survey of compensation packages (salary, bonus, stock options, golden parachutes) shows that nineteen business executives earned at least $50 million, and for the top six it was over $100 million, with one getting about three-quarters of a billion dollars (Reingold, 2000). Among the nineteen with the highest pay were:

Charles Wang (Computer Associates)	$665,424,000
Steven Case (America Online)	$117,085,000
Jack Welch (General Electric)	$ 93,138,000
Charles Schwab (Charles Schwab)	$ 69,096,000
Michael Eisner (Walt Disney)	$ 50,657,000

The average compensation for CEOs at the 362 largest American businesses was $12.4 million, an increase of 17 percent from the year before. The chief executive officers of the so-called "new economy" companies linked to the digital revolution averaged $27.5 million compared to $7.1 million for old economy firms (Leonhardt, 2000).

This compares with an average increase of 3.4 percent for factory workers and 3.5 percent for white-collar workers, further widening the gap between the people at the top and bottom of firms that has been developing for two decades. It is estimated that in 1980 top executives earned 42 times the income of the average factory worker, but that ratio had escalated to 209 times that of average factory workers in 1996 and reached a multiple of 475 times in 1999 (Bryne, 1996; Reingold, 1997, 2000). The magnitude of the gap in the United States dwarfs that found around the world as shown in Exhibit 5.2. Several Latin American and Southeast Asian countries pay executives 40 to 50 times their employees' earnings, but European and Japanese chiefs typically earn a multiple of only 10 to 25.

Widening the Gap between Rich and Poor

The majority of households occupy a broad middle-income range that allows families to enjoy a comfortable standard of living. However, the overall position of middle-income groups has actually declined as the share of income earned by the top earners has increased. Over the course of the 1990s the average real income of high-income families grew by 15 percent, while average income remained the same for low-income families and expanded by only 2 percent for middle-income families (Bernstein, et al., 2000).

The widening of the income gap has continued through periods of expansion and recession and during successive Republican and Democratic administrations,

EXHIBIT 5.2   Chief Executives' Pay Around the World, 1999

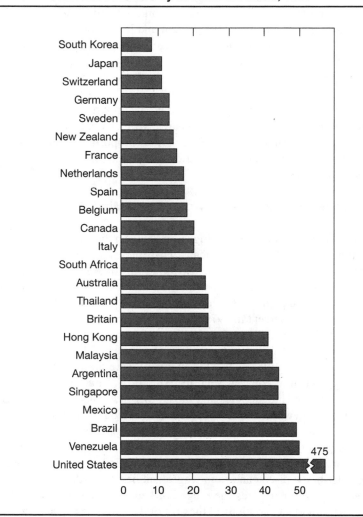

Note: Values are a multiple of manufacturing employees' pay.

Source: "Executive pay," *The Economist* (September 30): 110. © The Economist Newspaper Group, Inc. Reprinted with permission. Further reproduction prohibited. www.economist.com

suggesting that the widening gap is grounded in fundamental shifts in the economic system. Moreover, it is a pattern being repeated around the world, in Britain, Brazil, and Guatemala (Crossette, 1996). This trend is the product of a changing class structure. A disproportionate share of new jobs being created are either upper middle class, high-skill professional and managerial work or lower-end service and white collar work. The wages for jobs demanding high skills and low skills are diverging. To illustrate, wages for male high school graduates *declined* by 17 percent between

1979 and 1992, while earnings for college graduates *increased* by 5.2 percent during the same period (Kilborn, 1995). Female workers fared somewhat better, with college graduates' incomes rising by 19 percent and high school graduates improving marginally by .9 percent. In both cases, wages for the better educated are rising much faster than for the least educated.

The discrepancy between the extremes in the economic hierarchy is also accentuated by emergence of dual-income families with both spouses in professional and business positions. The expansion of occupational opportunities for college-educated women is a major consideration in this area. Women once excluded from well-paying careers by discrimination now hold a serious proportion of such jobs. If they are married to men in similar lucrative positions their combined earnings create very high income households.

The Earnings Gap: Lower Pay for Women and Minorities

There is a persistent and enduring **earnings gap** between the earnings of women and men, and among whites, African Americans, Hispanics, and other minority groups. To illustrate, median earnings for women working full-time in 1999 were $27,370, compared to $37,574 for men. A review of women's earnings over the last two decades reveals a mixed picture (Bowler, 1999). The magnitude of the earnings gap narrowed from about 62 percent in 1979 to about 76 percent at the end of the 1990s. The narrowing of the gap was due to an increase of 14 percent in women's earnings combined with a decline of 7 percent among male workers. The gap is narrower for younger women and for college-educated women. There are also conspicuous differences among women of color, as seen in Exhibit 5.3. Thus, although the gender gap is narrowing in the United States and most other industrial nations, it has yet to be fully eliminated anywhere. For example, a comparison of wages in manufacturing industries in twenty-seven nations show that women's pay in the early 1970s stood at 67 percent of men's and had improved to only 74 percent at the end of the twentieth century (Sivard, 1995). Women in Sweden called a one-day national strike to protest gender-based discrepancies in wages and benefits (Kalette, 1991).

The earnings gap compares the wages of year-round, full-time workers and therefore masks important variations in the size of the earnings gap at different class levels and in different demographic groups. The earnings gap is, for example, narrower for each younger age cohort, standing at about 90 percent for women under 25 compared to 73 percent for 35- to 44-year-olds and 68 percent for females aged 55 to 64 (Bowler, 1999). Younger women tend to have higher educational credentials than older workers, which makes them more competitive, but it also suggests that women beginning their careers are rewarded more equitably than those who entered the labor market earlier. The earnings gap is also narrower for racial and ethnic minorities. White women earn about 71 percent of white men, but the gap is 83 percent for African Americans and 96 percent for Hispanics.

There are also occupational differences. The most pronounced earnings gap is found in sales work, where women earn only 60 percent of men. Occupational

EXHIBIT 5.3 Women's Earnings as a Percentage of Men's Earnings, by Race and Ethnicity: The United States, 1960–1994

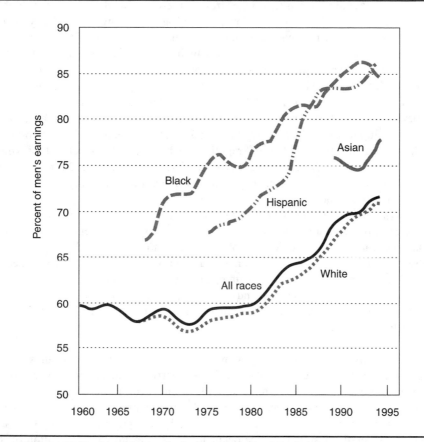

Source: Suzanne M. Bianchi and Daphne Spain, *Women, Work and Family in America*, Washington, DC: Population Reference Bureau, 1996, Figure 5 and Table 8, pages 24 and 25.

segregation plays a major role in explaining this situation because women are concentrated in retail sales while men are much more likely to be in more lucrative fields such as insurance and securities. The gap is also wide in working-class jobs, where women earn about 70 cents for every dollar earned by men and where there is also significant segregation. A similar discrepancy shows up in upper-middle-class managerial work, where men dominate higher levels in the managerial hierarchy. The gap is narrowest at the bottom of the stratification system in service workers and laborers, where women average between 85 percent and 90 percent of men's earnings.

When median earnings for blacks and whites are compared over time it is clear that measurable progress has been made since the 1950s. That was a decisive period for it signaled the beginning of the collapse of patterns of overt discrimination stretching back to the days of slavery. Exclusionary and discriminatory practices combined to exclude African Americans from white-collar work and the more highly paid professional and craft occupations, as well as producing unequal pay scales within similar jobs. Until that point blacks averaged less than half the earnings of whites. The data for 1939, the first year for which there are comprehensive statistics, document the burden of racism. Black men earned an average of 45 percent of what white males earned, and black women 38 percent of what white women earned (U.S. Bureau of the Census, 1979: 136). The earnings gap for black men narrowed to about 60 percent in the 1960s and reached 72 percent in 1979, but gains have been extremely sluggish since, currently standing at about 75 percent. The situation for black women has improved more rapidly, reaching about 90 percent of white women's earnings by the end of the 1970s, but has stagnated since. Moreover, they too are still burdened by the gender gap, meaning that they earn only about 83 percent of what black men earn.

No single factor explains the earnings gap. It is rather the result of a combination of conditions. Among the most significant are occupational segregation, educational levels, job tenure, and demographic considerations. Statistical analysis makes it possible to estimate the amount women and minorities would earn if they had comparable education and employment patterns, but such studies always reveal that there is an unexplained difference that must be interpreted as the result of discrimination—both overt and unintentional—which produces lower pay and hinders opportunities for advancement.

Occupational Segregation.   A major factor explaining the earnings gap is employment patterns. Despite the erosion of barriers that historically excluded women and people of color from some fields of endeavor, these groups still do not hold the same jobs. Both groups continue to be underrepresented in the better-paid professional, managerial, high-skill craft jobs, and overrepresented among low paying clerical, retail sales, and service occupations. For example, a tabulation of the principal occupations of women shows that four out of ten women are concentrated in just ten occupations (e.g., traditional women's occupations such as secretary, elementary school teacher, and nurse, as well as low-paying clerical jobs such as cashier) (Reskin & Padavic, 1994). This pattern holds true for Hispanic, Asian, and African-American women as well.

Occupational segregation is even more invidious than it might appear because not only do workers enter these occupations at low entry-level salaries, but they are less able to improve their earnings over time by the personal strategies which American ideology proclaims as the means to upward mobility—education and work experience. Economists are fond of referring to this as "returns on human capital," measuring the income increments associated with more education or longer work experience. The fact is that clerical, service, and sales work, and less skilled blue-collar work, do not yield significant financial returns to people who have formal education or longer work experience. In large part this is due to the fact that most of these are low-ceiling careers, lacking in meaningful promotion opportunities for higher-paying positions.

Education.   Formal educational credentials are a prerequisite to access to most higher-paying jobs in management and the professions. The earnings gap encompasses workers of several generations, and up until the 1970s fewer women earned college and professional degrees than men. Although women currently earn more than one-half of the bachelor's degrees, they still lag behind in professional degrees and Ph.D.s (necessary for careers in academics and the sciences). Advanced education opens doors to better-paying occupations but is no guarantee of more equitable wages because the earnings gap for women in the United States persists at every educational level. To illustrate, college-educated women earn $36,700 compared to $48,828 for men (Bowler, 1999). In short, despite diminishing differences in educational attainments, more formal education simply does not translate into better pay for women.

Differential educational attainments also handicap black workers (Tomaskovic-Devey, 1993b). Blacks generally bring lower levels of formal educational attainment to the labor market and are thus more likely to be channeled toward lower-paid work. However, it also important to emphasize that blacks simply do not earn the same economic rewards on education that whites do. It has long been observed that blacks are destined to earn less at every educational level compared to white workers. Some attribute this to an inferior quality of preparation in the schools attended by blacks, but it has also been argued that it may have less to do with the actual value of their education credentials and more likely may be attributed to employers' assumption that blacks' schools, curricula, and courses are less rigorous. This may be a disguised form of racial discrimination used as a rationale for limiting promotion opportunities or not paying wages similar to those for whites in comparable positions.

Intermittent Careers.   Also to be considered is the fact that women are more likely than men to interrupt their careers, usually to assume responsibility for young children or aging parents. Disruption of work careers can be costly. One study that compared American women with steady employment histories and comparable women with irregular careers indicated those returning to work initially earned about 33 percent less than women who never left the labor force (Jacobsen & Levin, 1995). Moreover, this gap persists for decades. Women experiencing a hiatus in their careers earn about 5 to 7 percent less twenty years later.

Many reasons account for this pattern. Intermittent work careers means that men accumulate more seniority and job-specific experience, which translate into higher wages. Loss of seniority also renders workers more vulnerable to layoffs under "last hired, first fired" rules. There is also the potential for job skills to atrophy during absence from the workplace. Many white-collar occupations, such as banking, which employs large numbers of women, are undergoing dramatic changes flowing from the introduction of electronic data processing, which places returning workers at a competitive disadvantage. Finally, absence from a job can penalize workers by the simple fact that they are not physically there to be considered for salary increments or more importantly, promotions to better positions. It is no coincidence that the peak years of child-bearing and child-rearing (twenty-five to thirty-five) coincide exactly with the years in which employers are making fateful decisions about the futures of its younger employees. There may also be a subtle form of employer bias at work in that supervisors may view gaps in work history as a sign that women may leave again and thus be less willing to promote them into positions with greater responsibility and rewards.

Demographic Factors.   Some of the earnings differential has its origin in the demographic characteristics of the African-American and Hispanic populations. Age is one consideration, for they are on the average younger, and youthful workers regardless of race or gender earn relatively less. The geography of residence also seems to work against African Americans. A large percentage reside in the South where earnings are on the whole lower than in other regions. In fact, some of the overall income gains reflect patterns of migration out of the South beginning in the 1960s, leading to some degree of optimism for the future. Urban residence also puts blacks at a disadvantage as job opportunities in the better-paying manufacturing sector are lost, being replaced by poorer-paying service work.

Earnings for black women have been approaching parity with that of white women much more rapidly than among male workers. In fact, in some areas median income is actually balanced in their favor, something almost never found among their male counterparts. As more and more black women have been able to break the barriers that held them in the traditional domain of domestic work in favor of blue-collar and lower white-collar jobs, their overall position has improved while African-American males have not made similar progress. It is possible that, by a sad and ironic twist, the improved position of black women may have its origins in the sociocultural heritage of American racism and discrimination. Young black women attach great importance to work as a part of their adult roles and anticipate a lengthy working career, probably because they can anticipate low earnings for themselves and their future husbands (Hudis, 1977). In the face of anticipated discrimination, women develop a powerful commitment to work and the income-producing aspects of labor, thus expending considerable effort to find and keep jobs which can be translated into greater rewards.

Discrimination.   Discrimination against women in the workplace, as elsewhere in society, has its origins in attitudes and beliefs prevalent in the larger society. One salient attitude is the very fundamental issue of whether or not women, especially those with young children, should even be in the labor market. It is a question that involves both money and social roles. The traditional division of labor that prevailed during much of this century imposed responsibility for the family upon women and responsibility for providing economic support upon men. This can have negative consequences for women if it causes employers to doubt the appropriateness of working females. It can mean that men will be given preference for jobs and promotions on the grounds that they must support families. The other dimension is parental, the belief that maternal employment detracts from time for the family and is a factor in the breakdown of the family. Studies confirm that many people believe that having a mother in the labor force is detrimental to their children (Greenberger, et al., 1988).

Another form of bias relates to the question of the correspondence between gender traits and occupational requirements. Simply put, traits attributed to women are assumed to be inconsistent with the traits necessary for success in the field. Such thinking generalizes to all members of a social category, ignoring individual differences and abilities. Moreover, it is often based on unverified assumptions about the traits needed to succeed in an occupation. For example, male police academy recruits preparing for the hazards of their work often equate their own personal safety with physical strength. Consequently, there is some reluctance to accept women as partners, despite the fact that the record shows injury or death is seldom a matter of physical prowess but rather a failure to follow established procedures (Remmington, 1981).

NET WORTH: MEASURING HOUSEHOLD ASSETS

An alternative way of measuring monetary inequality is to focus on the distribution of the finances and other resources of households. **Net worth** refers to the total value of privately held assets, including money in bank accounts; real estate; stocks, bonds, and securities; personal property in the form of vehicles, homes, and furnishings; the value of pension plans and life insurance; and equity in a business or profession after debts in the form of home mortgages, car loans, student loans, and credit card debt. The average value of household assets in the United States was $175,485 (the median was $39,146) in the mid 1990s, the last years for which reliable data are available (Keister & Moller, 2000). For most families, the largest share of their net worth is based on the equity in their homes. The household is also the unit of analysis in calculating private wealth because resources are typically held jointly between spouses.

The distribution of net worth is even more pronounced than that of annual income (Exhibit 5.4). The wealthiest one-fifth of households hold more than 80 percent of the total private assets in the society in the 1990s, and the top 1 percent alone holds more than 38 percent! That leaves less than 20 percent of wealth to be shared among 80 percent of the population. The bottom two-fifths of the society have less than one-half of one percent of the wealth. Moreover, a total of 19 percent of households either had no assets or had debts that exceeded assets.

Thus, it is possible to isolate a small segment of the society who have been able to amass great wealth, either on the basis of their own efforts or inheritance or some combination of the two. Wealth of this magnitude confers great advantages. It offers both long- and short-term financial security that can only be imagined among

**EXHIBIT 5.4   Share of Total Net Worth, by Position in the Distribution
of Wealth**

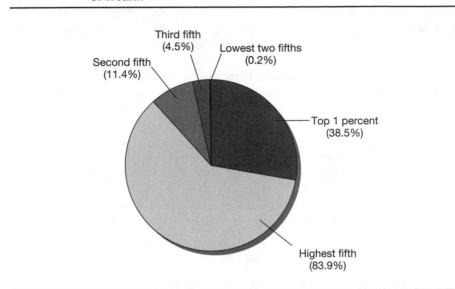

Source: Complied from government data reported by Lisa A. Keister and Stephanie Moller, "Wealth inequality in the United States." *Annual Review of Sociology*, 2000.

those who work for a living. In addition, wealth on this scale can be used to generate more wealth, and legal strategies are available to minimize taxes and pass assets to future generations. Wealth also means social prestige and can be translated into political influence (Keister & Moller, 2000). Thus, these inequalities in assets mean much more than mere purchasing power.

POVERTY

In 1962 Michael Harrington published *The Other America*, a scathing exposé of poverty in the midst of prosperity. The sad fact is that the book continues in print even today, decades later, standing as a stark reminder of the persistence of poverty in rich industrial nations. The number of the people living in poverty fluctuates over time, and specific individuals escape impoverishment, but the conditions that produce poverty seem intractable because those who break out of poverty are replaced by others.

In an abstract sense, the word **poverty** implies the lack of resources necessary to maintain a decent standard of living. However, it is difficult in practice to establish a dollar amount that defines poverty because it is an issue shaped by personal values and obscured by ideology and politics. One social scientist, for example, estimates that a family of four in the late 1990s needs an income of $27,000 for a minimally acceptable standard of living (Schwarz, 1997). Some European nations have attacked the problem by calculating a "decency threshold" that seeks to set a monetary value on sustaining a decent standard of living including proper food, clothing, shelter, and an occasional movie. It is set at 68 percent of average earnings and leaves 3 million British working women below the decency threshold (Hill, 1996).

The most widely used measure of poverty in the United States is the poverty threshold. **Poverty thresholds** are a continuation of original federal poverty measures first established in the 1960s by the federal government and updated annually to accommodate inflation.[1] This is the figure that typically shows up in official estimates of the number of Americans in poverty each year. The calculation of the poverty threshold began with establishing the cost of a minimal, nutritionally adequate, food budget and multiplied that figure by three (poorer families typically devoted one-third of their income to food) to allow for non-food items. It was based on an original plan developed by the Department of Agriculture as an emergency budget for families short of money, not one that would be satisfactory over long periods of time. A higher, alternative food budget was considered but rejected, in part because it would elevate the number of poor to a politically unacceptable level (Fisher, 1992). Poverty thresholds and guidelines are adjusted annually for increases in consumer prices, and in 1999 stood at $8,501 for a single individual and $17,029 for a family of four.[2]

The threat of poverty in America reached its peak in the Depression years of the 1930s when upwards of 25 percent of the labor force was unemployed. Estimates suggest that as many as two-thirds of the nation was mired in poverty in 1939 because the economy had not yet recovered from the worldwide depression that threw millions of people out of work (Ross, Danziger & Smolensky, 1987). World War II and postwar prosperity steadily reduced the proportion of poor Americans. The government began to tabulate official statistics in 1959, and Exhibit 5.5 shows that both the rate of poverty and the number of people living in poverty declined steadily through the 1960s and into the early 1970s. Beginning at that point the poverty rate stabilized at 10 to 15 percent. In contrast, population growth meant that the number of people in poverty began to increase, reaching a peak of about 40 million people early in the 1990s. The period of extended prosperity that began soon after was reflected in fewer people in poverty, but there are still over 30 million poor people in America.

---

[1]A number of other terms are frequently encountered in discussions of the nature and scope of poverty. *Poverty guidelines* are a simplification of poverty thresholds and are used for administrative purposes such as determining eligibility for certain federal programs such as Head Start. The *near poor* are people with incomes between 100 percent and 150 percent of the poverty level. They are the group most vulnerable to falling into poverty. *Extreme poverty* refers to those 15 million Americans (40 percent of the poverty population) with incomes of less than 50 percent of poverty thresholds. Children, people in female-headed households, and minorities are most likely to be living in extreme poverty (O'Hare, 1996: 29).

[2]Up-to-date poverty thresholds are available on line at http://www.census.gov/poverty/threshld/.

EXHIBIT 5.5   The Number of Poor and the Poverty Rate in the United States, 1959–1998

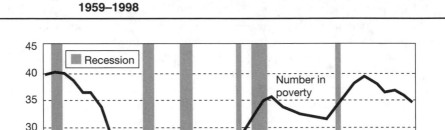

Note: Numbers in millions, rates in percent.

Source: U.S. Bureau of the Census, Current Population Reports, Series P60-207, *Poverty in the United States.* Washington, DC: U.S. Government Printing Office, 2000. Figure 1, page viii.

The Risk of Poverty

The data show that 30 million people have faced poverty in any given year. Some do climb out of poverty, only to be replaced by others who slip into poverty. The fact is, virtually no one is exempt from the threat of poverty. Any of a number of critical life transitions can suddenly thrust people into poverty. Joblessness is the most obvious cause, and the 1990s was a period of major restructuring and downsizing that caused millions of jobs to disappear. Births and drastic family disruptions brought about by death, divorce, or abandonment is the other major factor that can tip the balance between abundance and impoverishment.

Poverty is not an isolated event that happens only to members of an urban underclass. The majority of Americans will encounter poverty on a first-hand basis during their lives; either they or some member of their family or their friends and neighbors will fall into poverty. By age 35 nearly one-third of the population will have spent at least one year below the poverty line (Rank & Hirschi, 1999). By age 65 that proportion will rise to more than one-half and by age 85 will reach two-thirds. The racial discrepancy in poverty risk is even more striking (Exhibit 5.6).

EXHIBIT 5.6   Cumulative Lifetime Risk of Poverty, by Race

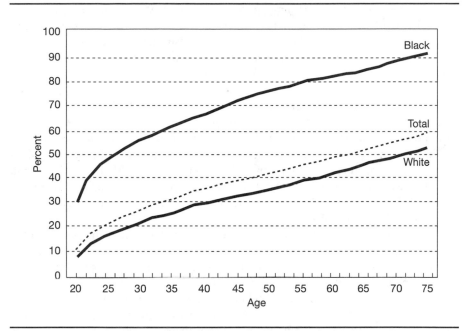

Source: Mark R. Rank and Thomas A. Hirschi. 1999. "The likelihood of poverty across the American life span." *Social Work* 44: 211, Figure 1. Copyright 1999, National Association of Social Workers, Inc.

More than one-half of the African-American population has faced an episode of poverty by age 26 and more than 90 percent by their mid-70s. Latinos also have a high risk of poverty, although data on cumulative risk are not available.

Gender and Poverty.   Women in America are at a somewhat greater risk of falling into poverty than men, and that has not changed significantly over the last several decades. It is a situation repeated in most industrial nations, although the discrepancy is narrower (Casper, McLanahan & Garfinkle, 1994). Women are at greater risk because the burdens of changes in family status such as births, divorce, or separation fall more heavily on them. Births increase the vulnerability to poverty by imposing additional financial burdens on parents, as well as causing some women to discontinue their schooling or leave the labor force to assume child care responsibilities. Divorced women usually suffer greater financial hardship than divorced men. Typically, the household income (per family member) of women declines by about 24 percent, while that for men drops by only 6 percent (Bianchi & Spain, 1997). Many different factors produce this disparity. Wives not in the paid labor force during the duration of the marriage are handicapped when subsequently seeking work, while husbands enjoy the financial benefits of work experience and seniority accumulated during marriage. Those in the paid labor force, or who enter it after divorce, confront the earnings gap that means they will earn approximately three-fourths of men's earnings. The death of a spouse also increases the risk of poverty for women. The chances are greater because they earned less on average during their working lives and because they are less likely to have private pension plans. Moreover, it is very difficult for older women to escape poverty through reemployment or remarriage.

The large number of female-headed families is another factor. While most will eventually marry, they must assume major responsibility for child care for some period of time. Moreover, many single mothers are teenagers, and the presence of children can increase the chances of terminating their education, thus limiting their futures and channeling them to lower-paying work. Women who do not finish high school have a much greater chance of being poor (38 percent) than men (27 percent). Single mothers with limited education often cannot find work that covers the cost of child care (O'Hare, 1996).

Alimony and child-support programs were, in part, originally designed to alleviate the financial burdens on nonemployed spouses after divorce. The program in practice falls short of its original goal because not all former spouses meet their financial obligations. Approximately one-half of all spouses receive full payment, but one-quarter get partial payment and one-quarter get nothing from absent fathers (U.S. Bureau of the Census, 1993). Mothers living with children of an absent father have a poverty rate of 35 percent, more than four times the rate for married couples with children.

Children and the Elderly.   A frequently overlooked characteristic of the poor is that less than half are of working age. About 40 percent of the poor are children and youths aged 18 and under. This translates into 13 million youngsters living in poverty, including some 5 million under age 6. Poverty exacts a heavy toll on children. Studies have shown that children raised in continual poverty have lower vocabulary and reading achievement and exhibit more behavior problems than the nonpoor or even those who experience shorter episodes of poverty (Duncan, Brookes-Gunn & Klebanov, 1994; Korenman, Miller & Sjaastad, 1995). Thus, childhood poverty weakens the chance of acquiring the cognitive skills necessary to succeed in school and the workplace.

The presence of children increases the risk of poverty for the family. The obvious reason is that children increase the financial burdens on families, but there are also child-care problems that cause many parents to leave the workforce. Quality child care is difficult to find for low-income people and can consume as much as 20 percent of their incomes. Thus, affordable child care is often the decisive factor in preventing low-income mothers from participating in the labor force.

About 10 percent of those living in poverty are aged 65 or older. In contrast to the problem of persistent poverty among the young there has been a pronounced decline in the proportion of the aged among the poor from 15 percent in the 1960s to less than 10 percent in the new century, despite the fact that more Americans are living longer. The expansion of federal programs such as Social Security and Medicare are responsible for much of the progress, along with the expansion of private pension plans. The risk of poverty among the aged has not been eliminated, but it has been reduced.

Rural Poverty.   Although urban, center-city poverty is the most visible, poverty is not exclusively a metropolitan problem but also reaches small towns and rural areas. In fact, rural areas have a very large share of poverty (22 percent) considering the relatively small number of people living in such areas. The reason is that many rural communities lack competitive educational systems and stable employment opportunities. Those jobs that do exist tend to be in low-paying manufacturing, service, and agricultural work.

The Working Poor.   The poor are repeatedly perceived as lacking the will to work or to take the actions necessary to escape poverty. Actually, many of the poor are either too young or too old to work, are disabled, or have child-care responsibilities. Focusing on the adult working-age poor (ages 22 to 64) shows that about one-half worked at some point during the year. Twenty percent of poor adults worked at year-round jobs, and 28 percent worked for at least some part of the year. These are the **working poor**, people in the labor force who do not earn enough to lift themselves or their families out of poverty. The working poor includes those unable to find regular, stable jobs and those who earn below poverty-level wages. The minimum wage (currently at $5.15 per hour) is a handy symbol of the problem for the working poor. Working forty hours a week for 52 weeks a year yields only $10,712, just about the poverty threshold for a two-person family.[3]

If there is any optimism in the poverty picture it is that most episodes of poverty are relatively short. Detailed analysis of the experiences of people in poverty shows that the median duration of poverty is 4.5 months (Naifeh, 1998). This means that most people are able to confront the problems that produced their poverty and reestablish their lives. Displaced workers find new jobs, the disruption of families is overcome, and child care is arranged. Unemployment insurance and social welfare programs such as Aid to Families with Dependent Children (AFDC) can facilitate the process. Unfortunately, poverty is a long-term problem for the remainder. Twenty-five percent are poor for more than a year, 13 percent are mired in poverty for more than two full years. A small group of the poor are trapped in long-term poverty. The term **persistent poverty** is often used to describe those who remain poor for long periods of time, usually at least five continuous years. This phrase highlights the fact that some people face the bleak prospect of unremitting poverty.

---

[3]Only about 5 percent of hourly workers' wages are at or below the minimum wage, and a large proportion of those are young single workers, but this group also includes many single parents, people over 65, and spouses supplementing family incomes.

CASE STUDY
The Chances of Escaping Poverty

Every year some people living in poverty are able to rise above the poverty threshold while some become poor. There are 5 to 6 million people in each category each year (Naifeh, 1998). Thus, poverty in America must be understood as a complex structural problem, with a continuous circulation of individuals and families falling into and escaping from poverty. The chances of escaping poverty are not equal, and studies reveal some interesting patterns (Exhibit 5.7). Minorities have less chance of leaving poverty than whites, as do the young and the old, who are more likely to be mired in poverty than the 19 to 64 age group. The group with the greatest chance of escaping poverty are young adults (18 to 24), most of whom are completing their education and seeking employment. And, as might be expected, employment is a major factor in understanding the dynamics of poverty. Over one-half of the adults who remain in poverty from one year to the next are unemployed in both years. Fifteen percent of those unemployed in both years escape poverty, usually as a result of a change in family status or increased earnings by another family member, but the most significant exit rates among those who worked occurred either by their getting a better-paying job or by working more hours.

EXHIBIT 5.7   People Escaping Poverty

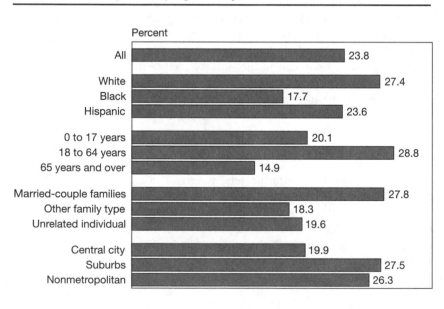

Source: Mary Naifeh. *Trap door? Revolving Door? Or Both?* U.S. Bureau of the Census, Current Population Reports, P-70-63. Washington, DC: U.S. Government Printing Office, 1998.

Social Welfare Programs

Federal, state, and local governments sponsor a wide variety of programs aimed at helping the poor and low-income Americans.[4] The first major wave of social welfare programs emerged out of the turmoil of the Great Depression in the 1930s with plans such as AFDC and unemployment insurance. Medicare and other programs came later as part of the "war on poverty" in the 1960s. By the mid-1990s the federal government devoted over $200 billion to some seventy welfare programs. Most federal money was designed to support people who are poor rather than help them out of poverty. Only 10 percent of means-tested money went to education and training programs that could foster self-sufficiency (O'Hare, 1996).

By the 1990s the welfare system had lost its legitimacy with major segments of the public and legislatures, resulting in strong political pressure to cut government spending. Many people doubted that the existing system could solve the problem of poverty, and some worried that it even perpetuated poverty and dependency. The result was the Personal Responsibility and Work Opportunity Reconciliation Act of 1996. The legislation cut spending, granted more responsibility to the states, and set restrictions on eligibility. Among the most notable restrictions are time limits on cash assistance, such as two years for able-bodied adults, and a five-year lifetime limit for 80 percent of a state's welfare recipients. One obvious goal is to move people off welfare and into the labor force, and therefore states are required to enroll 50 percent of welfare families in job training by the year 2002.

The welfare reform act generated much debate. On one side are those who believe it will motivate the poor to take the initiative and lift themselves out of poverty. Those who oppose it worry that the lack of meaningful opportunities will mean that the poor will be further impoverished. The full impact of welfare reform will not be felt for years as programs are developed and restrictions phased in, but it is clear that less money will be devoted to social welfare programs in the future, which could mean more people will fall below the poverty level and others could have their modest living standards further reduced.

HOMELESSNESS: LIFE ON THE STREETS

The most touching segment of the poor are the homeless. There is some debate over the specific number who go without shelter, either sporadically or continuously. No one knows precisely how many Americans are homeless, but estimates range up to 800,000 persons living in shelters or on the street on any given night. In addition, some homeless advocates warn that millions more are living on the edge, "one paycheck or one domestic argument from the streets." Whatever the exact number, the

---

[4]Programs specifically focused on low-income people are called "means-tested" because recipients must meet minimum income tests in order to qualify for benefits. For example, families with incomes 130 percent of the poverty threshold are eligible for food stamps.

homeless qualify as the poorest of the poor, for "not only do they lack material resources, but they lack human resources as well—friends or family who will take them in" (Piliavin, Sosin & Westerfelt, 1987–1988: 20).

What is striking about the street people is their diversity—young and old, black and white, families and individuals, women and men are without homes. The homeless population is somewhat different in each locality, a response to local social, economic and political conditions, but it is possible to sketch some broad overall patterns based on multiple city surveys done by various government and private agencies (Puente, 1993; Moss & Dickson, 1994; Burt & Aron, 1999).

More than two-thirds of the homeless are men, many of them single adult males. In some cities they make up more than half the homeless population. Many are Vietnam-era veterans, and many suffer from problems ranging from mental illness to substance abuse. Most are middle-aged or younger. There are very few older people—men or women—among the homeless for two reasons: first, because the elderly qualify for Social Security, Medicaid, and other age-related benefits, and second, because of the grim reality that the mortality rate for the long-term homeless is so high that few survive to old age.

About one-third are families with children, and a large group are young, lower-blue-collar families, typically thrown onto the streets by joblessness. Many are single parents, and 77 percent of the single parents are women, a large proportion of whom are abused or battered women, evicted or seeking to escape from violent domestic arrangements. The children in these families are at risk for psychological distress, unusually high rates of depression, anxiety, and reduced self-esteem. Most children are members of family units, but there is also a core of unaccompanied children (about 4 or 5 percent, with equal numbers of boys and girls) counted among the homeless. They are typically runaways or "throwaways" (abandoned or evicted children) fleeing abusive homes, and all-too-often reduced to crime or prostitution to survive. There are also high rates of pregnancy and substance abuse among these youths.

Members of two minority groups are dramatically over-represented among the homeless. African Americans comprise about 11 percent of the total population, but somewhere between 40 and 45 percent of the homeless are black, with rates even higher in some cities. In New York City, blacks are 17 times more likely to be homeless than whites, while in Philadelphia it is a factor of 21 (*The Economist*, 1997a). In New York, black children under age 5 are 33 times more likely to end up in a shelter than white children. Native Americans form 1 percent of the population, but 8 percent of the homeless.

Sources of Homelessness

Homelessness is the result of the interplay among a number of social and economic forces. Among the most important are poverty, unemployment, increases in the incidence of troubled individuals, abusive and broken families, and the limited availability of low-income housing.

As would be expected, poverty and unemployment drives many people onto the streets. However, some of the homeless (one in five) are the working poor, employed, but unable to find or afford housing. Another segment is driven to the streets and shelters by domestic circumstances. These are usually female single parents and teenagers. Divorce, abandonment, or the need to escape domestic abuse throws them on their own resources. Research shows that those most likely to become homeless are socially isolated, lacking supportive social relationships with family or friends who might be able to aid them. For example, an unusual proportion had spent some period of time in foster-care during their childhood (Piliavin, Sosin, & Westerfelt, 1987–88).

A substantial proportion of the homeless do have psychological or behavioral problems that contribute to their plight. More than 60 percent have substance abuse and/or mental health difficulties. Vietnam-era veterans are overrepresented, some suffering service-related disabilities. Substance abuse is frequent, with almost half misusing drugs and alcohol or some combination of substances. About one-quarter of the homeless have a history of mental illness. Their plight represents an ironic twist in the evolution of the care of the mentally ill, a process called **deinstitution-alization** that opened the doors of mental institutions but failed to provide alternative sources of care (Dear & Wolch, 1987). Several factors contributed to this situation. First, the assertion of patients' civil rights have made it virtually impossible for police, psychiatrists, or family members to hold people in hospitals against their will, unless they are very seriously impaired. Second, reforms in the treatment of chronic mental patients shifted the emphasis from institutional care to the idea of returning patients to the communities where they must live. Although the idea was worthy, governments failed to provide the necessary community-based outpatient facilities to help those released from institutions. Those not able to successfully adapt are left to fend for themselves on the streets.

Ultimately, the most obvious problem is inadequate affordable housing for low-income people. The average income of the homeless in the previous month in one survey was $367, compared to a U. S. average of $2,840 (Burt & Aron, 1999). Gentrification and urban renewal raze low-income housing and low-rent hotels to make way for middle-class homes, roads, and shopping centers. In other cases, property owners in inner cities allow buildings to deteriorate to a point that sets in motion the decline of whole neighborhoods. Neither governmental efforts nor private construction has kept pace with the demand for low-income housing since the 1970s. Estimates indicate there was a shortage of 4.7 million low-rent homes (6.5 million units for 11.2 low-income renters) in the United States in 1993 (Barry, 1996).

Responses to the Homeless

Americans exhibit contradictory and ambivalent attitudes toward the homeless. Compassion and caring are unmistakable in efforts to alleviate the suffering. Cities open shelters, governments devote millions of dollars to the creation of affordable housing for them, and private and religious charitable institutions and individuals provide meals. Most Americans agree that homelessness is a serious problem and worry that the problem is getting worse, and the vast majority feel there is something fundamentally wrong with a society with so many homeless people (Taylor, 1996).

In contrast, there is also a mean-spirited streak. Many places have prohibited sleeping in public places such as parks, and Chicago fenced off an underpass where the homeless had openly congregated since the Great Depression of the 1930s (Cohen & Tharp, 1999). At least two dozen communities have used the police to forcibly remove the homeless from certain sections of town. Others have enacted limits on activities associated with homelessness (Ybarra, 1996). Among them were bans on sitting on sidewalks, begging, and standing too near cash machines.

There is no single explanation of the sources of such negative responses to the impoverished, but several factors seem to operate. There are, first, practical considerations that arouse negative feelings. Aggressive begging or soliciting at cash machines, especially after dark, is admittedly intimidating within an environment of widespread urban violence. In addition, business owners complain that beggars clog the sidewalks and deter potential customers. In the courts it has become a clash between the public order and the rights of the homeless to occupy public parks and abandoned buildings, to sleep on the streets, and to beg in the streets. At a deeper level it may also reflect the pervasive effect of the dominant ideology of individualism that locates responsibility for misfortune with the individual rather than with structural problems. For example, it is not uncommon for one-third of the population to invoke personal choices and failings (aversion to work, laziness) for poverty and homelessness (Lee, Jones & Lewis, 1990).

CONCLUSION: FAVORING GREATER EQUALITY

Financial resources are, by any criteria, unequally distributed across the society. A few hundred thousand citizens enjoy substantial wealth at the same time that more than 30 million people live in poverty. Most Americans express some reservations about the current distribution of money and wealth. A full 62 percent of Americans feel that money and wealth "should be more evenly distributed among a larger percentage of the people" (Gallup Poll, 1996). The rest feel that current economic patterns are "fair" or have no opinion.

As would be expected, opinions on the fairness of the current system are shaped by class, race, and gender. Women are somewhat less likely to endorse the fairness of the current situation, as are minorities. Judgments of fairness are directly related to the size of income, with one-half the people in families earning more than $40,000 seeing the distribution of financial resources as fair, with the percentages declining to only 16 percent of those in the $10,000 or less income bracket. It is not surprising that perceptions of the fairness of the stratification system are defined by the size of the rewards people earn from the existing system.

KEY CONCEPTS

annual income	homelessness	poverty
deinstitutionalization	net worth	poverty thresholds
earnings gap	persistent poverty	working poor

SUGGESTED READING

DENNY BRAUN. *The Rich Get Richer: The Rise of Income Inequality in the United States and the World*, 2nd ed. Chicago, IL: Nelson-Hall, 1997. A critical analysis of the widening gap between rich and poor around the world and the threat to the basic fabric of societies that accompany this development.

CYNTHIA M. DUNCAN, ed. *Rural Poverty in America*. Westport, CT: Praeger, 1992. An analysis of the breadth of rural poverty and the special problems that arise in attempting to deal with it.

MICHAEL HARRINGTON. *The Other America: Poverty in the United States*. New York: Macmillian, 1962. This book was instrumental in bringing the problems of poverty into the national spotlight and helped to stimulate President Lyndon Johnson's war on poverty in the 1960s.

CHRISTOPHER JENCKS. *The Homeless*. Cambridge, MA: Harvard University Press, 1994. Professor Jencks' book stresses the structural sources of homelessness—deinstitutionalization, the drug culture, and the loss of low-income housing.

MICHAEL B. KATZ. *The Undeserving Poor: From the War on Poverty to the War on Welfare*. New York: Pantheon, 1989. An examination of divergent attitudes toward the poor in American history.

WILLIAM P. O'HARE. *A New Look at Poverty in America*. Washington, DC: Population Reference Bureau, 1996. An up-to-date and comprehensive overview of the nature and scope of poverty, and the implications of recent welfare legislation.

USEFUL WEB SITES

Forbes magazine (**www.forbes.com**) publishes annual reports on the largest businesses and the 400 richest persons.

The National Coalition for the Homeless maintains this site (**http://nch.ari.net/**) with information on the sources and extent of homelessness and provides a useful bibliography to assist further research.

The U. S. Bureau of the Census (**http://www.census.gov**) is a primary source of data on income, net worth, and poverty in America. Current Populations Reports in the P-60 and P-70 series are especially valuable.

The Institute for Research on Poverty at the University of Wisconsin (**http://www.ssc.wisc.edu/irp/**) supports research on the causes and consequences of poverty. It offers an extensive publication list.

The Northwestern University/University of Chicago Joint Center for Poverty Research (**http://www.jcpr.org**) publishes a newsletter reporting on many facets of the study of poverty.

CHAPTER SIX

Social Evaluations
and Social Relations

SOCIAL EVALUATIONS

Sociologist Max Weber pointed out that individuals, families, communities, and occupations are ranked on hierarchies of social status by members of society. **Social status** is the term used to describe the combined social judgment of relative superiority or inferiority, respectability or disdain, desirability or rejection. Everyday synonyms for the same phenomena are prestige, social standing, social honor, respect, or esteem. Status represents the subjective evaluation of members of society by other members of that society using contemporary standards, values, and beliefs.

Some evaluations are based on personal performance. American society, for example, places great emphasis on musical talent and athletic prowess. Individuals with these skills can earn huge incomes and become cultural icons. Social evaluations are also based on structural position (occupation, social class, family) and social attributes (race, ethnicity, gender, age). It is fair to conclude that occupation is the most salient source of social status in urban industrial societies because occupation is used to anticipate a wealth of information about a person or family—their income, education, lifestyle, and personal attributes—and to a large extent it proves to be an accurate estimate (Nock & Rossi, 1979).

The subjective evaluation of others is important to people because they are sensitive to the judgments of those around them and prize the admiration and positive evaluation of others. Therefore, social status has the ability to influence the way individuals act, how they see themselves, and how they feel about themselves. It is obvious that people strive to improve their social status in subtle and not so subtle ways. The most transparent is conspicuous consumption in cars, clothes and accessories, and electronic gadgets in an attempt to impress others, and advertisers are quick to exploit the status value of their sneakers, pens, cars, wristwatches, and designer clothing.

The implications of social standing extend beyond the mere approbation of others, although that is important in and of itself. Social status is also an important factor in social relations. People who occupy a similar rank on status hierarchies tend to define themselves, and to be defined by others, as social equals. Therefore, in a number of situations social interaction is segregated by social status, with association concentrated among people at the same social level. This shows up in friendships and marriage patterns as well as in residential choices and membership in social clubs. It may be voluntary or the result of deliberate attempts to exclude those judged to be below them in the status hierarchy. In extreme cases people at the same class level will attempt to form exclusive communities, limiting all forms of social contact to others at the same level. Such behavior stands as a reminder that status is ultimately a judgment of social superiority and inferiority.

SOCIAL CLASS AND SOCIAL STATUS

Americans tend to divide members of society into a number of social classes, with the number depending on the way in which the question is posed. Few people see less than three classes—wealthy, middle class, and poor. Others think in terms of four classes, inserting the working class between the middle class and the poor, or five classes by making a distinction between an upper and a lower middle class. It is clear that social classes are ranked in terms of increasing social status from the poor at the bottom to the wealthy at the top. Consider the feelings of people at the upper levels toward people at lower levels. Members of more advantaged classes may exhibit indifference, compassion, or pity toward the less affluent, but it is unlikely that they envy people at the lower reaches of the stratification system.

The ranking of social classes is a complex process, involving a number of considerations. The ideology of individualism plays a role, as does income, occupation, and lifestyle (MacKenzie, 1973; Coleman & Rainwater, 1978; Jackman, 1979). Each has an independent effect and overlaps with the others.

The Ideology of Individualism

The ideology of individualism is a major factor underlying social status at both the individual and class levels. The belief that occupational success follows individual effort translates into the idea that members of higher classes deserve the respect of others for their performance. The more affluent also enjoy a more comfortable and desirable lifestyle. By the same standard, members of the lower classes are viewed as mired at the bottom of the system due to their own failures. Many of the negative attitudes toward the poor are embodied in the phrase "poor white trash" (Case Study).

Income and Lifestyle

There is no question that earnings enhance social status, and the reason is straightforward. Income determines access to necessities and luxuries. Members of the elite are without economic concerns although their wealth may decline with fluctuations in the stock market. They can enjoy virtually any home, sports car or SUV, travel, or indulgence they choose. In contrast, everyday life is a constant struggle for the poor. The things many middle-class people take for granted—decent food, a place to live, a vehicle, a vacation—are always at risk, threatened by the loss of a job or the breakup of a relationship. Middle-income families can enjoy a comfortable lifestyle because they can own a car or two, keep up mortgage payments, take vacations, and nicely furnish their homes. Yet they must often choose among access to a number of important things—entertainment, the latest electronics, child care, savings for retirement, and their children's education.

Occupation and Social Status

Occupation is perhaps the most powerful status consideration in industrial societies. Occupation is also one of the principal consideration in class placement, and social classes are thus composed of occupations of roughly similar social status. Members of occupations, sensitive to their public status, regularly devote themselves to improving or protecting the prestige of their work. For example, when the issue of lawyer advertising first reached the United States Supreme Court, opponents of professional advertising claimed that advertising would cause commercialization, undermine the lawyer's sense of dignity and self-worth, and tarnish the dignified image of the profession. It also shows up in groups' attempts to upgrade their prestige by inventing new titles for their work, as is evident in the evolution of names for those who handle the dead, from "undertaker" to "mortician" to "funeral director."

Blue-collar versus White-collar Work.   Perhaps the most fundamental division among occupations in contemporary American society is the distinction between blue-collar and white-collar work. The origin of these labels and their implications can be traced to the early stages of industrialization. Craft workers, machine operators, and laborers who toiled in the factories and mills came to be identified symbolically by the sturdy dark clothing they wore. In contrast, the owners and managers, clerks, and record keepers worked in the offices and could wear lighter-colored outfits, which confirmed that they did not soil their hands or their clothing as they worked.

Blue-collar and white-collar thus came to signify a range of differences. Office workers enjoyed cleaner and safer working conditions than those who worked the

CASE STUDY
Blaming the Poor for Being Poor: Poor White Trash

The phrase **poor white trash** combines racial and social class imagery in the form of a group of stupid and lazy families. It is a stereotype with a long history and is used to describe a number of different groups of people. It appears that the term originated early in the nineteenth century among African-American slaves who used the term to denigrate white domestic servants (Wray & Newitz, 1997). The point was that blacks' poverty was forcibly imposed by their servitude, but whites' destitution was due to their own failures, their own lack of effort. By the end of the century the term was used to identify the rural poor as degenerate hillbillies—promiscuous, lazy, violent, alcoholic, ignorant, and mentally defective due to incestuous sexual unions.[1] Eugenic researchers were actually successful in sterilizing poor rural whites on the grounds that they were "genetic defectives" (Duster, 1990).

In the 1950s the stereotype was enlarged to include the lower-middle and working-class residents of trailer parks (Berube & Berube, 1997). Inhabitants were defined as people with modest aspirations and limited occupational accomplishments, and various forms of social deviance—sexual promiscuity, domestic violence, and substance abuse—were attributed to them. Consequently, many communities passed zoning laws that banished trailer parks to the remote outskirts of cities. Today, their taste in home furnishings is the stereotypical velvet Elvis portrait, a choice readily ridiculed by the middle classes. One critic of former President Bill Clinton's family's fondness for pizza, steaks, and burgers labeled it an example of "the Clintons' trailer park tastes" (Sweeney, 1997).

Poor white trash is thus a handy stereotype for some members of the middle class. The poor are portrayed as victims of their own limitations and self-defeating behavior rather than focusing on structural limitations that inhibit the rural poor. The term conveys the idea that some whites are biologically defective and all are stupid. This, combined with their improvident behavior—substance abuse, indolence, lack of ambition—explains their position at the bottom of the stratification system and confirms the dominant ideology that rewards flow directly from hard work and talent.

---

[1] There is perhaps no better characterization than that found in James Dickey's book and the film *Deliverance*. In addition, comedian Jeff Foxworthy parodies the lifestyle of the rural Southerner.

land or operated machines. They were also likely to have more formal education because their jobs required communication skills. However, the most basic distinction then and now is the difference between manual and mental labor. Electricians, carpenters, janitors, auto mechanics, truck drivers, assembly line workers, machine operators, and laborers work with their hands; they perform manual labor. In contrast, managers, accountants, secretaries, lawyers, teachers, and salespeople perform mental or social tasks. Phrases such as "working with people" or "working with ideas or information" (rather than things) are commonly used to distinguish white-collar work from blue-collar work. A oil refinery worker has no problem making the distinction, "it's when you work with your hands rather than your brain. It's physical work, it's not mental work" (Halle, 1984: 210).

As a general rule white-collar work enjoys higher status than manual work. Historians point out that the relative prestige of the two kinds of work is deeply embedded in Western cultural traditions (Tilger, 1930). It originated with the ancient Greeks, who believed that manual work was the curse of capricious gods. Physical labor was demeaning and inferior compared to the exercise of the intellect. Therefore, work with one's hands was, whenever possible, to be avoided and relegated to subordinate classes, peasants, or slaves. Work using the mind and the intellect became the cultural ideal, a claim to respectability, and ultimately the basis of powerful status distinctions.

This status distinction continues to have relevance for the way people think about social class and themselves. White collar workers tend to depreciate those who do physical labor and feel that it is somehow demeaning to work with one's hands (Sennett & Cobb, 1977). Blue-collar workers depreciate white-collar workers, believing they do not work very hard or produce anything tangible or useful (LeMasters, 1975; Halle, 1984). Members of the working class are acutely aware of their relatively lowly position in the status hierarchy. Blue-collar workers tend to view themselves as doing decent, important, and honest work, but are very sensitive to the fact that their work does not carry the same social prestige as white-collar work. There is not much question in their minds that office work carries more status than factory work. However, they are frustrated by a lack of respect for their work and by the derogatory stereotypes used to identify them.

People tend to prefer to interact with others at the same class level. This is, in part, because people feel more comfortable associating with others at the same social level. A comment by a white-collar manager's spouse clearly reveals the relationship between social class and social relationships,

> I consider myself middle class. My husband works for a construction company in the office. Many of the construction workers make a lot more money than he does. But when we have parties at my husband's company, the ones with less education feel out of place and not at ease with the ones with more education. I think of them as working class (Coleman & Rainwater, 1978: 184).

OCCUPATIONAL PRESTIGE RANKINGS

The systematic study of the prestige of occupations originated in the 1920s among vocational counselors seeking to determine the relative social standing of different jobs. Today there is a rich and comprehensive literature on the subject. This tradition of research confirms that occupations are located on relatively stable hierarchies of prestige. Despite some individual variation, there is a high level of consensus on the relative placement of most occupations, both within nations and even in nations with markedly different religious, political, and cultural traditions (Treiman, 1977; Fredrickson, Lin & Xing, 1992).[2] Admittedly, people do tend to inflate the social standing of their own occupations and similar ones. There is also some variation in the relative weight given to different criteria, with, for example, economic rewards being a more salient criteria for people at the lower end of the stratification system while educational attainment is given more weight by those at the upper end.

Occupational prestige rankings for fifty different jobs are reported in Exhibit 6.1. This hierarchy is consistent with other studies spanning several decades and reveals some broad general patterns. Members of the upper middle class dominate the top of the scale. These are the highly educated professionals (physician, lawyer, college professor) and those holding positions of institutional power (mayor, superintendent of schools), all having scores in the 80s and 90s. Political positions in state and federal government such as governors, cabinet members, and Supreme Court justices also have high scores although they are not included in this particular study.

There is a clear point of demarcation separating lower-level, upper-middle-class occupations from the upper reaches of lower-middle-class clerical and sales workers. Clerical occupations are clearly sorted by income and skill, with private secretary rated well above general secretary, keypunch operator, and file clerk. The craft sector of the working class tends to occupy the same range of scores in the 50s and 60s as the more skilled lower middle class, although they have significantly higher earnings, which confirms that manual workers get less respect. The scores of the less skilled members of the working class fall into the 20s. The bottom of the prestige hierarchy is anchored by unskilled labor and low-paying service occupations such as janitor and domestic household workers. Not only do they suffer problems associated with financial insecurity, they are viewed with disdain.

The relative prestige accorded occupations by members of a society appears to be influenced by two analytically distinct processes. One is rooted in socialization experiences beginning in childhood and carrying on through the life cycle that teach each new generation that some occupations have more prestige than others. This is called **ascribed prestige.** In contrast, occupations also earn prestige on the basis of an evaluation process in which they are ranked on the basis of the perceived characteristics of the work. For example, as a general rule prestige is related to levels of income and education, indicating that people take these two factors into account in rating occupations. This is called **achieved prestige.**

---

[2]There are, however, conceptual and methodological considerations which demand that this research be approached with some caution. Some general titles actually encompass quite different circumstances. "Lawyer," for example, includes corporate lawyers and solo practitioners, public defenders and costly celebrity attorneys. The question of comparability of occupations in different societies is also an important consideration. For example, the role of "judge" is often organized quite differently and carries somewhat different cultural meanings in different societies. There is, in addition, a potential sampling bias in these studies because urban and educated populations tend to be overrepresented.

EXHIBIT 6.1   Social Class and Occupational Prestige

Social Class	Representative Occupations	Score
Upper Middle	Physician	96
	Mayor	92
	Lawyer	90
	College professor	90
	Superintendent of schools	88
	Stock broker	82
	Factory owner employing 2000	82
	Registered nurse	75
	High school teacher	70
	Office manager	68
	Elementary school teacher	65
	Hotel manager	64
	Social worker	63
Lower Middle	Private secretary	61
	Warehouse supervisor	56
	Dental assistant	55
	Stenographer	53
	Office secretary	51
	Bookkeeper	50
	Telephone operator	46
	Typist	45
	Post office clerk	42
	File clerk	34
Working class	Electrician	63
	Police officer	58
	Carpenter	54
	Auto mechanic	45
	Beautician	42
	Butcher	39
	Cotton farmer	32
	Assembly line worker	28
	Textile machine operator	28
	Delivery truck driver	27
	Coal miner	24
	Garbage collector	16
The Poor	Stock clerk	24
	Waitress or waiter	22
	Box packer	15
	Laundry worker	15
	Janitor	13
	Maid or household worker	12
	Salad maker in a hotel	14
	Parking lot attendant	8

Note: The range of possible scores is 0 to 100.

Source: Christine E. Bose and Peter H. Rossi, "Gender and jobs." *American Sociological Review* 48 (June, 1983): 327–328.

Ascribed Prestige.   Occupational prestige hierarchies are part of the cultural traditions of societies and are transmitted during socialization. The power of ascribed prestige is demonstrated unmistakably in the fact that very young children with little direct contact with the nature and dynamics of social stratification are sensitive to gradations of inequality and social status. It is no problem for preschoolers or first graders to distinguish between "rich" and "poor" people based on visual clues (Ramsey, 1991). Third graders give virtually the same rankings to jobs as adults do (Simmons & Rosenberg, 1971). These findings suggest that children are exposed to clues to the ranking of groups in society very early in the socialization process. The culture of a society offers many clues to the relative worth of different occupations, clues embedded in everyday social interaction and media representations. The ascription of occupational prestige is, as in the case with other forms of social learning, a combination of both conscious and deliberate attempts to convey a particular point of view, and the unintentional learning which evolves from exposure to the values and preferences shared among members of the society.

Children begin to meet representatives of many occupations very early in their lives. Jobs such as mail carrier, police officer, supermarket clerk, teacher, principal, garbage collector, and school janitor are a very real part of their social environment. Consequently, they are able to observe how people in such jobs are treated and at the same time see that they themselves are encouraged in direct and subtle ways to show more respect to some than others. People tend to exhibit deference toward members of some occupations but not others. Deference may take the form of exaggerated politeness, the use of courtesy titles ("Doctor," "Ms," "Sir," "Your honor"), providing favors, repressing disagreement, or acquiescence. In contrast, others are treated less well, conveying their relative social standing. Adults may, for example, be rude and demeaning to servers in restaurants, but respectful and deferential to their religious leaders. The sum of these interpersonal interactions will tend to reproduce the existing hierarchy of prestige. An awareness of the prestige ascribed by others seems to exert a significant influence on subsequent personal judgments about prestige (Haug & Widdison, 1975).

It seems that adults are constantly posing the question, "What are you going to be when you grow up?" Parents and grandparents, teachers, peers, and even strangers always want to know what careers children aspire to when they are old enough to enter the workforce. Adult reactions to choices such as prison guard, which might seem exciting to children, are not met with much enthusiasm and are likely to be accompanied by lectures listing the disadvantages and handicaps of such work. The prestige of other occupations is enhanced by their definition as good career choices, typified by the cliché of the proud parent, "My daughter the doctor."

The media also play a major role in shaping conceptions of occupational prestige. Children are exposed to many hours of television, and what they see molds their view of the world of work. In fact, television sometimes provides their only image of certain occupations. Most children have no direct personal contact with the work of judges, lawyers, reporters, military personnel, or corporate executives, yet these are among the roles most frequently found in TV programming, and there is some evidence that most occupational knowledge of these roles originates with television (Jeffries-Fox & Signorielli, 1978). Media portrayals thus have the potential to shape perceptions and stereotypes of jobs and shape characterizations of workers.

Much of the population is in blue-collar or service work, but such occupations are rarely seen, with their invisibility suggesting a lack of importance and value. Professionals and executives make up about one-quarter of the workforce but are 60 percent of television characters (Gable, 1993). Moreover, those blue-collar and lower white-collar workers who do appear look different—they are more likely to be overweight—and behave differently—they drink more, commit more crimes, tell more lies. However, the real villains in television are business people (Lichter, Lichter, & Rothman, 1991). They are consistently portrayed as unsavory and engaged in criminal conduct.

The role of police in society may, more than any other single occupation, be shaped by the media, and polling data suggest an ongoing decline in respect for the police. This is in part a reflection of changing fictional portrayals of the police over the last several decades (Lichter, Lichter & Rothman, 1991). Television police of the 1950s through 1970s tended to be admirable characters. The police in "Adam 12," "Dragnet," "Kojak" and "The Streets of San Francisco" were honest, hard-working, bright, likable people. By the 1980s the image of law enforcement began to include more incidents of police misconduct and violations of civil rights. At the same time, video tapes of apparent police misconduct surfaced in court cases and the news. Thus, television (via news and programming) helped convince the majority (68 percent) of Americans that police brutality is a frequent occurrence, despite the fact that only 20 percent have direct personal knowledge of anyone mistreated or abused by the police (Gallup Poll, 1991).

Achieved Prestige.   Achieved prestige focuses on a more deliberate evaluative process in which jobs are compared on various standards such as income or working conditions. It focuses on the factors that people report using in judging occupations. The underlying view is that occupations earn prestige on the basis of having desirable characteristics. This approach suggests that four broad kinds of criteria influence collective judgments. Some are self-evident and obvious, but others are more subtle and complex.

Several of the qualifications for admission to a particular kind of work are considered in determining prestige. Educational requirements are the single most significant factor in prestige scores in industrial systems (MacKinnon & Langford, 1994). This accounts for the high ranking of the professions, all of which involve lengthy formal education. Moreover, as a general rule professions which require graduate education or training (college professor, physician, scientist, lawyer) are placed above those requiring a bachelor's degree (teacher, architect, accountant). The fact that in the United States most of the crafts involve apprenticeships or extensive experience contributes to their standing above those blue-collar jobs viewed as not requiring any extensive occupational training. Jobs not having any particular educational qualifications—unskilled and service work—have the lowest prestige.

The question of the scarcity of qualified personnel may also be a factor; recall that structural-functional theory places considerable importance on this factor. Although it is difficult to assess scarcity in any objective sense, it may help to account for the generally high prestige of occupations perceived as demanding rare and special attributes such as the physical dexterity of the athlete, the analytic ability of the scientist, the humanitarianism of the social worker, or the creative impulse of the artist.

Occupations earn prestige on the basis of the tasks involved and working conditions. Physically dirty (janitor) or unsafe (coal miner) work tends to be devaluated. Routine and repetitive work (assembly line jobs) has less prestige than work which is interesting and creative (electrician). Jobs involving the supervision, evaluation, and direction of subordinates place higher than those under the control of superiors and which allow little individual discretion. Consequently, supervisors rank above those they oversee.

There is a good deal of debate over the concept of the functional importance of jobs. Structural functional theory argues that certain types of occupations are essential to the survival and welfare of all societies (Davis & Moore, 1945). Clergy, for example, occupy a central role because religion serves to integrate members of a society through a common value system, and scientific and technical occupations develop the technique and hardware to achieve national goals such as the exploration of space or the eradication of disease. Functional theory claims that it is imperative that these roles be filled and that people are motivated to perform these essential services. Prestige is among the major rewards which can be used to motivate people, and thus prestige becomes one of the rewards attached to the more important positions in society. Prestige is thus an "unconsciously evolved device by which societies insure that the most important positions are conscientiously filled by the most qualified persons." It is not at all clear that people utilize this abstract concept of functional importance in considering the prestige of occupations, but they are able to rate occupations along a continuum of "importance to society" (Haug & Widdison, 1975).

CLASS, RACE, AND SOCIAL RELATIONSHIPS

One of the most common—and relatively obvious—characteristics of social relationships is the tendency for people with similar attributes to associate with one another. Friendships illustrate this since they are usually grouped on the basis of qualities such as age, religion, race, and social class. People at the same class level are more likely to associate with other people in the same class than with people who rank above or below them in the stratification system. This pattern has long been documented in many different kinds of social relationships including friendships, residence, social club membership, dating, and marriage (Warner & Lunt, 1941; Laumann, 1966; Fischer, 1982).

Class-based patterns of association are, in part, based on occupation because social relationships are very often extensions of the workplace. Many workers, whether lawyers, teachers, or construction workers, often participate in special-purpose social clubs, trade unions, or professional associations that bring them together off the job. Less formal links are established because people congregate beyond the workplace to share the unique rewards and problems of their work. It is, for example, frequently noted that police officers' friends are usually other police officers because it is only members of this group that can appreciate and understand the dynamics of policing. Thus, in a very real sense bars, clubs, and other social situations are a continuation of the workday.

Perhaps the most dramatic instance of exclusionary social relationships developed during the nineteenth century among members of the emerging capitalist class in the United States (Baltzell, 1958; 1964). In the 1880s, wealthy white British Protestant industrialists and bankers, prompted by concern over the mass immigration that was bringing literally millions of foreign workers to the United States, began a conscious attempt to formalize an exclusive social network. Exclusive country clubs sprang up, expensive boarding schools such as Groton (1894) proliferated, and groups such as the Sons of the Revolution (1883) that traced their ancestors to the colonial period were formed. Members of this class soon congregated in exclusive neighborhoods and in 1887 published the *Social Register*, a volume that listed the names (and addresses, alma maters, country homes, club memberships, and yacht names) of socially acceptable families in major American cities. Members of this self-defined social elite lived and partied together and sent their sons and daughters to exclusive Ivy League universities (Yale and Harvard) where they dated and eventually married the children of other elite families. Members of the social elite dominated business, industry, the arts, and politics during the early decades of the twentieth century.

The *Social Register* continues to be published, and the 1998 edition contains some 30,000 names (Sargent, 1997). However, the boundaries of the original capitalist social elite are blurred. It has been impossible for members to maintain their exclusive domain in the face of dramatic social changes. New millionaires are being created, marriage across social class lines is more common, and although members of this social elite are still influential, power is more widely distributed. That does not mean that the new rich institutional elite are all readily accepted by members of the old capitalist elite. All of Donald Trump's money could not, for example, gain him access to their homes or exclusive clubs (Kunen, 1990).

Social Distance and Intergroup Contacts

Studies of social relations among diverse groups in societies often employ the idea of **social distance**, a concept originated in the 1920s to measure whites' willingness to accept racial and ethnic minorities in different social situations. Although developed to explore association with minorities, it can be expanded to include social class. Social distance scales are designed to tap underlying attitudes by focusing on the extent to which people welcome members of dissimilar people into increasingly more intimate social situations. Respondents are asked if they would be willing to accept group members:

as residents of the country,
as visitors to the country,
as speaking acquaintances,
in the same work group,
into the neighborhood,
as very good friends,
as marriage partners.

Studies show that most people express the highest tolerance for groups that are the most similar and least accepting of peoples that are the most dissimilar. Americans, for example, are consistently most accepting of Canadians, a close geographic neighbor with a long history of peaceful relations and sharing many common socio-cultural, linguistic, and political elements. In contrast, there is the least acceptance of Chinese, Japanese, and Arabs, groups separated by geography, culture, religion, and language (Crull & Bruton, 1985). It is a pattern repeated in other western countries such as Australia (McAllister & Moore, 1991). The overall model holds true for both men and women, but as a general rule females are more tolerant than males in studies of social distance.

Social distance scales reveal preferences for maintaining physical and social separation. These attitudes contribute to observed patterns of social segregation in many different contexts—residential, occupational, educational, and interpersonal.

Residential Segregation

It typical for neighborhoods to be segregated along class and racial lines. Clearly, economics is a factor because housing prices tend to be similar within neighborhoods, excluding people with lower incomes. In addition, there is a voluntary dimension since people prefer to live among people sharing similar lifestyles (Exhibit 6.2). When asked to express neighborhood preferences, nine out of ten people give a class-based answer, and there is strong preference for a neighborhood composed of people of the same or a higher class (Jackman & Jackman, 1983: 195). The expressed preference for living among people of the same class is most powerful among the working and middle classes. Not unexpectedly, it is weakest among the poor, who would probably rather escape areas that are often deteriorating and unsafe.

Voluntary class preferences are only part of the explanation of patterns of residential segregation for the practice of deliberately, physically excluding groups of people has a long history. The word "ghetto" appears to have originated with the sixteenth-century Italian practice of isolating Jews in certain parts of cities. The United States government relegated American Indians to reservations and banished trailer parks to urban fringes, while immigrants congregated in Chinatowns, Little Italys, and Hispanic barrios in urban communities. Residential segregation is a

EXHIBIT 6.2   Social Class and Neighborhood Preferences

	Preference for a neighborhood with:	
Class	own class only	own/higher class
Poor	20.3%	68.3%
Working	52.5	35.1
Middle	57.3	13.2
Upper middle	40.5	5.5

Source: Mary R. Jackman and Robert W. Jackman. *Class Awareness in the United States.* Berkeley, CA: University of California Press, 1983, Table 9.1, p. 195. Copyright © 1983 by the University of California Press.

complex phenomenon because there are always financial constraints on people's housing choices. In addition, some segregation has a voluntary dimension because immigrants may be attracted to areas where their native language and culture are maintained.

As is well known, there were separate churches, schools, bathrooms, restaurants, and places on buses for blacks in America well into the 1960s. In fact, early in the 1940s four out of five urban whites openly endorsed separate sections of towns for "Negroes." Among the most bizarre remnants of the segregated system surfaced in 1996 in a small southern town when church deacons asked that a mixed-race infant be exhumed and removed from their graveyard because they wished it to remain exclusively white (Bragg, 1996). The request generated massive media attention, and the church deacons subsequently relented and apologized publicly.

Exclusionary practices based on color continue to play a role in residential segregation. For a long time African Americans and whites lived in separate communities. Whites' racial attitudes have softened over the years, and blatant racial discrimination is now prohibited by the Fair Housing Act of 1968, although enforcement is uneven, and the growth of the black middle class has expanded the economic options of more families. Consequently, residential segregation is slowly declining in major cities, but the rate and the magnitude of change is modest.

A convenient way of conceptualizing residential segregation is to look at the typical neighborhood of racial and ethnic groups. The 2000 census suggests little improvement in community integration despite growing ethnic diversity in the nation. The average white person lives in a neighborhood that is 83 percent white, while the average Latino's neighborhood is 42 percent Latino, and the average black's neighborhood is 54 percent black (Exhibit 6.3). Whites are likely to live in areas with few minorities, while blacks, Latinos, and Asians live in more integrated neighborhoods (Logan, 2001).

Dual Housing Markets.   Only a small portion of the racial segregation that occurs within suburban areas can be explained by black-white income differences

EXHIBIT 6.3   Neighborhood Diversity in Metropolitan Areas, United States, 2000

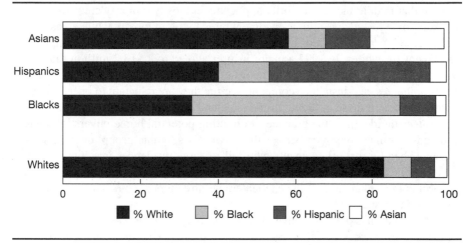

Source: John Logan, *Neighborhood Integration Is at a Standstill.* Albany, NY: Lewis Mumford Center for Comparative Urban and Regional Research. The University at Albany, 2001. On-line at www.albany.edu/mumford/census.

(Stearns & Logan, 1986; Bobo & Zubrinsky, 1996). Nor can it be explained by minority preferences for minority neighborhoods since most blacks favor integrated neighborhoods (Streitweiser & Goodman, 1983). Discrimination helps to preserve residential segregation because individuals' choices are limited by the workings of a **dual housing market** in which a variety of individuals and agencies, including realtors, lending institutions, and insurance companies—both overtly and quietly—limit the housing opportunities of the poor and racial groups. Several prevalent, but illegal, practices perpetuate residential segregation.

Outright discrimination occurs when minorities are excluded from housing more frequently than whites. It occurs, for example, when minorities are denied mortgages more frequently than whites with similar incomes. In New York City, one study found the rejection rate for African Americans was 21 percent compared to 11.4 percent for whites (Lambert, 2000). Discrimination also shows up when minorities and women have different experiences than whites in the rental market. To illustrate, men and women callers speaking either white middle-class English, black accented English, or black vernacular English telephoned rental agents about the availability of advertised apartments (Massey, 2000). White middle-class males were twice as likely as female callers posing as poor blacks to be told that rentals were available. Not only were black women more frequently refused, they were also often badly treated, including hints about drug use and indiscriminate sexual activity.

More direct exclusionary practices include redlining and steering. *Redlining* refers to the unwillingness to grant loans or insurance for property in poor or minority neighborhoods. The term originated when bankers physically drew red lines around such areas on community maps. One review of mortgage applications showed that middle-income minority applicants in mostly minority areas were twice as likely to be rejected as middle-income whites living in mostly white areas (Loeb, Cohen & Johnson, 1995). For blacks the rejection rate was 37 percent compared to 18 percent for whites. In 1997 a major insurer agreed to a $13.2 million settlement with the Justice Department for allegations of redlining (Dugas, 1997). Banks, mortgage companies, and insurance companies argue they are reluctant to operate in poor neighborhoods because of higher crime rates and unstable property values.

Steering identifies the practice of directing potential home buyers into neighborhoods dominated by members of their own class, ethnic group, or race. This is accomplished by real estate agents who fail to show residences in white neighborhoods to black potential home buyers. There is evidence that some degree of steering occurs in as many as half the encounters with realtors in some cities, both North and South (Glaster, 1990).

Most families prefer to move to neighborhoods with better resources (schools) and amenities (parks) as their class position improves. The predicament is that it is more difficult for African Americans to move out of segregated and low-income neighborhoods as their income rises. Consequently, blacks at the same income level as middle-class whites are more likely to live in neighborhoods with fewer resources for themselves and their children (Massey, Condran & Denton, 1987). The combination of racial segregation and poverty has many unhappy consequences for individuals living in poorer neighborhoods, not the least of which is ill health. Less access to health services, alienation, and social stress all contribute to susceptibility to illness and mortality (Krieger, et al., 1993; Collins & Williams, 1999).

Marriage Patterns

Marriage is the most intimate social relationship, and some people argue that intermarriage among people of different classes and racial and ethnic groups is the best measure of the breakdown of social distance. It is clear that marriages are sorted by race and social class, even in a heterogeneous and geographically mobile urban society like the United States. Ninety-five percent of American marriages unite men and women who are members of the same ethnic group, and a study in Detroit showed that a majority (58 percent) of people married someone in the same social class (Whyte, 1990). A conspicuous part of this pattern is that parents generally prefer their children to marry someone of the same or higher social class. People often express such feelings very directly. Speculating on future marriage partners for a child, an upper-middle-class parent comments,

> What sort of a husband would a carpenter be. . . . My viewpoint would not jibe with a carpenter. Marriage is based on equals. I would want my daughter to marry in her own class. She would go to college and would want her husband to be educated. I would want to be able to mix with in-laws and converse with them (Laumann, 1966: 29).

This quotation points to an underlying dimension of class and social relations, the common belief that members of different social classes have different perspectives and values. All other thing being equal, many people simply feel more comfortable with others having similar styles of life.

At one time, forty American states had laws that expressly prohibited marriages between people of different races. The U. S. Supreme Court ruled miscegenation laws unconstitutional in 1967, but the constitution of the state of Alabama contained this phrase until it was repealed by referendum in November of 2000:

> The legislature shall never pass any law or authorize or legalize any marriage between any white person and a Negro, or descendent of a Negro (Sengupta, 2000).

A majority of Americans now say that it is acceptable for blacks and whites to date, and a Gallup poll of teenagers found that 57 percent had dated someone of another race (Peterson, 1997). However, interracial marriages are still the exception in America, representing only 5 percent of all unions. The percentage is small but the numbers have been increasing for three decades. In 1970 there were 900,000 interracial couples, but by 1998 the number had grown to nearly 3 million couples (Pollard & O'Hare, 1999). More than one-half (52 percent) of these marriages involve Hispanic and non-Hispanic couples, suggesting that these two groups are separated by the lowest level of social distance. Nineteen percent of the marriages are between whites and Asians and 12 percent between whites and Native Americans. African Americans are the minority group least likely to marry across racial lines (9 percent). This pattern, combined with research on social distance, suggests that blacks tend to exhibit high levels of social distance toward other groups (Hraba, Radloff & Gray-Ray, 1999).

Increases in interracial marriages mean an increase in the number of multiracial children. Not all birth certificates record the race of both parents so all estimates are low, but at least 5 percent of all babies have parents of different races (Pollard & O'Hare, 1999). Many celebrities are in this category—Mariah Carey (African American, Venezuelan, white), Tiger Woods (African American, Thai, Native American, white), Keanu Reeves (Chinese, Hawaiian, white), and Cameron Diaz (Cuban, white). The expansion of the number of Americans having interracial roots will certainly demand a reconsideration of the very idea of race, which has the potential to weaken the importance of race in American society.

Discrimination and the Contact Hypothesis

It is often predicted that increasing interpersonal contacts among members of diverse groups promote positive attitudes and reduce intolerance and prejudice, an idea called the **contact hypothesis.** This belief supports attempts to integrate jobs, neighborhoods, and schools. The lack of social contacts produced by various forms of segregation allows ignorance to flourish and stereotypes to prevail. The contact hypothesis proposes a self-perpetuating process of intolerance where isolation separates people from the interpersonal contacts that have the potential to disprove stereotypes. Among both blacks and whites, prejudice is more likely among the less educated, lower and working classes (Farley, et al., 1994). Research has produced mixed results, but interracial social contacts generally do contribute to more positive racial attitudes, especially among whites (Smith, 1994; Sigelman et al., 1996). Although the magnitude of results is sometimes modest, the weakening of negative attitudes is cause for some optimism for the future of an increasingly diverse society.

A Melting Pot or Multiculturalism

In 1909 a Jewish immigrant authored a play called *The Melting Pot* that affixed a new identity to the United States. The imagery of a **melting pot** defines America as a crucible in which the various immigrant nationalities blend to create a unique new American culture. In practice, generations of immigrants during the nineteenth and twentieth centuries usually adopted and reinforced the dominant western European Protestant culture. Thus, they *assimilated* the prevailing culture, rather than dramatically recasting it, although many third-generation white Americans do retain some elements of their ethnic heritage.

An increasing tolerance of racial and ethnic difference and a new appreciation of cultural diversity emerged in the 1960s as a reaction to the discrimination and exclusionary practices that were then common. This has evolved into an alternative societal model—**multiculturalism**, the image of a pluralistic nation of many racial and ethnic groups maintaining their unique identities and enjoying mutual acceptance and respect. The importance of a multicultural model is accelerated by recognition that whites will become a numerical minority sometime after the year 2050. Bilingual education to assist the children of immigrants, laws that protect non-Western religions and customs, and classroom programs that emphasize the social and political contributions of minorities in American history are tangible manifestations of multiculturalism.

Proponents of multiculturalism or pluralism emphasize that it encourages understanding and appreciation of the values and beliefs of the many groups that contribute to the creation of the nation. Critics of multiculturalism believe that it threatens the social cohesion of the nation by fostering divisions among peoples. Many critics favor integration and assimilation. They worry that multiculturalism might foster the social and physical resegregation of racial and ethnic groups. They recall extreme instances around the world where racial and ethnic divisions led to wars and ethnic cleansing. Debates about multiculturalism are also about political power, because the growth of racial and ethnic identity can be translated into political power and shows up in the form of the increased number of minority candidates for office and the increased response to the needs of groups that form cohesive voting blocs.

CLASS AND CHARACTER JUDGMENTS

The public may never know what, if anything, happened at the Excelsior Hotel in Little Rock on May 8, 1991. Paula Jones, a lower-middle-class white-collar worker, claimed that then governor of Arkansas Bill Clinton made improper sexual advances, which he denied. Her allegations were ridiculed by members of the press, who quickly fastened on her modest social class position to attack her character. She was dismissed as "some sleazy woman with big hair coming out of the trailer parks" by a columnist at a major newsmagazine (who later apologized). "Drag a $100 bill through a trailer park and there's no telling what you'll find," added a high-profile political consultant.

This is not an isolated incident, merely one manifestation of the way that people may construct judgments about one's character on the basis of a person's location in the class system. Americans are likely to believe, for example, that traits such as intelligence, competence, and responsibility increase at each higher class level (More & Suchner, 1976; Jackman & Senter, 1982; Baron, Albright & Malloy, 1995). One study reveals that college students feel that mothers in low-prestige occupations are less competent than higher status mothers (Etaugh & Poertner, 1991). A major sneaker company used that strategy when it claimed that buyers at a discount store could not distinguish their brand from a similar looking but less expensive model. The judge rejected the claim as "elitist," and added, "the fact that a consumer may prefer to purchase low-price footwear (or have no other option) does not transform them into an unsophisticated, careless shopper" (Pines, 1994). It may be assumed that such character judgments help to explain certain patterns of interaction such as mock jury deliberations, where it is consistently found that people at the bottom of the stratification system—unskilled workers—have the least influence on deliberations and are viewed as least helpful and least likely to be chosen as foreperson (Berger, et al., 1977).

The link between class and character is ultimately embedded in the ideologies of class, race, and gender. The dynamics of the ideology of individualism leads members of society to attribute generally negative character traits to members of the lower classes and more positive traits to higher classes, reasoning that location in the class structure is the outcome of individual abilities and effort. While such judgments identify specific traits, they do not necessarily solidify into totally positive or negative stereotypes (Skafte, 1989). Higher-class persons may be rated smarter, more intelligent, healthier, and happier than the poor, but they are also thought of as more self-centered and selfish. The poor may be judged as less intelligent and to be more likely to steal and have lower self-esteem, but also are seen as hard working, generous, and able to handle money wisely. In short, although the poor may be perceived as less able, this does not extend to the notion that they are lazy and unmotivated. Instead, it suggests recognition that social position shapes character rather than that character determines position. This may be interpreted as further evidence of the weakening of the salience of the ideology of individualism and opportunity.

CONCLUSION: CLASS AND SELF-ESTEEM

The existence of occupational and class hierarchies of social status has the ability to influence the way that people think about and evaluate themselves. Social scientists ordinarily use the generic term *self-concept* to describe individuals' overall thoughts and feelings about themselves (Rosenberg, 1989). Self-concepts are complex social and psychological phenomena that include several different dimensions, but the one that has received the most attention in recent years is self-esteem. **Self-esteem** is a person's self-evaluation of their social or moral worth. Self-esteem is shaped by many factors, with physical appearance among the most significant, especially among adolescents, and is, at least in part, forged in interaction with other people. People's judgment about themselves is influenced by their perception of what they believe others think of them.

Among adults, work is a significant consideration. Those in the least prestigious work typically seek to counter judgments of inferiority, reflected in these words of a man who digs graves:

> Not anybody can be a grave digger. . . . You have to make a neat job. . . . A human body is goin' into this grave. That's why you need skill when you're gonna dig a grave. . . . It's like a trade. It's the same as a mechanic or a doctor. . . . A grave digger is a very important person (Terkel, 1972: 658–660).

Unfortunately, personal claims that work is good and useful and meaningful can neither erase nor neutralize broader social judgments.

In most cases, research confirms a positive link between social class ranking and self-esteem (Rosenberg & Pearlin, 1978; Francis & Jones, 1996). The poor, usually the most socially depreciated members of society, exhibit the least positive self-concepts (Faunce, 1989). The link between class and self-esteem can show up as early as adolescence (Rosenberg, Schooler & Schoenbach, 1989). Adolescent self-esteem is especially important because low self-esteem is often associated with poor grades, psychological depression, and juvenile delinquency. All are factors that can have serious long-term implications. Bad grades in school or a record of delinquency can permanently limit the occupational options of these youngsters later in life, relegating them to the lower rungs of the class system.

African-American children and young adults have somewhat higher average self-esteem scores than their white counterparts (Goodstein & Ponterotto, 1997; Gray-Little & Hafdahl, 2000). The sources of such differences are unclear, but one plausible interpretation is that blacks in contemporary America have the advantage of a reference group which can be a source of identity and respect that is not available to whites.

Social class position is also associated with other indications of psychological well-being, including "happiness" and generalized "satisfaction with life" (Gallup Poll, 1995). Such measures of quality of life may represent the interplay between the multiple consequences of class—social as well as economic. People are sensitive to their social environment, and social hierarchies carry the potential to harm or enhance self-image because status and prestige convey others' judgments of inferiority and superiority. This basic fact and related issues such as ideas about class and character and preferences for including or excluding people from social relations combine to shape people's self-esteem and self-concepts.

KEY CONCEPTS

achieved prestige	melting pot	social distance
ascribed prestige	multiculturalism	social status
contact hypothesis	poor white trash	
dual housing market	self-esteem	

SUGGESTED READING

E. Digby Baltzel. *The Protestant Establishment*. New York: Random House, 1964. The primary study of the origins and wide-ranging influence of the capitalist elite in the first half of the twentieth century.

Robert D. Bullard, J. Eugene Grigsby III, and Charles Lee, eds. *Residential Apartheid*. Los Angeles, CA: CAAS Publications, 1994. A collection of essays that explores the many dimensions of residential segregation.

William J. Goode. *The Celebration of Heroes: Prestige as a Social Control System*. Berkeley: University of California Press, 1978. The idea of cultural heroes as the embodiment of society's basic values and ideals.

Donald J. Treiman. *Occupational Prestige in Comparative Perspective*. New York: Academic Press, 1977. This survey of research on occupational prestige around the globe is dated but remains the best single source on the topic.

Matt Wray and Annalee Newitz, eds. *White Trash: Race and Class in America*. New York: Routledge, 1997. An intriguing collection of essays that explores the nature of the "white trash" stereotype, including several papers by people who grew up in modest circumstances.

USEFUL WEB SITES

The goal of Racial Legacies and Learning sponsored by the Public Broadcasting Service and the American Association of Colleges and Universities (**www.pbs.org/adultlearningals/race**) is to foster meaningful dialogue and to improve race relations through the exchange of information.

Americans Against Discrimination and Preferences (**www.aadap.org**) include a bibliography and abstracts of articles focusing on discrimination.

CHAPTER SEVEN

The Shape
of Political Power
and Influence

POLITICAL POWER: CONCENTRATED OR DISPERSED?

Developments in democratic industrial nations over the course of the twentieth century have concentrated enormous power and authority in the hands of national, state, and local governments. Among the most conspicuous governmental responsibilities are policing and prosecution of criminal behavior; collecting taxes; building and maintaining public works (roads, public buildings); regulating the professions, business, and industry; educating children; sustaining social insurance programs (Social Security, Medicare); and protecting and defending the nation's vital interests around the world. Thus, the activities of government touch every facet of the lives of its citizens.

The broad reach of government raises a number of important questions. For example, who are the men and women who serve in the government and how are they chosen? Who contributes the money necessary to contest elections in the television age? Does the government serve the interests of all groups and classes or are some groups dominant? Who participates in the elections and the political process? In short, who exercises political power and influence? There are two basic models or theories that attempt to unravel the role of class, race, and gender in the political process. The elite model holds that the interests of the elite class generally overwhelm all others in the political arena. Pluralists take the position that power is distributed among a number of different organized groups pursuing their own interests. Neither model explains all that occurs in the political sphere.

The Elite Model: The Concentration of Power

The origins of the elite model are found in the writings of Marx and Engels in the nineteenth century. They argued that members of the ruling class control the government and the other major societal institutions. **Elite theory** was first formally laid out by C. Wright Mills (1956). Mills, writing in the 1950s, pointed out that three institutional sectors—corporations, the federal government, and the military—had grown to the point that they exercised undue influence over society. He emphasized that such growth signaled a major transformation in industrial societies. Ever-larger corporations that displaced small businesses, as well as the Great Depression and World War II, expanded the scope of the federal government and created a massive military bureaucracy. He envisioned three levels of power. Singular power was thus vested in the people who directed these structures—corporate executives, the president and his staff and cabinet, and generals and admirals. He labeled this group of people the **power elite**.[1]

Mills argued that the power elite exercised largely uncontested control of decisions in two key areas: establishing economic policy and the conduct of foreign policy. Political activity at the next level involved various interest groups seeking to influence Congress. Those groups—labor unions, business interests, professional associations, environmental groups—competed with each other, but it was impossible for any one to really succeed. The majority of people at the bottom of the system were impotent because the power elite was beyond their reach; hence they were passive witnesses to the flow of events.

Mills also believed that the members of the power elite formed a single more or less unified elite. These people shared a common perspective because, he argued, they were overwhelmingly recruited from similar backgrounds and went to the same small circle of elite schools, colleges, and universities. Not only did they share a common value system, but there was a constant interchange of people circulating among the military, industry, and the government. Dwight David Eisenhower was, at the time Mills was writing, the epitome of the process since he had left the military as a five star general, became a college president (Columbia), and then was elected President of the United States.

The goals of the elite class in this model center on the expansion and protection of individual and corporate wealth and power. There are several different contemporary perspectives within the elite model who disagree over the composition of the controlling elite and details of the exercise of power, but they are united on the key points that an inordinate amount of power and influence resides in the hands of

---

[1]President Dwight Eisenhower was discussing the same process when he warned of the emerging influence of the "military-industrial complex" as he left office in 1961.

a narrow and unrepresentative segment of society, and that the majority of the population has minimal influence over political events (Greider, 1992; Dye, 1995; Parenti, 1995; Domhoff, 1998).

The Pluralist Model: The Dispersion of Power

In contrast, **pluralist theory** asserts that the ability to influence the government is widely shared among different groups and at different levels of the stratification system. Pluralists argue that governments in democratic industrial societies respond to countless different pressure groups, each pursuing their own interests and agendas (Richardson, 1993). Examples of these groups include working-class trade unions (e.g., International Brotherhood of Electricians), business groups (e.g., American Bankers Association), upper-middle-class professional associations (e.g., Association of Trial Lawyers), lower-middle-class employee groups (e.g., Letter Carriers), women's advocacy groups (e.g., National Organization for Women), and groups promoting the objectives of minority groups (e.g., NAACP). In addition, there are more broadly based pressure groups such as the Sierra Club (environmental issues), the American Association of Retired People, and the National Rifle Association that cut across class, race, and gender lines. Pluralists contend that each presses for legislation that promotes their agenda, but that no one group is ever able to prevail in all cases and on all issues because they are in competition with other interest groups (Dahl, 1958). In fact, some pluralists worry that so many powerful pressure groups are at work that they prevent elected officials from pursuing legislation aimed at the best interests of society as a whole (Rauch, 1994).

Not all pressure groups are equal, and pluralists usually concede that representatives of the wealthy and business interests dominated politics in the early years of the republic, but they insist that paths to success are increasingly open to merit and that no one class dominates all institutions. Rather, society is characterized by shifting combinations of groups that temporarily join together on specific issues. Moreover, although business groups are influential, they lack a common focus because there are major differences among such groups; high-tech telecommunications firms obviously have much different interests than traditional banks or retailers.

Individuals and groups influence the political process in democratic societies in several ways. They participate directly in the political process by joining political parties, voting, and holding political office. Moreover, they have the right to try to determine policy through influencing their representatives by active lobbying (either individually or through interest groups), public demonstrations, petitions, letter-writing campaigns, making financial contributions to political candidates, and other forms of behind-the-scenes persuasion. In many ways, financial contributions to political parties are the major road to influence.

These models focus attention on the key issues in understanding the role of class, race, and gender in the political sphere. There are differences in the form and intensity of participation among social classes, races, and gender. In addition, these groups have dissimilar experiences in the system and different attitudes toward the political process.

THE ELITE: PATTERNS OF INFLUENCE

Political influence is exercised in different ways in democratic societies. There is the open and public dimension that includes holding public office, working on behalf of candidates, and making financial contributions to individuals and political parties. Such activities are a matter of public record and commented on in the media, but political influence is also regularly exercised away from public scrutiny. It is exerted in private meetings, in quiet lobbying and the activities of obscure special interest groups, and in the circulation of individuals between government and industry. Many people believe that exercise of influence by the elite class must be shrouded in secrecy because it is the only way to maintain the legitimacy of the political system in the minds of the rest of the population. The subtlety of the exercise of upper-class control means that it is sometimes difficult to document, but it cannot be underestimated or ignored.

Direct Participation in Government

It is not uncommon for members of the elite class to hold high political office, and it is logical to assume that they are more responsive to the interests of people like themselves than to others whom they do not know or understand. The earliest American presidents such as Washington, Adams, and Jefferson were drawn from the wealthy land-owning classes, and twentieth-century presidents such as Franklin Roosevelt, John F. Kennedy, and George Herbert Walker Bush were born to privileged upper-class families. The 2000 presidential campaign offered Americans a choice between two members of the elite. President George W. Bush is the Yale-educated son of a president, grandson of a senator, and great-grandson of George Herbert Walker, a wealthy financier. Democrat Al Gore is the son of a long-term Tennessee senator and was educated at private schools and Harvard.

Once elected, Presidents often bring members of the upper classes into their administrations. Studies show that cabinet-level appointees from the 1890s onward followed this pattern (Mintz, 1975). Well over one-half, and possibly two-thirds, of the appointments went to people with links to the upper classes. Even judicial appointments tend to go to people of unusual wealth. It is estimated that 34 percent of President Clinton's nominations for federal judgeships and 32 percent of George Herbert Bush's selections were millionaires (Willing, 1997). To illustrate, twenty-five people with average assets of $1,798,000 were nominated in 1997 and fifteen were millionaires. Those with wealth enjoy lifestyles that distance them from the rest of society, as is suggested by the fact that one candidate earned $13,800 by renting her luxurious home as a location for filming Hollywood movies.

Campaign Contributions

The cost of seeking political office rises with each election, with the bulk of it going to buy television time. Therefore, fund-raising is a constant concern. "Money is," as political consultants like to say, "the mother's milk of politics." It is estimated that the November, 2000, elections cost a total of $3 billion (FEC, 2000). Calculations suggest that the average Senate race costs about $4.5 million (*The Economist*, 1997b). That means a U.S. Senator must raise $14,000 a week every week of a six-year term to finance a reelection campaign. Campaigns in some large states cost even more; between them Rick Lazio and Hillary Rodham Clinton spent $69 million in their 2000 New York senatorial contest (McCaffrey, 2000). In neighboring New Jersey, Democrat Jon Corzine alone spent $61 million, most of it from his own fortune amassed as a Wall Street banker.

Wealthy individuals and families were once the major contributors to election campaigns, but a series of campaign financing reforms enacted in the 1970s weakened the influence of wealthy citizens and radically altered campaign financing. Individuals' donations are currently limited to $1,000 per candidate per election, and there is a ceiling of $25,000 annually for all national elections. There are, however, no real limits on so-called **soft money** contributions to political parties, rather than specific candidates, to be used for "party-building" activities. The original idea behind soft money was that the money would be used for nonpartisan political activities such as citizen education or voter registration drives, but some of the money is diverted to clearly partisan purposes in violation of the law. Hundreds of millions of dollars in soft money is donated to political parties in that way, often in exchange for the opportunity to meet with political decision-makers. Large soft money donors enjoy cocktail parties, golf weekends, fishing trips, Super Bowl parties, and elegant dinners where they can socialize with office holders (Wayne, 1997; Broder & Van Natta, 2000). The sheer size of campaign contributions raised during the 2000 elections prompted calls for campaign finance reform in the new Congress.

Corporate executives and other members of the elite often donate money to both major parties to assure some return on their investment (Greider, 1992). There is an element of status enhancement at work here, for contributed money means that donors are invited to political events and have photo opportunities with the President. More typically, large contributions offer donors access to members of Congress or the executive branch, where they can press their agendas and influence decisions. Obviously, important decisions are to be made—government appointments to courts and regulatory agencies that decide antitrust enforcement, environmental protection, tax policy, and other actions that affect the elite. Ambassadorships to foreign nations are a good example of political favors for large donors. For example, a New York City investment banker who contributed some $600,000 to party coffers became ambassador to France. However, in most cases large contributions alone are not enough to guarantee a favorable outcome, largely because decisions are so complex (Birnbaum, 2000).

Corporate PACs.   Campaign financing reform legislation in the 1970s endorsed **Political Action Committees (PACs)** designed to encourage smaller donors to pool their money and thus have more influence than they could have individually. Any group or organization may form a PAC, and most major class-, race-, and gender-based interest groups originate them to compete in the political process. Corporations or unions may not contribute directly to PACs, but they can organize them and facilitate contributions by their members. Each PAC is limited to donations of $5,000 per candidate per election. There are over 4,000 PACs registered with the Federal Election Commission (FEC), and they account for one-third of all contributions. Political Action Committees are thus a critical source of funds for politicians. PACs support the pluralist model to the extent that the needs of major groups in society are represented.

PAC contributions are distributed in different ways. Sometimes they are used to bolster the candidacy of a specific individual or a particular party, based on the belief that they will pursue a specific political agenda once in office. Business leaders, for example, tend to favor the Republican party because they anticipate more favorable treatment from them. However, PACs are usually much more pragmatic; they tend to target incumbents because nine out of ten typically retain their seats, and more often than not money is spread among all major candidates to ensure supporting the candidate who eventually wins. To illustrate, the largest corporate PACs in a recent election distributed 53 percent of their money to Republicans and 47 percent to Democrats (Clawson, Neustadt & Scott, 1992). In that way contributors guarantee themselves access to whoever is the office holder. It is very simple; "The PAC gives you access. It makes you a player," explains the chair of a business PAC.

Corporations are aware that they cannot ordinarily prevent legislation that is popular, even if it is detrimental to their interests. For example, things like corporate taxes, occupational safety, and clean air are too popular with American voters to ever be eliminated entirely. Rather, the usual goal of corporate PACs is to win special benefits for their particular company or industry (Case Study). They seek to weaken legislation that is costly or cumbersome or win exemptions, extensions, or exclusions from laws that they cannot prevent. Such exemptions are often hidden or buried in obscure sections of bills and thus escape public scrutiny. A 1986 law increasing corporate tax rates stands as a classic example of how corporate welfare works. The law was over 800 pages long, and Section 739, subsection J, paragraph iii, contained an exemption that limited the tax liability of one company. The firm was identified only as "a corporation incorporated on June 13, 1917, which has its principal place of business in Bartlesville, Oklahoma" (Clawson, Neustadtl & Scott, 1992: 91).[2]

---

[2]The only firm that fits this description is Philips Petroleum.

CASE STUDY
Corporate Welfare

The success of business groups in the political sector shows up clearly in **corporate welfare**, the tangle of tariffs, subsidies, laws and regulations, tax breaks, and exemptions that benefit business and cost taxpayers millions of dollars each year in lost revenues or higher prices. It is difficult to know the precise cost of corporate welfare, but the tab is high by any estimate. One research center calculates corporate welfare at about $60 billion in industry-specific tax breaks and another $75 billion in government spending that directly benefits business (Borrus, 1997). The extent of corporate welfare shows up in things such as higher drug prices, subsidies for foreign advertising, the federal census of the population, and tax credits for business development.

Drug Prices.   Pharmaceutical companies face the prospect of price competition from generic drugs when their patents on products expire. Consequently, they engage in extensive lobbying campaigns to extend their patents and thus prevent competition. The absence of competition translates into higher prices for consumers. For example, in 1996 a quiet amendment to a budget bill extended the patent on the anti-inflammatory drug "Daypro" (with $280 million in annual sales), shielding the maker from competition for an extra two years (Glastris, et al., 1997). The company's political contributions amounted to $256,875.

In 1994, a bureaucratic miscalculation turned into a major windfall for pharmaceutical companies. A technical error in a trade agreement inadvertently granted a group of 109 drugs special protection from generic competition. Some senators sought to rectify the error when they realized that consumers and insurers would pay some $6 billion in higher prices. However, drug companies were able to convince enough senators not to correct the error. A spokesperson for a drug company that stood to gain $2 billion by maintaining high prices, and one that subsequently contributed $487,000 to the Republican National Committee, insists that lawmakers' votes were based on the merits of the bill, not politics (Glastris, et al., 1997).

Foreign Advertising.   American companies typically compete in the global marketplace. The government annually contributes about $100 million a year to help American companies advertise their products abroad. That means taxpayers are helping to subsidize the advertising budgets of corporate giants like McDonald's, Campbell's soups, Mars candy, Miller beer, and Gallo wine, among others. The companies who receive these subsidies defend them on the grounds that the money allows them to sell their products in the highly competitive foreign market for food and beverages, which translates into jobs for Americans. Critics argue that in a true market economy businesses should succeed or fail on their own merits rather than being supported by taxpayers.

The Census. The Constitution mandates that the government count the population every decade to determine representation in Congress, and the results are also used for allocating various forms of federal aid. The census is strongly defended by corporate America because the census also collects a vast amount of information on consumer habits and demographic data that is very useful to retailers, although of questionable value to the government considering the costs. Lobbyists for J. C. Penney, Sears, and other stores were able to frustrate attempts by the census to cut costs by reducing the collection of such data (Peyser, 1997). The census costs taxpayers $4 billion and provides business with enormous benefits, free of charge.

Business Expansion. Corporate welfare also flourishes at the state and municipal levels, often in the form of lavish tax credits to business to encourage expansion and create jobs. Sometimes the outlay is high. Kentucky, for example granted tax credits of $132 million for the expansion of a paper and pulp mill (Leroy, 1999). Fifteen jobs were involved, meaning the state sacrificed $8.8 million in tax revenues over fifteen years for each new job! Companies may also threaten to physically move their operations elsewhere if tax breaks are not forthcoming. New York City reportedly granted the New York Stock Exchange $600 million in tax relief to avert a possible relocation of several thousand jobs.

Business Lobbies

There are also much more obscure but powerful business-sponsored groups such as the Business Roundtable, the Business Council, the National Chamber of Commerce, and the National Planning Association that seek to shape foreign policy and social welfare programs and to forestall antibusiness legislation (Useem, 1983). The work of the Business Roundtable, founded in 1972, exemplifies the inner workings of political influence. It is composed of about two hundred top executives from some of the largest industrial corporations. The group works through a dozen "task forces" that develop policy recommendations that are distributed to members of Congress and the executive branch, and individual members personally lobby law-makers. The Business Roundtable is generally credited with successfully obstructing attempts to create a federal Consumer Protection Agency that would have meant more regulation for business and industry.

Informal Forms of Influence

It does not always require campaign donations for members of the elite to contact government officials because they often move in the same social circles as political decision-makers. There is, for instance, a network of national clubs and resorts where the elite socialize informally with members of the government (Domhoff,

1974). Among the most well-known is the Bohemian Grove, an exclusive camp in northern California with a membership that includes corporate executives (officers of forty of the fifty largest) and bankers (twenty of the largest twenty-five). The guest list at one of their meetings suggest that these sessions create the opportunity for business people to mingle with other powerful segments of society; several major university presidents were there, as were two members of the President's cabinet, the Chairman of the Joint Chiefs of Staff, the president of United Press International, and the Governor of California.

The boundary between government and business is often blurred by the regular interchange of personnel between government, industry, and lobbying groups. This process of movement among jobs is referred to as the **revolving door** of power, money, and politics. The revolving door finds people leaving government jobs and moving into the private sector, and sometimes eventually back into government. Federal law prevents them from lobbying Congress for one year after leaving government, but they are free to make contact after that point. A total of 138 former members of Congress were registered lobbyists in 1998 (Center for Responsive Politics, 1999). To illustrate, soon after former senator Bob Dole failed in his run for the Presidency he accepted a $600,000 position with a major Washington law firm that lobbies the government on behalf of corporate clients (Lavelle, 1997). Other members of the same firm include former Treasury Secretary Lloyd Bentsen, former Texas Governor Ann Richards, and former Senate majority leader George Mitchell. Other former government officials accept lucrative positions on corporate boards of directors. Former Secretary of Commerce Barbara Hackman Franklin earned $619,000 in 1999 from directorships at companies such as Aetna and Dow Chemical (Strauss, 2000). Onetime governmental officials have sensitive information about pending legislation and a host of personal contacts that can prove useful in influencing the course of future government actions. It is also argued that the lure of potential high-paying jobs after retiring from politics could encourage government officials to be more cooperative with business and industry during their tenure in Washington.

WHITE-COLLAR AND BLUE-COLLAR POLITICAL ACTIVITY

The broad middle class of white- and blue-collar workers grouped between the elite and the poor are a numerical majority and therefore have the potential to be the key to victory or defeat in elections. Members of these middle classes seek to shape political policies by working for political candidates, contributing money, and joining organized interest groups. Some are active participants in government at the national, state, and local levels. There are, however, important class differences within this broad category, and the most consistent finding is that almost all forms of political activity and participation decrease at each lower class level.

The Upper Middle Class in Government

A large proportion of the people who hold seats in Congress and the state legislatures are upper middle class, having come from careers in the professions or private business. About one-third of all state legislators come from these occupations (Perez-Pena, 1999). The single largest occupational category is lawyer. This is true at the national and state level, although the proportion has been shrinking over the last three decades. Forty-three percent of the 106th Congress in 1999 were attorneys. People in upper-middle-class occupations have major advantages in the political arena—education, income, social prestige, lifestyle, managerial experience, and social contacts—all of which are factors that enable them to become active in local civic and political enterprises. Candidates for public office are typically recruited from this pool of people. One consequence of this situation is that upper-middle-class interests receive special attention in the Congress as reflected in some elements of the tax laws such as the ability to deduct interest on mortgages for second homes and tax-sheltered retirement income.

In contrast, direct participation in the sense of holding political office is rare among members of the lower-middle or working classes. Time and resources are a factor, but so too is the work situation. Clerical and blue-collar jobs often fail to provide people with the opportunities for activities such as public speaking and directing and managing people, which are valuable skills in the political sphere (Kohn & Schooler, 1983). However, it must be remembered that labor unions are an exception since they do provide opportunities for gaining political experience.

Lobbying and PACs

Many of the wealthiest PACs are organized around upper-middle-class or working-class occupations. For example, PACs of attorneys, teachers, physicians, automobile dealers, real estate agents, and accountants all dispensed over one million dollars to candidates in the 2000 election cycle (Exhibit 7.1) and still have sizable amounts on hand for future campaigns. Over a million dollars was also disbursed by labor unions such as those of machinists and auto workers. EMILY's List and Black America fight for the interests of women and African Americans. There are, in addition, many special interest PACs such as the National Rifle Association and Right to Life whose objectives are more general. The work of PACs for these groups enables them to protect and enhance the interests of their own members, and this often puts them in competition with one another on some issues. Thus, trial lawyers are often at odds with business groups because they frequently press lawsuits on behalf of individuals against companies for dangerous or defective products. Notable cases in recent years include challenges to the tobacco industry, breast implant manufacturers, and SUV tire-makers. It is situations exactly like this that lead pluralists to argue that no one group is ever able to prevail in all cases.

Trial lawyers also find themselves pitted against corporate interests because

EXHIBIT 7.1   Financial Disbursements, Political Action Committees

PAC	Disbursements
International Brotherhood of Electrical Workers	$4,169,317
Association of Trial Lawyers	3,307,769
National Automobile Dealers Association	2,480,749
American Federation of State, County, and Municipal Employees	2,473,874
Realtors	2,168,588
American Federation of Teachers	2,157,646
National Education Association	2,043,361
American Medical Association	1,753,921

Note: Includes the period January 1, 1999 to June 30, 2000.

Source: Federal Election Commission, *Top Fifty PAC's: Disbursements.* www.fec.gov/press/pacdis1800.htm

the lawyers often pursue product liability cases against businesses. The President of the U. S. Chamber of Commerce, the nation's largest lobbyist on behalf of business, openly targets trial lawyers whose "main objective is to get money for themselves, not for the plaintiffs," he claims (Belton, 1997). And manufacturers point out that the cost of lawsuits against them are ultimately passed on to consumers in the form of higher prices. Lawsuits add $23 to the $120 price of aluminum ladders and $3,000 to the $18,000 cost of heart pacemakers.

Labor Unions

Labor unions are among the largest contributors to political campaigns despite the fact that union membership in the United States has been declining, currently enrolling about 15 percent of the workforce. Teamsters, the United Auto Workers, and government workers are the best financed. Labor unions have had mixed results over the last decade in winning legislation benefiting members of the working class. Probably the most decisive defeat occurred with the passage of the NAFTA, which labor unions opposed because they believed that American jobs would be lost.

VOTING AND POLITICAL PARTICIPATION

It is estimated that one-half the world's population lives in countries that restrict voting rights in some way. Those people reside in nations at war or under the control of autocratic regimes that control the selection of candidates for elected office or outlaw rival political parties. Citizens in the rest of the world have the prerogative to elect lawmakers. Enjoying the right to vote, to exert some influence over the course of governmental action by choosing among candidates for political office, does not mean that people will necessarily exercise that right. Despite its powerful democratic traditions, the United States has a relatively low level of participation in the electoral process when compared to other industrial democracies. Voter turnout typically hovers around 50 percent of eligible voters. The 1996 presidential election brought out 49 percent of eligible voters, and that proportion slipped to 45 percent in the congressional elections of 1998. Voter turnout rose to about 51 percent in 2000 due to voter mobilization drives in key states and the closely divided public opinion on the candidates. Voting among Americans lags well behind other industrialized nations such as Italy, the Netherlands, Belgium, Australia, Sweden, Germany, and Norway.

There are also significant class differences in voting. There is a clear relationship between social class level and voting, with the highest rates of participation found among the upper middle class where approximately six out of ten people can be counted on to turn out. Voting among members of the lower middle class stands at about 50 percent. Turnout slips to about one in three eligible voters among the working class and service workers, and the lowest level of voting is found among the unskilled segment of the poor where only about one in five cast ballots.

CASE STUDY
Why Do College Age Adults Fail to Vote?

The Twenty-sixth Amendment to the Constitution lowered the voting age to 18 more than two decades ago. However, 18- to 24-year-olds are the least likely of any age group to vote. The turnout of young adults typically hovers around 30 to 35 percent, compared to more than 65 to 70 percent among people aged 55 and older. Gender and education make some difference within the younger group. Women are about 5 percent more likely to vote than men, and students are about 15 percent more likely to turn out than those not in school.

It is clear that young adults were not deeply engaged in the political process in 2000. They were, first of all, not very well informed; less than 75 percent could name the 2000 Presidential candidates and less than 35 percent could name the vice-presidential candidates (Collins, 2000). Many were not very knowledgeable; one-half of those asked to identify the most important issue *not* being discussed by the candidates could not come up with an answer. Large numbers feel untouched by the process; over 40 percent felt the election would have a minor impact on them and 27 percent felt it would have no impact. And, when asked directly why they don't go to the polls, the largest group reported it was because they felt their vote would not make a difference.

The poor turnout among young adults raises the question of the origins of their apparent apathy. Pragmatic political candidates point out that they target the groups most likely to vote and consequently not much time or campaign money is devoted to young adults. Young adults counter that they don't vote because politicians ignore them, failing to devote serious resources to voter education on college campuses or mounting registration drives similar to those aimed at immigrants and retirees. The result is that the two sides continue to blame each other, and ignore each other.

EXHIBIT 7.2   Patterns of Voter Turnout, Percentage of Eligible Voters in 1998

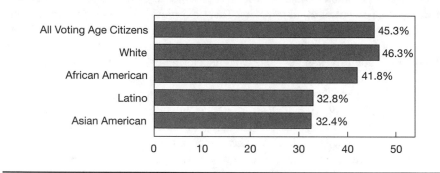

Source: U.S. Bureau of the Census, *Voting and Registration in the Election of November 1998.* Current Population Survey P20-523. Washington, DC: U.S. Government Printing Office, 2000. Table 2.

Gender and color are also relevant factors. As a general rule women are more likely to cast ballots than men by about 4 or 5 percent. Voter turnout among minority groups is below that of whites, as shown in Exhibit 7.2. African Americans' voting record has tended to lag behind that of whites for decades, but the gap is shrinking, standing at about 42 percent in 1998 (U. S. Census Bureau, 2000). Both Asian Americans and Latinos have relatively low levels of voter turnout, about 32 percent. Overall, the pattern of class-related voting is repeated among women and minorities.

Voter turnout is but one measure of involvement in the political process. Others include keeping abreast of political matters, contributing money, and becoming actively involved in political campaigns. All follow the same general pattern found in voter turnout, viz., each form of participation increases at each higher level in the class system, with the very lowest levels of participation found at the lowest levels of the stratification hierarchy. In response, states are experimenting with a variety of techniques to encourage and simplify voting. Oregon, for example, has gone to statewide mail-in ballots. California, Arizona, and Washington recently have begun testing on-line voting. This method offers the advantage of easy accessibility, but raises some unresolved questions about privacy and security.

GENDER IN THE POLITICAL SPHERE

Organized women's suffrage movements date from the middle of the nineteenth century, and in 1893 New Zealand became the first nation to grant women the same voting rights as men. Scandinavian countries (Norway, Denmark, and Finland) followed early in the twentieth century, and the United States in 1920. It took until the 1940s for women in France and Italy to win the right to vote, and until 1971 in Switzerland. Today, women have the legal right to vote and hold office everywhere except in a few nations in the Middle East and Asia. Reliable global data on voting by gender is not always available, but in the United States women are currently somewhat more likely to vote than men, a trend which first appeared late in the 1970s. Prior to that point men were more likely to turn out to vote.

The Gender Gap in Voting

Since women vote in somewhat greater numbers than men, their votes can be decisive in a close election. This is especially important in the political calculus because American women tend to favor the Democratic Party over the Republican Party, a situation that is referred to as the **gender gap**. The gender gap has been evident in elections for national office since the 1960s.[3] For example, in the 2000 Presidential election men favored Republican George W. Bush by a 53 percent to 42 percent margin, but women supported Democrat Al Gore 54 percent to 43 percent (Connelly, 2000).

The gender gap is shaped by a combination of factors, including differing attitudes of men and women toward government and political issues in general, the stance of the parties on specific social and economic issues, and socioeconomic inequalities. To begin with, there is some indication that women, when compared to men, tend to be more critical of business, face greater economic insecurity, and are more favorably disposed to an activist role for government in addressing social issues. It is an outlook that is generally closer to the political philosophy of the Democratic party than Republicans (Kaufmann & Petrocik, 1999).

Moreover, the position of the Republican party on a number of specific issues contributed to the alienation of some women. Many see 1980 as a watershed year because that was when the party adopted a platform that supported a constitutional ban on abortions and decided to oppose the Equal Rights Amendment, thus abandoning several decades of support for that goal (Melich, 1996). Although not all women favored either initiative, it did serve to separate many women (and men) from the party. The Republican party also became identified with opposition to social programs that benefit families and women more than men: Medicaid, Social Security, parental leave, and nutritional programs for women and children. In contrast, the Democratic party has endorsed positions that resonate with significant numbers of women: gun control, environmental protection, health issues, education, and job training.

Gender inequalities in socioeconomic attainments are also a factor. Women at the lower end of the stratification system are, just as are men, more disposed to the

---

[3]Women have been more likely to support Democratic presidential candidates since 1964, and consistently more likely to support Democratic congressional candidates since 1982. Women have been more likely to identify with the Democratic party since 1964 (Seltzer, Newman & Leighton, 1997).

EXHIBIT 7.3   Partisanship and Gender, Congressional Elections, 1990–1994 (percent voting Democratic)

Income level	Women	Men	Gap
Overall	52.7%	41.6%	11.1%
Under $15,000	66.6	55.8	10.8
$15,000 to $30,000	54.1	47.2	6.9
$30,000 to $50,000	50.4	39.7	10.7
$50,000 plus	49.5	36.3	13.2

Source: Richard A. Seltzer, Jody Newman, and Melissa Voorhees Leighton, *Sex as a Political Variable*, Boulder, CO: Lynne Rienner, 1997, Table 3.10, pages 58–60.

Democratic party. Women at that level are plagued by economic insecurity, even in periods of prosperity, because they are more sensitive to the consequences of low wages and the threat of unemployment. Their concerns tend to focus on very basic issues—health insurance, child care, schools. The Democratic party over the years has been identified with creating and protecting a safety net of social welfare programs for the more vulnerable members of society such as the poverty program, Medicare and Medicaid, Social Security, unemployment insurance, and the minimum wage. Consequently, women in general are more likely to support Democratic candidates, as shown in Exhibit 7.3, and the difference is much more pronounced at lower levels of the income hierarchy.

Gender, Race, and the Gender Gap. It appears that voter turnout among Hispanics may be an exception to the gender gap found among other groups. No significant differences between women and men have shown up since the 1970s (Montoya, Hardy-Fanta & Garcia, 2000). Hispanic women are, like women in general, more likely to identify with the Democratic party. However, partisanship among Latinas differs by national origin. Puerto Rican women are definitely more likely to identify with Democrats, but the gap for Mexican women is slight. In contrast, Cuban women are more likely to be Republicans than Cuban men. This pattern of Cuban-American support for Republicans can be traced to the Kennedy administration's handling of the communist takeover of the island in the 1960s.

African-American women typically support Democrats by a margin of about nine to one. Race and class intersect for the large numbers of black women who hold (or whose husbands hold) low-paying blue-collar and service jobs. However, race is also an independent factor because Democrats have long been identified with the interests of racial and ethnic minorities. It dates from the coalition of working-class and minority voters forged by President Franklin Roosevelt in the 1930s. Therefore, the party is associated with support for civil rights legislation, voting rights, and affirmative action. African Americans voted for Al Gore in 2000 by a margin of nine to one.

Women in Government: The Representational Gap

Individual women have gained leadership roles in government in the years since they won the right to hold political office. Margaret Thatcher in Great Britain, Golda Meir in Israel, and Gro Harlem Brundtland in Norway exerted a powerful influence over the affairs of their nations. However, women as a group hold a relatively modest share of positions in government compared to their numbers in the general population. Women around the world hold an average of just 10 percent of the seats in national legislatures, and some political analysts estimate that any group must have at least 30 percent representation if it is to exert a substantial influence on politics (Kenworthy & Malami, 1999). Scandinavian countries such as Finland and Sweden have the highest levels of women's political participation, while countries such as Japan and Jordan exhibit much more modest levels. Some examples of the proportion of political participation is shown in Exhibit 7.4.

These numbers confirm that women are underrepresented in government in the United States, but they simultaneously signal significant progress since the 1960s when government was almost exclusively a male domain. There are currently 59 women in the House of Representatives and 13 Senators. Women have had to overcome a whole host of obstacles. There was, for one, the social division of labor between home and work, which extended to the political arena. As late as 1972 a majority of Americans felt that women should concentrate their energies on the home and family and "leave running the country up to men" (Lipman-Bluman, 1984). Prevailing gender stereotypes suggested they lacked the traits needed for political leadership. Then, too, women's social class position worked to their disadvantage, with relatively small numbers of women holding the upper-middle-class occupations that are the traditional recruiting ground for political candidates. Finally, it is always difficult for newcomers (women or men) to unseat incumbents, who are reelected about 90 percent of the time.

These disadvantages were challenged on a large scale beginning in the 1960s. Participation in the civil rights movement and the women's movement led to broader political involvement and political action. For example, women played a major role in grassroots attempts to revitalize communities and influence local governments on issues ranging from industrial pollution, poverty, the declining qualities of schools, and the deterioration of neighborhoods (Miller, 2000). Such movements appear to have mobilized both middle- and working-class women.

By the 1970s a number of groups such as the National Women's Political Caucus were formed to promote and foster political participation. Women increased their involvement in party politics at the community and state levels and began seeking elective office in ever greater numbers. The combination of grassroots experiences and success in local politics provided the seasoning and credibility necessary to seek higher political office. Money also entered into the calculus at that point with the creation of fund-raising groups such as EMILY's List (Early Money Is Like Yeast), formed to provide campaign funds to women very early in the electoral process when it is essential to sustain support. Interestingly, by the 1999–2000 election, the

EXHIBIT 7.4   Women in Government, Share (Percentage) of Seats in National Legislatures

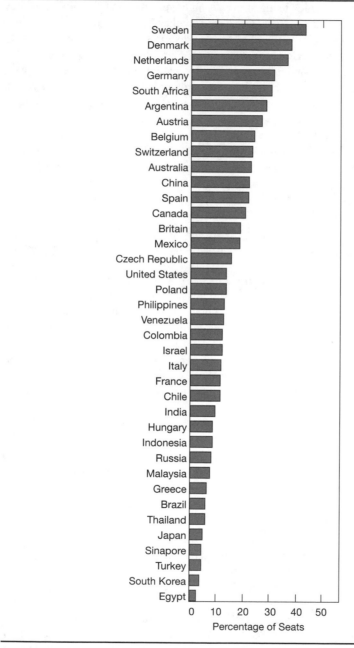

Source: "Women in Politics." *The Economist,* March 11, 2000, p. 116. © The Economist Newspaper Group, Inc. Reprinted with permission. Further reproduction prohibited. www.economist.com

EMILY's List PAC was the largest single contributor to candidates, distributing over $13 million. Thus, during the 1980s women were able to make significant progress in gaining access to positions of political power, both elected and appointive. Women currently hold positions in Congress and the Cabinet in Washington and in every state legislature, and many are governors and mayors.

Gender in Elections. As more women have entered the political arena, gender has lost some of its saliency as a factor in choosing among candidates. This is illustrated by public opinion polls. In 1937 this question was posed, "If your party nominated a women for president, would you vote for her if she were qualified for the job?" At that point less than one-third (31 percent) admitted they would support a women, but by the 1990s the same question elicited agreement by over 90 percent of both men and women (Seltzer, Newman & Leighton, 1997).

Some reluctance to support female candidates for political office remains, and gender stereotypes play a role in explaining those attitudes. There is a tendency to believe that assumed female gender traits render women less suitable for the demands of higher political offices than men. Definitions of a "good" or "ideal" candidate for President still favor masculine traits (Rosenwasser & Dean, 1989; Leeper, 1991; Huddy & Terkildsen, 1994). Perceived male traits such as strength, self-confidence, determination, and decisiveness are considered more helpful in dealing with issues such as the economy, defense, or the military. Women's perceived strengths (warmth, gentleness, compassion) are viewed as more suitable for the needs of legislative or judicial posts. In contrast, those typical female traits are considered more suitable for lower, nonexecutive positions, especially the judiciary. Thus, women who contest for national office must confront bias among some voters.

There is also some indication that women and men are treated differently by the media (Kahn, 1992; Kahn & Goldenberg, 1991; McQuillan, 1999). Analysis of Senate races shows that women tend to receive less coverage than men, and the coverage is likely to remind voters of candidates' gender. Journalists more often include women's age, marital status, and number of children than they do for men. The media tend to downplay issues and devote their efforts to the process, i.e., questions of the ability of women candidates to win, and emphasize their effectiveness in stereotypical policy areas—education, health, poverty.

Obviously, polls and attitude surveys have limits, and the question of actual gender bias in the voting booth is much more difficult to measure. Comparing the success of women candidates pitted against men is never easy because so many factors impinge upon voters' decisions that it is difficult to apportion the exact influence of gender. There is some evidence that women voters are more likely to support women candidates (Huddy & Terkildsen, 1994). However, gender is not always the decisive factor for most voters. Party preference is a major factor in voting, but voters will cross party lines for a candidate perceived as strong—woman or man—or against a weak candidate—woman or man (Zipp & Plutzer, 1985). On the whole it appears that men and women candidates are evaluated in the same manner and have an equal chance of being elected (Seltzer, Newman & Leighton, 1997).

Gender and Social Policy.   Recent electoral victories place increasing numbers of women in positions where they are able to influence public policy by introducing legislation and by supporting or opposing bills. Legislative decisions are complicated and shaped by many factors, including ideology, the characteristics of the constituencies, individual priorities, the position of the political party, and persuasion from interest groups (Barnello, 1999). Gender is one of the factors that enters into legislative behavior. Female legislators tend to have more liberal voting records and give higher priority to issues relating to women, children, and families[4] than males, who are more likely to focus on business and economic legislation (Thomas, 1994). African-American women in legislatures stand with non-black women on most issues and with African-American legislators on minority issues. If there is any single difference it is that black women exhibit an unusual degree of consensus on policy priorities (Barrett, 1995). For African-American women policy makers, the most pressing issues are clear—education, health care, and employment.

To illustrate, party affiliation is decisive on most votes in the U. S. Congress, with men and women voting with their parties on issues such as foreign aid, campaign reform, and governmental reorganization (Segal & Bruzy, 1995). However, on certain key pieces of legislation women (both Democrat and Republican) vote much differently than men. They oppose the prohibition of publicly funded abortions, support handgun control, and endorse the Family and Medical Leave Act. Thus, gender becomes a salient factor on issues that focus directly on women's rights but also on broader issues that deter violence, promote health and safety, protect the environment, support the family and child care, and upgrade education. It suggests that the increase in the proportion of women in political office has the potential to produce a discernible impact on the shape of public policy.

MINORITIES IN THE POLITICAL SPHERE

The 1960s are remembered for the violence that accompanied attempts to end barriers to African-American participation in the political process. Prohibitive poll taxes, stringent literacy tests, closed primaries, and outright intimidation were employed to deny the vote and access to public office. Massive voter registration drives encouraged by the Voting Rights Act of 1965 enfranchised hundreds of thousands of new voters. At the same time, whites' attitudes toward African-American candidates softened. Tangible evidence of this is found in public opinion polls tracking attitudes toward a black candidate for President. In 1958, almost 80 percent of blacks, compared to only 35 percent of whites, expressed readiness to support a black candidate, but by 1997 more than 90 percent of both groups expressed a willingness to endorse a black for President (Holmes, 1997). The result is that African Americans, Latinos, and other minorities now hold office at all levels of government ranging from local

---

[4]These are sometimes defined as "women's issues," but that is misleading because they transcend gender and include education, safety, health, and workplace matters that benefit all members of society.

school boards to big-city mayors, from state legislatures to state governors and cabinet officers in Washington. The election of minority candidates to public office is of inestimable symbolic value, validating the increasing openness of the political system.

People of Color and Voting

Turnout among minorities often lags behind that of whites, as emphasized in Exhibit 7.2. The discrepancy between the proportion of African Americans and whites who vote is narrowing. In 1976, when overall turnout was higher, the gap was 12 percent (61 percent for whites to 49 percent among blacks) but by 1998 the gap was five percent (46 percent to 41 percent). Part of the explanation is socioeconomic progress among the African-American population that influences political participation. Increases in educational attainment and income are all associated with higher voter turnout among all races, and black Americans have made significant progress in these areas over the last two decades.

The low Hispanic vote is a complex phenomenon and has a number of sources (del Pinal & Singer, 1997). It must be remembered that approximately one-third of the Hispanic population in the United States is ineligible because they are not yet citizens, but even eligible citizens have a low turnout. Hispanics are overrepresented among the poor and the less skilled segments of the working class, and these groups always have lower rates of voter turnout than members of white-collar occupations. Language is a barrier for others, distancing them from involvement in the process, and in some cases literacy tests are conducted in English. In addition, a high proportion of Hispanics are young, and political participation is consistently low among younger people in all groups.

Comparatively low turnout does not mean that these groups are not a significant political force, especially in those areas where they form a meaningful segment of the electorate. This is because the minority vote can be decisive in close elections. For example, 90 percent of black voters are concentrated in twenty states, including key states such as Florida, Michigan, and Pennsylvania. The six states with the largest Hispanic populations—California, Texas, Florida, New York, Illinois, and New Jersey—control over 170 of the 270 electoral votes needed to elect a President. Demographics are on the side of Latinos because they are destined to become the largest minority group and an ever-larger proportion will be eligible to vote, so that they will enjoy even greater political leverage in the twenty-first century. Consequently, both parties openly and aggressively court African-American and Latino voters.

The Democratic party stands to benefit the most from a heavy turnout of African-American voters. In every presidential election since 1964 more than 80 percent of their votes have gone to the Democratic candidate (Lee, 2000). Two of the three largest Latino populations also tend to favor the Democratic party (Hero, et al., 2000). Two-thirds of Mexican Americans and 71 percent of Puerto Ricans identify themselves as Democrats or Democratic leaning. In contrast, seven out of ten Cuban

Americans favor Republicans. Latino voters tend to be attracted by the broad civil rights stance of the Democratic party, and by its support for the preservation of Latino culture through bilingual education.

Race and Social Policy. Political representation among minorities has positive benefits for minority citizens. Among African Americans there has been an expansion of minority businesses. Most elected black officials give very high priority to fostering black-owned business, and they are in a position to accomplish this through the distribution of contracts and government purchasing practices (Jaynes & Williams, 1989). In addition, some municipalities initiated set-asides for minority businesses. The result is that black-owned businesses tend to be larger and more successful in cities with black mayors than in those with white mayors (Bates & Williams, 1993).

Cities with African-American mayors also seem to influence participation in the political process, probably because they can see the benefits of personal involvement (Bobo & Gilliam, 1990). Policing is also affected by black representation. Policing is an issue of long-standing concern to African-American citizens because some police departments, like many other organizations, once systematically discriminated against minority employment and were often socially distanced from minority communities. Moreover, incidents of white police mistreatment of black citizens continue to surface all too frequently. Hence progress in this area would seem to be a vital component in fostering interracial tolerance.

A comprehensive review of police department activities suggests that certain kinds of innovations in policing practices are more likely to emerge in communities with black political involvement (Saltzstein, 1989). For example, cities with large black populations of potential voters are more likely to have community outreach programs (storefront offices, meetings with black community groups) and a policy of measured responses (mediation as opposed to arrest) to disturbances of the peace. Communities with black mayors make more progress with minority representation on the police force and in the creation of civilian review boards that oversee police conduct.

The situation is similar for Latinos. Increases in Hispanic office holding has positive consequences in government employment, recruiting of Latino teachers, and representation on civic boards and public commissions (Hero, et al., 2000). Thus, it appears that political strength in the form of votes or elected representation does have the potential under the right circumstances to translate into specific programs benefiting minority constituents.

CONCLUSION: POLITICAL ALIENATION

One of the most troubling political trends emerging in the later decades of the twentieth century and continuing today is the widespread erosion of public support and confidence in the American political system. Moreover, political alienation is a worldwide phenomena; opinion polls in Germany, Britain, Italy, Canada, Sweden, and Austria all confirm an increasing sense of disillusionment with politicians and governmental institutions (Putman, Pharr & Dalton, 2000). Only in the Netherlands, among mature political democracies, is there clear evidence of rising public confidence.

It is convenient to describe this process with the general term **political alienation.** In practice, the term actually encompasses two separate but interrelated perceptions of the workings of government. One is a sense of "estrangement" from government expressed in a lack of faith or trust in government. The decline in trust in government over the last half of the twentieth century is dramatic. Between the mid-1950s and the 1990s the proportion of Americans who felt that "you can trust the government to do what is right most of the time" fell from 75 percent to 22 percent (Seltzer, Newman & Leighton, 1997). The numbers are even more dismal when the question focuses on a specific branch of government. In the 1990s, only 7 percent of the public expressed a "great deal" of trust in Congress, and 10 percent in the executive branch (Smith, 1997).

Estrangement focuses on feelings of trust, but there is also the more pragmatic issue of efficacy, the feeling that ordinary citizens can have an impact on governmental decisions and the direction of public policy. A lack of efficacy produces a feeling of powerlessness. Powerlessness is unmistakable in feelings that special interest groups have too much control and that political leaders are out of touch with the people. Americans tend to believe that special interest groups exercise disproportionate influence. Three of five people agree with this statement, "No matter what laws are passed, special interests will always find a way to maintain their power in Washington" (Gallup Poll, 1997).

Increases in political alienation are shaped by many factors, including some that touch all levels of the stratification system. Recurring presidential scandals (Watergate, Iran-Contra, Lewinski) contribute to negative images of government leaders. The increasing importance of soft money and PACs in financing election campaigns implies a diminishing role for individual citizens. Many people believe there are no real differences in the major political parties, suggesting an unresponsive government. Finally, the sheer complexity of contemporary political issues can overwhelm voters.

Ultimately, the presence of competing interest groups will mean that virtually any governmental action that favors one group will produce disappointment among other segments of the population. Reductions in social welfare spending or the defeat of minimum wage increments increase political alienation among the poor, while members of the middle classes are more likely to be alienated by corporate welfare, government subsidies to industry, and tax breaks for the wealthy. Thus, government actions that bring benefits to one class are likely to engender dissatisfaction among other segments of society.

As would be expected, feelings of estrangement and powerlessness tend to be linked, and the general pattern that emerges is that people at each lower level in the stratification system feel more alienated, with greater feelings of disaffection and lower perceptions of effectiveness (Verba, Nie, and Kim, 1978). Class position shapes alienation in many subtle ways. More education means greater familiarity with the dynamics of the political process, and having more money to contribute to candidates increases a sense of involvement and direction. It has also been suggested that the work of most people below the level of the upper-middle class does not give them much experience with the exercise of power and thus may contribute to feelings of powerlessness in the political sector.

The irony is that political alienation can be self-perpetuating in the sense that it may foster apathy and the failure to engage in the very activities—voting, sending money, lobbying, political organization—that might have an impact on political leaders and produce some benefits for them. At a minimum, political participation would produce a feeling of having some influence over the political process. Consequently, class position contributes to feelings of alienation, which in turn reduces the effectiveness of the least advantaged classes.

KEY CONCEPTS

corporate welfare	pluralist theory	political alienation
elite theory	Political Action	revolving door
gender gap	Committees (PACs)	soft money

SUGGESTED READING

TERRY NICHOLS CLARK and SEYMOUR MARTIN LIPSET, eds. *The Breakdown of Class Politics: A Debate on Post Industrial Stratification*. Baltimore, MD: Johns Hopkins University Press, 2000. This collection of essays exploring the impact of social class on political activity is a valuable tool for advanced analysis of this controversial topic.

DAN CLAWSON, ALAN NEUSTADT, and DENISE SCOTT. *Money Talks: Corporate PACs and Political Influence*. New York: Basic Books, 1992. A far-reaching analysis of the organization and operation of business PACs, including interviews with corporate officials.

ELEANOR CLIFT and TOM BRAZAITIS. *Madam President: Shattering the Last Glass Ceiling*. New York: A Lisa Drew Book/Scribner, 2000. Two Washington, DC, journalists examine the status of women in contemporary politics and the problems they confront.

ELIZABETH DREW. *Whatever It Takes*. New York: Viking Penguin, 1997. A disturbing portrait of the role of money in shaping the elections of 1996.

JOSEPH S. NYE, PHILIP D. ZELIKOV, and DAVID C. KING, eds. *Why People Don't Trust Government*. Cambridge, MA: Harvard University Press, 1996. A collection of essays suitable for advanced students that explore the sources of political alienation.

RICHARD A. SELTZER, JODY NEWMAN, and MELISSA VOORHEES LEIGHTON. *Sex as a Political Variable*. Boulder, CO: Lynne Rienner, 1997. This broad analysis of voting for and by women in the United States dispels a number of misconceptions about the role of gender in the political process.

PHILIP M. STERN. *Still the Best Congress Money Can Buy*. Washington, DC: Regnery Gateway, 1992. A highly critical appraisal of the influence of special interests on financing congressional campaigns.

SUE THOMAS. *How Women Legislate*. New York: Oxford University Press, 1994. A comparison of women's and men's legislative priorities and approach to the law making process.

MICHAEL USEEM. *The Inner Circle: Large Corporations and the Rise of Political Activity in the U.S. and U.K*. New York: Oxford University Press, 1983. This study emphasizes the links among corporate executives.

USEFUL WEB SITES

The Center for Responsive Politics (**www.opensecrets.org**) tracks the role of money in the political process.

EMILY's List (**www.emilyslist.org**) is dedicated to fostering women's participation in the political process through funding and education.

The Federal Election Commission (**www.fec.gov**) collects and collates voting data and reports financial contributions by individuals and political action committees.

The John F. Kennedy School of Government at Harvard maintains this web site (**www.vanishingvoter.org**) which focuses on Americans who ignore the electoral process.

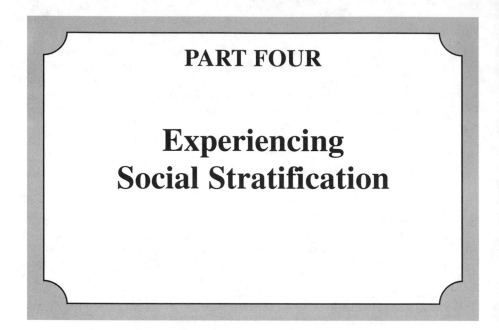

PART FOUR

Experiencing Social Stratification

Class, race, and gender shape the manner in which people experience their social and physical environment in both direct and subtle ways, determining their access to the pleasures of life and influencing the way they perceive the world and organize their lives. Chapter 8 surveys the broad issue of life chances with special attention to the way in which one's place in the stratification system structures experiences in the criminal justice system, impacts health and illness, and determines environmental justice. Chapter 9 explores the social organization of life at different class levels. Chapter 10 focuses on how people think about class, race, and gender, and their place in society.

CHAPTER EIGHT

Class, Race, Gender, and Life Chances

THE CONCEPT OF LIFE CHANCES

Class, race, and gender have broad and significant implications for individuals. It is clear that striking income, status, and political differences separate bankers, bakers, beauticians, brokers, and bookkeepers, but the consequences extend well beyond earnings and politics. Max Weber introduced the concept of life chances in connection with social classes to focus attention on the comprehensive consequences of social class. He explained **life chances** as "the typical chances for a supply of goods, external living conditions, and personal life experiences" (Weber, 1946: 180). The concept of life chances thus focuses on the quality of life and the way that class, race, and gender expands or limits access to the benefits society has to offer.

The impact is often direct and conspicuous, as when the modest financial resources of the poor or the working class impose some limits on the educational attainments of children, or their ability to afford luxury SUVs. However, the financial implications of class are also less obvious, more subtle. The operation of the tax system nicely reveals the idea of life chances. To illustrate, class influences whether or not people pay taxes, with 2,574 Americans earning more than $200,000 not paying any income tax in a recent year (Mastio, 1998). Class also shapes the risk of being audited by the IRS, with poorer people (earning less than $25,000) checked more frequently than those making $100,000 or more (David Johnston, 2000). The effect of class even survives death; Although millionaires in a recent year left estates of $202 million, only $75 million (37 percent) of that wealth was taxed (Drew & Johnston, 1996). In short, any individual's experiences with taxation are clearly linked to class position.

It is possible to compile an extensive list of life chances sorted by class, race, and gender. Some examples are infant mortality, victimization in a violent crime, going to jail, obesity, use of birth control and the practice of safe sex, educational attainments and lifetime earnings, and political orientation and chances of holding political office. The idea of life chances can be best illustrated by focusing on several extremely salient areas of life: the digital divide; experiences in the criminal justice system; and opportunities for health, the risks of illness, and exposure to subtle forms of environmental hazards.

THE DIGITAL DIVIDE

The digital revolution is reshaping many facets of modern life, and the creation of the Internet must be ranked as one of the most exciting developments, giving people access to unprecedented sources of information. The gulf between those who have access to computers and the Internet and those who do not is called the **digital divide** and has profound implications. People are able to use the Internet to do research, find health-related information, search for a job, do their banking, shop for a book or a car or a house, visit a chat room, and communicate with virtually anyone anywhere with access to a computer. Obviously, those lacking access are at a disadvantage, especially children, who can use the Internet to help them learn to count and read, to do research for homework, or simply peruse an encyclopedia.

By the beginning of 2001 over one-half of all American households have a computer and over 40 percent have an Internet hookup. The digital divide is constantly narrowing as more and more schools and libraries offer electronic access, but there is no substitute for a home computer, and the digital divide can be measured by class, racial, and ethnic differences. As Exhibit 8.1 clearly shows, wealthy upper-middle-class parents far outdistance the poor in being able to provide online access at home. Barely one in ten poor homes can afford such access. There are also racial and ethnic differences, with more than one-half of Asian-American families connected to the Internet compared to less than one-quarter of African-American or Latino households.

It would be a mistake to think that the digital divide is merely a matter of access. Rather, it is also a matter of skills and the availability of online resources. People at all levels use the web to locate employment opportunities and housing and health-care information, but the Internet is dominated by information for the most advantaged segments of the population. Few sites deliver practical information for the poor. For example, fewer than 1 percent of sites direct users to local, entry-level jobs (Rodger, 2000). Likewise, only 1 percent of sites focus on low-income housing. Add to that the fact that sites for beginning English speakers or those with marginal literacy are extremely uncommon. Thus, the digital divide encompasses both access and content.

EXHIBIT 8.1   Percentage of U.S. Households with Internet Access

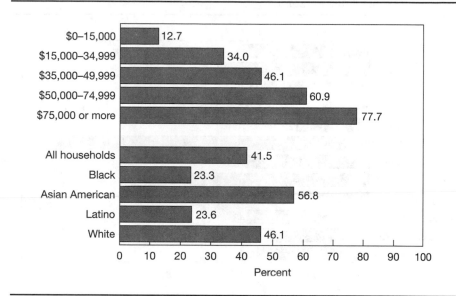

Source: U.S. Department of Commerce. *Falling Through the Net: Toward Digital Inclusion.* Washington, DC: U.S. Government Printing Office, 2000.

... AND THE POOR GET JAIL: THE CRIMINAL JUSTICE SYSTEM

Crime is an all too common problem in the United States, and the chances of being a victim are shaped by class, race, and gender, as shown in Exhibit 8.2. An average of 50 people per 1,000 in the United States are victims of violent crimes[1] each year, but the poor, people of color (especially American Indians), and men are at the greatest risk. Moreover, class and race combine to produce the very highest rates of victimization among poor members of all racial and ethnic groups.

There is a widespread perception that crime is the almost exclusive province of the poor, especially young, urban, black males. It is an image fueled by media coverage of criminal activity, and the force of the image echoes in the words attributed to Reverend Jesse Jackson, "There is nothing more painful to me at this stage of my life to walk down the street and hear footsteps and start thinking about robbery—and then look around and see someone white and feel relieved" (Will, 1993). It is true that African Americans, who make up no more than 12 percent of the total population, comprise a disproportionate share of prison populations (32 percent of

---

[1]Violent crimes include simple and aggravated assault, robbery, and rape and sexual assault against people aged 12 and older.

EXHIBIT 8.2   Average Annual Number of Violent Victimizations per 1,000 Persons

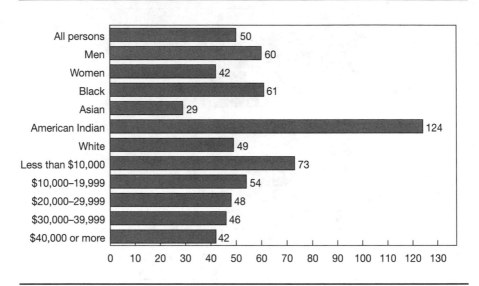

Source: Sourcebook of Criminal Justice Statistics. U.S. Department of Justice, Bureau of Justice Statistics, NCJ 171147. Washington, DC: U.S. Government Printing Office, 1998.

federal prisoners and 50 percent of state prisoners).[2] However, it must be remembered that ending up in jail is the end result of a long process and that the poor and minorities have different experiences at every stage of the process. Statistics show that the poor are more likely than the more affluent to be detained, arrested, charged, convicted, and if convicted, more likely to be sentenced to prison. In short, prison populations represent the end result of a series of decisions by people in the criminal justice system: police officers, prosecutors, juries, judges, and parole boards (Reiman, 1996).

Crime and Social Structure.   Social scientists have long been interested in clarifying the role of social structure in explaining criminal behavior. The external conditions that foster crime are extremely complex, but there is some evidence that inferior economic conditions—the environment that the poor confront on a regular basis—is associated with higher crime rates. For example, factors such as unemployment rates, income inequality, and the availability of entry-level jobs have been linked to higher rates of some kinds of property and violent crimes (Crutchfield &

---

[2]There is some evidence that this is not a uniquely American situation. Minorities in Canada, Australia, England, and Wales are also overrepresented in prison populations (Tonry, 1994).

Pitchford, 1997; Shihadeh & Ousey, 1998). This research suggests that economic deprivation in all its forms creates an environment that can increase the incidence of crime.

Defining Crime.   The very act of identifying and defining crime is a social act, but the issue of the social construction of crime is beyond the scope of this volume. It can simply be noted that while certain acts are criminal by virtually any contemporary American definition of deviance—homicide, rape, child abuse, arson—others are subject to different interpretations. Prostitution is one such case, largely illegal in the United States, but lawful and licensed elsewhere. Prostitution remains illicit because the idea of sex for pay violates the values and beliefs of powerful segments of society. However, there are also many who favor decriminalizing prostitution because it is seen as a "victimless crime," a consensual act among adults. Prostitution is also frequently the province of poor and uneducated women, exploited by procurers and organized crime. Human rights groups claim that millions of poor women and children have fallen victim to global networks of sex traffickers since the 1970s (Pope, 1997). The women come from impoverished Asian nations and the former Soviet Union; they eventually emerge in Los Angeles, New York, and Washington, DC. The basic thesis is that the behavior of the poor is more likely to be defined as illegal by middle-class decision-makers (legislators, law enforcement officials, and judges).

The Incidence of Crime.   Criminologists continue to debate whether or not men, the poor, and minorities initially commit a disproportionate share of crimes (Tittle & Meier, 1990). It is difficult to arrive at a definitive answer to the question because not all crimes come to the attention of the police and subsequently show up in official statistics. The fact is, when asked, the majority of Americans at *all* social class levels admit that they have done things that could get them in trouble with the law—petty theft, disorderly conduct, tax evasion, assault, auto theft, and carrying concealed weapons are among the most common crimes. It is also clear that members of the middle classes commit many of the same crimes usually attributed to the urban poor—drugs, armed robbery, breaking and entering, and vandalism (Reiman, 1996). Most social scientists conclude that illegal behavior is relatively common at all levels in the stratification system, but that members of the criminal justice system respond differently to different groups at every point in the criminal justice process.

Detaining and Questioning.   In 1997 Patricia Appleton, an African-American Chicago travel agent was stopped upon arriving at O'Hare airport and subjected to a strip search for no apparent reason other than her race (Howlett, 2000). Her experience was apparently all too typical because black women are nine times more likely than other passengers to be x-rayed or subjected to intrusive searches by customs officers (GAO, 2000). This conduct is known as **racial profiling**, targeting people for heightened law enforcement scrutiny based on their race. Research confirms that blacks are more likely to be stopped by the police, although usually for the same kinds of offenses (suspicion of drug possession, traffic violations, drunkenness) and are not always treated differently during the encounter (Norris et al., 1992). Police departments around the country are currently facing charges of racial profiling in making traffic stops. Police departments counter that they have a clear policy prohibiting the use of race as a factor in stops, and deny discrimination.

Arrest and Charging. It has long been known that for equally serious offenses, poor people are more likely to be arrested and if arrested, more likely to be charged than those from higher social classes (Gold, 1966). The police are often singled out for censure on this point, with critics claiming that the police openly discriminate. Concentrating on individual biased police officers ignores the broader context in which crime occurs and the realities of policing. Police officers' actions are often determined by suspects' behavior or judgments of their character (Piliavin & Briar, 1964). To illustrate, the police (and most members of the public) are likely to respond differently to a belligerent drunk at an elegant country club or a campus fraternity house than to the same behavior at a saloon adjacent to an urban housing project. Moreover, contacts between police and civilians are more likely to end in arrest when the encounter becomes confrontational, and poor men are more likely to challenge police officers. Police also respond differently to different classes of people because they can anticipate different consequences on the basis of previous experiences in similar situations. For example, when dealing with juvenile suspects, police officers can logically anticipate that the parents of wealthy youths are more likely to be aware of their Constitutional rights, will hire attorneys to defend themselves, and may consider lawsuits. The same kind of considerations influence the decisions of prosecutors who make the decision to bring formal charges.

The race of suspects complicates matters for African-American males. Minority suspects are also exposed to more rigorous prosecution, including more severe charges, stiffer penalties, and full-scale prosecutions (Editors, 1988). These numbers confirm the opinion of many people. More than 40 percent of Americans, and more than 70 percent of African Americans, believe that minorities are treated less fairly than others in the criminal justice system (Aronson, Rovella & Van Voris, 1998).

Plea Bargaining and Convictions. The most salient incident in the criminal justice process is conviction. Looking at all individuals accused of the same crime and having similar prior records shows that poor defendants are more frequently found guilty than the more well-to-do (Reiman, 1996). Two major factors combine to produce this result: the availability of bail and the quality of legal counsel, and both are influenced by finances.

Those released on bail are at an advantage because they are able to actively contribute to their own defense by collecting evidence and seeking out witnesses and supportive testimony. In contrast, the poor lacking the resources to meet bail are kept in prison, which is in itself a form of punishment. Moreover, those stranded in jail may also be more vulnerable to prosecutorial pressure and thus willing to accept plea

bargains that will gain them shorter sentences or immediate release from custody.[3]
The result is that they may be tempted to plead guilty to lesser charges (such as
breaking and entering rather than burglary) which will set them free. Unfortunately,
that freedom is bought at the cost of a criminal record that later makes it more difficult to find employment and contributes to their continued poverty.

Legal Defense for the Indigent. All citizens accused of serious crimes are
entitled to legal representation, and those too poor to afford a lawyer are granted a
court-appointed attorney. Statistics show that about 80 percent of defendants charged
with felonies in the nation's seventy-five largest counties relied upon court-
appointed counsel for legal representation (Smith & DeFrances, 1996).[4] It is clear
that assigned counsel is not always as effective as that provided by private attorneys.
In one study, public defenders won dismissals for their clients in only 11 percent of
cases compared to 48 percent of the clients of private attorneys (Champion, 1989).
Seventy-five percent of the inmates in state prisons were represented by assigned
counsel. A significant proportion of the fault must lie with the system rather than
individual court-appointed lawyers or public defenders. They are often young and
inexperienced in criminal work, and they frequently have very limited financial
resources to devote to the collection of evidence and hiring expert witnesses. For
example, in Virginia, they earn $40 to $60 per hour up to a maximum $845 for
felonies (except homicide) that are punishable by more than twenty years in prison
(Cauchon, 1999). In addition, public defenders usually have heavy caseloads that
preclude devoting enough time to each and every case. An American Bar Association study found that some public defenders have annual caseloads of more than 500
cases with up to 300 of them juveniles (Puritz, 1995).

Sentencing and Imprisonment. Some two million American men and
women are behind bars. Predictions based on these numbers mean the chances of
any person going to prison during their lifetime is 5.1 percent, but the racial divide
for males is dramatic. White males have a 4.4 percent chance compared to the risk
for black males of 28.5 percent (Bonzcar & Beck, 1997). Wide variations prevail in
sentences imposed on whites and blacks or women and men for similar offenses,
showing that some jurisdictions deliver justice more equally than others (Crutchfield, Bridges & Pitchford, 1994). Therefore, the overrepresentation of African
Americans in prisons is influenced by that consideration. Race appears to continue
to play a role in certain situations, especially physical attacks (homicides, assaults,

---

[3]The vast majority of criminal convictions in the United States are the result of negotiated pleas,
somewhere between 75 and 90 percent.

[4]There are three basic systems for providing legal representation for the indigent (Smith &
DeFrances, 1996). Thirty states rely primarily on a public defender office staffed by full or part-time
salaried staff. Assigned counsel programs utilize private lawyers appointed by the courts as needed and
reimburse some fees and expenses. Contract attorney systems are agreements with lawyers and bar associations to provide representation in return for fees specified in advance.

CASE STUDY
The Death Penalty Question

The death penalty is a controversial issue. The death penalty is banned in 108 nations, with only the United States, India, and Japan among industrial democracies continuing the practice (*The Economist*, 2000c). Over three thousand persons currently await execution in America's prisons, 98 percent of whom are men. A majority of Americans favor the idea of the death penalty, although support seems to be slipping. Those who support it generally feel that it is appropriate punishment for serious crimes such as murder, and they believe it acts as a deterrent to other potential offenders. Opponents of the death penalty argue that it is morally wrong for the government to take a life and that the system regularly makes mistakes and convicts innocent people. There is room for disagreement on most of these issues, but it cannot be disputed that errors occur.

The United States Supreme Court has repeatedly ruled that the threat of the death penalty puts a citizen at special risk, and consequently the legal system must be especially attentive in capital cases. One consequence is the requirement that convictions are automatically appealed. Another is the rule that states are obligated to provide legal aid for those too poor to afford an attorney. Unfortunately, it is often the case that the criminal justice system is flawed and that defendants on trial for their lives, especially the indigent, are frequently represented by inferior or poorly trained lawyers lacking the legal and financial resources needed to adequately handle capital cases (Coyle, Strasser & Lavelle, 1990).

It is estimated that a proper defense in a death penalty case requires months of research and preparation and costs $250,000 or more, but in many cases defendants are represented by lawyers who are paid a few thousand dollars and devote only a few days to the case (Dirk Johnston, 2000). The families of defendants with limited means are usually unable to afford top quality legal representation and are forced to settle for any lawyer willing to take the case. The result is often inept lawyering. The *Chicago Tribune* in 1999 found that thirty-three death row inmates were represented by an attorney who had been disbarred or suspended. In Texas, the discipline rate for lawyers representing death row inmates is eight times higher than for lawyers overall.

Clearly, the allocation of economic resources is a major part of the problem, either as a result of inattention or a disregard for the legal needs of the poor. States set unrealistically low limits on compensation for the lawyer's time and expenses, and moneys for investigations, expert witnesses, and appeals are often in short supply. For example, despite the obvious value of DNA evidence, only New York and Illinois pay for DNA testing in old cases where the guilt of the accused is challenged. Lawyers assigned to death penalty cases may be ill-equipped to handle the complexities of a major trial. Public defenders are overworked, court-appointed lawyers are often young and inexperienced, and not all states provide pretrial training for court-appointed lawyers preparing for capital cases. The result is that the indigent are denied the right to an effective and credible defense. The process in Illinois had so many flaws that the governor called a moratorium on executions after new evidence cleared thirteen men who had been convicted and sent to death row between 1977 and 2000.

and sexual violence) against whites by blacks (Spohn & Cederblom, 1994). In such situations blacks consistently receive harsher sentences than whites. Between 1976 and 1994, 275 convicts were executed, and 84 percent of their victims were white, although less than one-half of all murder victims are white. It is still a society that reacts quickly to acts of interpersonal violence by minorities.

Another consistent pattern of differential sentencing shows up in white-collar crimes. They are crimes of the upper middle class and are punished less severely than the crimes of the poor and minorities (Case Study).

CASE STUDY
Sentencing White-Collar Criminals

The very nature of some upper middle class occupations puts people in a position to engage in illegal activity called white-collar crime. **White-collar crimes** are offenses committed by people acting in their legitimate occupational roles. The offenders are professionals, businesspersons, government officials, who , by virtue of their jobs, have the opportunity to engage in a variety of illegal or unethical acts. The crimes include accepting or paying bribes, fraud, tax evasion, and embezzlement. Billions of dollars are lost through white-collar crime. They are crimes that can only be committed by people in positions of authority and trust. Embezzlement (misappropriating funds that are entrusted to one's care) is a case in point (Exhibit 8.3). The people that have responsibility for clients' funds are lawyers, union officers, realtors, or stock brokers, not teachers, janitors, or plumbers. The proportion of all workers who embezzle or commit white-collar crimes is small, but these criminals are clearly treated differently than lower-class people who commit property crimes.

EXHIBIT 8.3   Sentencing Patterns for Different Forms of Crime

	Sentenced to Prison (Percentage)	Average Sentence (in Months)	Average Time Served (in Months)
Crimes of the poor			
Robbery	99%	101.1	60.2
Burglary	82	62.8	26.0
Larceny/theft	39	17.9	15.2
White-collar crimes			
Fraud	48	22.2	15.6
Tax law violation	43	25.2	11.6
Embezzlement	31	15.7	11.0

Source: Original data in *Sourcebook of Criminal Justice Statistics*, compiled by Jeffrey Reiman, *The Rich Get Richer and the Poor Get Prison*. Boston, MA: Allyn and Bacon, 1995, Table 5, page 125.

A STRATIFIED HEALTH CARE SYSTEM

The specter of ill health threatens everyone, but the risk of sickness, injury, and even death is not equally distributed across societies. One of the most consistent and disturbing findings in the health care field in the United States and elsewhere is that women and men, racial and ethnic groups, and people at different levels in the stratification system have unequal chances of suffering from virtually every disease, have different experiences in the health care system, and have different mortality rates (Adler, et al., 1993). Among the medical conditions and risks unevenly distributed in societies are asthma, certain kinds of cancer, diabetes, high blood pressure, heart disease, homicides, infant mortality, and psychological distress. Consequently, there are revealing differences in life expectancy. A white female born in the United States has a life expectancy of 79.6 years, five years longer than a white male (73.3) and a black female (73.9), and almost fifteen years longer than an African-American male (64.9) (Singh, et al., 1994). There is no single explanation for the stratification of health care. Rather, it reflects the interaction of many different factors, including socioeconomic conditions such as poverty, the availability of health insurance, access to medical facilities and treatment by health care professionals, unequal safety and health risks on the job, and variations in lifestyle, all of which play a part in the outcome.

Health Insurance

No one is exempt from illness, but the presence of insurance coverage can buffer some of the financial and emotional stress. Those living without health insurance constantly worry that unexpected illness or injury will strike and huge medical bills accumulate. In 1999, more than 42 million Americans (15 percent of the population) were without health insurance. It must be remembered that the vast majority of working people in the United States obtain health insurance through their jobs or the work of some member of their family. The lack of health insurance translates into constant worry and causes people to miss the kinds of treatments that would prevent more serious illness. For instance, one in twenty-five of the uninsured are unable to fill their prescriptions, and 30 percent report failing to get the care they need (*The Economist*, 1997c).

Not surprisingly, the poor face a much greater risk of being uninsured, with about one-third lacking medical coverage. Americans are also divided by race and ethnicity; 35 percent of Latinos are uninsured, 22 percent of African Americans, 21 percent of Asian Americans, and 15 percent of whites (Campbell, 1998). Thanks to Medicare coverage for the elderly and Medicaid for the disadvantaged, only 13 percent of adults not in the labor force go without insurance. However, children fare badly. Ten million children (almost 14 percent) lack insurance. Health insurance is an important consideration, especially for children, but universal coverage does not eliminate the link between class and health. There was, for example, no overall improvement in health indicators when Britain introduced its National Health Service, and Scandinavian countries that protect all their citizens with universal health insurance have been able to weaken but not eliminate the link between social class and illness (Adler, et al., 1993).

Among the most vulnerable groups are new immigrants. Isolated by language and culture, restrained by a lack of insurance, unfamiliar with modern drugs and technology, and worried that the medical bureaucracy is somehow linked to immigration authorities, many turn to an underground health care system (Steinhauer, 2000). The result is that some immigrants avoid conventional medicine entirely and some depend upon herbal remedies, outdated and black market medicines unwisely administered, and even mystical treatments such as amulets to ward off evil sprits and exorcisms. While these practices may cause no immediate harm, they produce delays in seeking help until people become so ill they must turn to hospital emergency rooms.

Discrepancies in Treatment

Making contact with health care professionals is but the first step in the direction of rehabilitation. There are a number of areas in which differences in diagnosis and treatment based on class, race, and gender appear. These differences range from relatively small things to patterns of life and death. For example, it may be of relatively minor importance to find that African Americans and Latinos with broken bones are less likely than whites to be given pain medication in emergency rooms (Healy, 1999). However, heart disease and infant morality are much more salient issues.

Cardiac Care.   Heart disease is the leading cause of death in industrial nations around the world (Ratzan, Filerman & LeSar, 2000). Survival from heart attacks depends upon diagnosis, speed of reaction, and type of treatment. Race and gender influence response to patients with chest pains (Shulman, et al., 1999; Rathore, et al., 2000; Pope, et al., 2000). African-American and women patients describing severe chest pain are much less likely to be referred for cardiac catheterization—the best diagnostic tool—than whites and men. The disparity is greatest for black women, who are 60 percent less likely to be referred than white men. Among people admitted to hospitals with diagnosed heart problems, men and white patients are much more likely to undergo major life-saving procedures such as angioplasty, coronary bypass surgery, or cardiac catheterization (Pope, et al, 2000). This pattern prevails regardless of age, overall health status, and insurance coverage.

Infant Mortality.   One of the best single indicators of the health status of a population is the infant mortality rate, which reflects the convergence of key social and economic factors such as the status of public health, climate and natural resources, health care expenditures, the availability of medical professionals and technology, and other factors. The world average rate of infant mortality is 57 deaths per 1,000 live births (PRB, 2000). The situation is acute in countries such as Ethiopia

EXHIBIT 8.4   Infant Mortality Rates by Race and Ethnicity

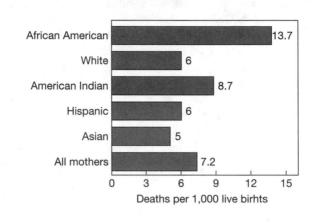

Source: CDC/NCHS: *Infant Mortality Statistics*, www.cdc.gov/nchs, August, 2000.

(116), Iraq (127), Laos (104), Sierra Leone (157), places racked by war or famine or AIDs. The number of infant deaths at childbirth stands at 7.0 per 1,000 births for the United States. Although there has been steady improvement in the United States over the years, the rate still remains above that of some other industrial nations such as Austria, Britain, Canada, France, Germany, and Japan.

There are meaningful differences among racial and ethnic groups in American society, as shown in Exhibit 8.4. African-American infants are at the greatest risk, having a rate well above all other groups. Native American babies also have a rate above the national average while white, Asian Americans, and Latinos fare much better.

Infants are put in danger by a combination of socioeconomic and lifestyle factors. One of the greatest problems is the lack of adequate prenatal care for the mother. Minorities and the poor experience more health problems under any circumstances and are less likely to have health insurance. Consequently, less than three-quarters of Latino, African-American, and American Indian women report receiving prenatal care during the first trimester (Pollard & O'Hare, 1999: 18). Poor women are also more frequently undernourished. To this must be added lifestyle behaviors such as smoking that increase the risk of underdeveloped babies.

A much less well-known but related issue is the problem of maternal deaths associated with childbirth. Each year over 300 mothers die during delivery or soon thereafter. African-American women are four times as likely to die in childbirth as white women, a pattern that has remained unchanged since the 1960s (Stolberg, 1999). The sources of this discrepancy are not well understood, but certainly the fact that black women more commonly suffer from hypertension and diabetes, which can produce complications during labor, is a relevant factor.

Occupational Safety and Health

Occupational safety and health is a major workplace issue because many people labor in environments that are dangerous. Six thousand people are killed at work each year, and another 6 million workers suffer injuries and illnesses, including more than 2 million injuries that involve lost workdays (U.S. Bureau of Labor Statistics, 1995). These figures do not include long-term latent illnesses such as cancers that are difficult to link to specific workplace toxins and are consequently typically underreported. As a general rule, the occupations of the working class, the poor, and minorities are more hazardous than white-collar work. Factories, mines, mills, ship-yards, meat packing plants, auto assembly lines, and construction sites are danger-ous places, teeming with moving machinery, power tools, electrical shocks, and toxic substances from which the effects may not appear for years.

The number of occupational illnesses has been on the increase since the mid-1980s, and the bulk of that increase can be attributed to one cause, "repetitive trauma," which includes conditions due to repeated pressure, vibration, or motion. Workers facing this risk factor are clerical workers, truck drivers, meat packers and poultry processors, sewing machine operators, and assembly line workers of all kinds. In all of these occupations the job demands repeated movements or exposes people to frequent impact or shock that can cause disabling illness over time. The most well-known form of repetitive trauma is carpal tunnel syndrome, a painful wrist inflammation associated with working with computers.

Stress.   Despite the widespread emphasis on the dangers of the fast-paced, high-stress life of corporate executives, investment bankers, and neurosurgeons, the evidence suggests that lower white-collar and blue-collar workers are the most likely to experience stress and consequently be at heightened risk of heart disease. Some of the highest stress jobs are: secretary, waitress, police officer, editor, medical interns, and air traffic controllers (Armour, 1998). Stress is generated by a combina-tion of factors, including repetitive tasks (assembly line workers), unremitting pace (interns, secretaries), and continual deadlines (editors, waitresses, bus drivers). In addition, a key factor in the incidence of stress is the lack of control over the situa-tion, which certainly describes the majority of manual and service jobs.

Workplace Violence.   Eleven percent of French male workers and 9 percent of French female workers report being assaulted on the job (McNamee, 1998). American workers are less likely to be physically attacked (1 percent of men and 4 percent of women), yet 2 million people are assaulted and over 1,000 are killed at work each year. In fact, homicide became the second leading cause of fatalities in the workplace during the 1990s. Working-class and lower-middle-class people are most vulnerable because their work routines expose them to crime, usually rob-beries. Taxi drivers, gas station attendants, convenience store clerks, and fast-food restaurant workers are all at relatively high risk. Mehrle Reeker, a 60-year-old con-venience store clerk in Florida is a classic case, murdered during a robbery that yielded the bandit a mere $52. The overrepresentation of women in many of these jobs helps to explain why homicide is the leading cause of death for women on the job and the third leading cause for men (Anfusco, 1994).

Lifestyles

Social class differences in lifestyles also have implications for well-being. Upper-middle-class persons appear to have been quicker to reject unhealthy lifestyles. This includes behaviors such as cigarette smoking, lack of regular exercise, and poor nutritional habits, all of which are more common at lower levels in the stratification system and are behaviors associated with heart disease and some forms of cancer. Lower-class people are also less likely to engage in preventive care. To illustrate, women at each higher social class level are more likely to have Pap tests and mammograms. It appears that the poor are unlikely to develop a self-management approach to health care; rather, they seek help for specific illnesses but tend not to adopt the lifestyles that help to prevent illness (Cockerham, et al., 1986).

Outreach and patient education programs can weaken but not eliminate the class–lifestyle link. However, it is important to note that lifestyles are not always simply a matter of individual choice, but are also a matter of opportunities. For example, there are class differences in the way health programs are offered and organized. While employees are increasingly encouraged or forced into managed-care plans, some executives continue to enjoy no-cost coverage and unlimited access to physicians and specialists (Myerson, 1996). Corporate-supported wellness and health programs are also much more likely to be aimed at members of the executive and managerial levels than the production workers on the factory floor (Rundle, 1987). In some businesses, health facilities remain an executive prerogative, a status symbol. Moreover, even where programs and facilities are available to all workers, blue-collar workers will find it more difficult to gain access to the facilities. It is, for example, difficult for large numbers to use company fitness facilities during the same fixed lunch break, and lower-level workers do not have the flexibility of scheduling that executives do.

It is also evident that men tend to participate in a lifestyle that involves more risk than women. A large part of this is due to the fact that men are more commonly working in high-risk occupations such as agriculture, construction, and truck driving. Men also more frequently engage in behaviors that increase the risk of illness and accidents such as smoking, drinking, and driving over the speed limit. Women in the United States are on average more sensitive to the advantages of good nutrition, and they put that knowledge into practice.

Environmental Justice

Most poor people face a continuing struggle. They struggle to find work, to feed their families, to maintain their homes, to educate their children, to survive on a daily basis in substandard housing and in poor neighborhoods where crime rates are high. Still another problem surfaced in the 1980s, when it was recognized that poor and minority neighborhoods were too often located near toxic waste sites or adjacent to polluting industries (Stretesky & Hogan, 1998). Proximity to toxic wastes and emissions is linked to birth defects, cancer, lupus, and a whole host of other health problems. A combination of grass-roots activism, legal challenges, and government action is aimed at **environmental justice,** identifying and addressing the potentially adverse health effects of governmental and commercial actions on minority and low-income populations.

Both industry and government must share the criticism for putting people at risk. Plants that spew toxic wastes into the air are commonly found adjacent to poor or minority neighborhoods. One example can be found in the Manchester area of Houston, Texas (Potok, 1997). The community surrounding a sulfuric acid regeneration plant has a per capita income of $6,031, and one-third of the residents live in poverty. Ninety-eight percent of the residents are minorities, largely Hispanic. The federal government is not exempt from similar charges. It devotes millions of dollars to providing subsidized housing to the poor, and a Texas newspaper found that 40 percent of public housing nationwide is located within one mile of a toxic waste site or a toxic air pollution source (Flournoy & Loftis, 2000). That translates into more than 850,000 federally subsidized apartments for America's poorest that are located near one, two, three, or even a dozen factories that emit noxious air pollution.

Several factors combine to help explain building near toxic waste sites or locating chemical factories in predominately poor and minority areas (Stretesky & Hogan, 1998; Hird & Reese, 1998). Overt or thoughtless discrimination must be weighed as a factor, considering the disproportionate impact on racial and ethnic groups, although it is difficult to document. The economics of cheaper land adjacent to poor communities also plays a role. Research shows comparatively low levels of political mobilization in threatened communities, which means that they are not well equipped to fight proposed industrial sites and hazardous plants.

Endangered communities are not without resources and support in their struggle for environmental justice. Since 1994 federal agencies have been required to assess the impact of construction and land use on both the physical and the socioeconomic environment, including factors such as literacy, lifestyles, occupations, property values, and community values (Millan, 1997) Consequently, a number of different projects have been successfully challenged. In Kansas, a federal highway project was stalled because of potential damage to wetlands and the cultural life of the Haskell Indian Nations University (Lavelle, 1997). In another case, licensing for a uranium plant was denied because it was adjacent to two small African-American communities (Millan, 1997). Much of the pressure at the local level for environmental justice comes from a grassroots movement largely populated by women lacking prior scientific expertise (Brown & Ferguson, 1995).

CONCLUSION: SHAPING LIFE CHANCES

Individuals' chances of equitable treatment in matters of taxation, the criminal justice system, and the health care system are shaped by class, race, and gender, but there is no single source of the discrepancies. Rather, they reflect the convergence of a complicated set of social and structural factors.

Flawed Delivery Systems.   Institutional systems designed for the delivery of justice and health care often exhibit shortcomings that work to the disadvantage of the poor and minorities. Health insurance is not universally available, creating a two-tiered health care system in which those without insurance must depend upon over-burdened clinics and emergency rooms, where the care is often aimed at crisis management rather than long-term care. For example, uninsured children suffering asthma attacks or seizures may receive medications for the immediate problem but no long-term health management (Shearer, 2000). In the same way, the criminal justice system lacks the economic resources to provide adequate legal services for all disadvantaged persons accused of crimes. More than one state legislature is unwilling or unable to devote enough money to court-appointed attorneys or take steps to ensure that people have effective counsel.

Racial, Ethnic, Gender Bias.   Members of some groups may be the victims of intentional or unintentional forms of discrimination. It is clear from a number of studies that African Americans, Hispanics, and women are apt to have experiences in diagnosis and treatment that are unfavorable. Racial and gender profiling is more likely to introduce blacks and women into the criminal justice system. In these cases the discriminatory behavior may be based on outright prejudice, unexamined stereotypes, or mere ignorance of differences among groups.

Socioeconomic Environment.   People of color and the poor often live in neighborhoods that offer limited resources or are dangerous, or both. Not only are many communities exposed to ongoing environmental hazards, but everyday life is also uncertain. Many retail stores and major grocery chains are unwilling to locate in poor neighborhoods, and pharmacies are less likely to stock basic medicines (Morrison, et al., 2000). Poorer neighborhoods have poorer living conditions and higher rates of crime, meaning that people are at greater risk of illness and of becoming the victim of a serious crime. Families at the bottom of the class system are twice as likely to be targets of a crime as people at the top. The most serious forms of crime are assaults and homicides, and the results measured by projected life spans are disheartening. Almost two-thirds of African-American teenagers living in poor areas of Chicago and New York are not expected to live to age 65 (Koretz, 1999)! This compares with a national average of 38 percent for all black males. About one-third of poor white youths in Cleveland and Detroit are expected to die before their sixty-fifth birthday, and the national average is 23 percent. Thus the combination of poverty and race has deadly consequences.

Lifestyles. It must be recognized that poor people are more commonly engaged in unhealthy lifestyles. Smoking, alcohol consumption, and obesity are more frequently found at lower levels in the stratification system and each is associated with a greater risk of illnesses such as heart disease and diabetes. The poor also are more likely to have low birth weight babies, a major contributing factor in infant mortality.

KEY CONCEPTS

digital divide

environmental justice

life chances

racial profiling

white-collar crime

SUGGESTED READING

DAVID COLE. *No Equal Justice: Race and Class in the American Criminal Justice System.* New York: New Press, 1999. The author argues that we tolerate a criminal justice system that exploits minorities and the poor.

JOHN IRWIN and JAMES AUSTIN. *It's About Time: America'sImprisonment Binge,* 2nd ed. Belmont, CA: Wadsworth, 1997. The authors offer a critical analysis of the way the American criminal justice system responds to criminal behavior.

DEBORAH PROTHROW-STITH. *Deadly Consequences.* New York: Harper, 1991. A disturbing look at the epidemic of violence that puts young black males at serious risk of premature death.

JEFFREY REIMAN. . . .*and the Poor Get Prison: Economic Bias in American Criminal Justice.* Boston, MA: Allyn and Bacon, 1996. This analysis demonstrates that the poor and minorities are at a disadvantage at every stage of the criminal justice process from arrest to incarceration.

GAIL SCHEARER. *The Health Care Divide.* Washington, DC: Consumer's Union, 2000. This research shows that the financial burden of heath care weighs heavily on the sick, the middle class, and the poor.

SAMUEL WALKER, CASSIA SPOHN, and MIRIAM DELONE. *The Color of Justice.* Belmont, CA: Wadsworth, 1996. An indictment of racial and ethnic discrimination in the criminal justice system.

USEFUL WED SITES

The National Institutes of Health (**www.nih.gov/**) support research on illness and health, and this site offers access to a wealth of information.

The Office of Minority Health Resources Center (**www.omhrc.gov**) is a useful source of information on the social and economic status of minority populations.

The Bureau of Justice Statistics (**www.ojp.uddoj.gov.bjs/**) offers a broad range of statistics on crime and various aspects of the criminal justice system.

The U.S. Department of Housing and Urban Development offers online maps of air quality and hazardous waste for all American ZIP codes (**www.hud.gov/emaps**).

The U.S. Department of Commerce (**www.commerce.gov**) conducts an ongoing survey of digital access among Americans sorted by income, education, race, gender, and other factors.

CHAPTER NINE

Class and Lifestyles

THE CONCEPT OF LIFESTYLES

Members of social classes often display distinctive patterns of thought and behavior that distinguish them from members of other classes. The term **lifestyles** refers to the common values, attitudes, beliefs, and behaviors that are shaped by position in the stratification system. Distinctive lifestyles are conditioned by the shared social and physical environments of different classes. Among the most salient considerations in understanding class-linked styles of life are economic, political, and social inequalities combined with the work environment. Members of the elite occupy a position of financial security and have considerable political influence and high social status. This situation molds their approach to the world and the future. In contrast, the poor face constant financial insecurity, degraded social status, and limited political influence. Their world view and perceptions of the future are likewise molded by their situation. However, the role of the work environment is more subtle.

WORK, VALUES, AND PERSONALITY

People's social class and occupation locate them in a system of authority and power on the job that have implications for the way people perceive their world and behave in it. In addition, jobs offer unequal promotion opportunities. Most upper-middle-class professional and managerial positions involve career paths that present structured opportunities for people to improve their situation through individual effort. In contrast, other occupations, especially unskilled labor and service work, offer few (if any) chances for upward movement regardless of the level of industriousness. Occupations also differ in the stability of work, offering relative security to some while confronting others with the unending threat of unemployment and financial devastation.

Experiences encountered at work not only shape individuals' responses to their specific job, but also may extend beyond daily routines to the point of helping to shape their lifestyles and perceptions of the larger society and their place in it. Occupations locate individuals in a system of hierarchical authority, placing them under the jurisdiction of others and imposing limits on their autonomy, initiative, and control over the pace and performance of their tasks. For example, work environments for members of the upper-middle class professions tend to be intellectually challenging, to offer the chance to exercise personal discretion and direct the activities of subordinates, which contributes to an emphasis on self-direction and self-control. Alternatively, those occupying lower levels of the class system are typically faced with narrow, repetitive tasks under close and punitive supervision, which contributes to an emphasis on conformity and instills a more constrained and less optimistic view of the world. This insight was, of course, a key aspect of the work of Marx and Engels, and has been more recently elaborated by Eric Olin Wright.

Sociologists have systematically explored the implications of authority relations at work on perspectives and attitudes away from the job. Their basic thesis, referred to as the **learning-generalization hypothesis**, argues that lessons learned in one sphere of life are carried over into other areas of life (Kohn & Schooler, 1983). Consequently, experiences encountered on the job may come to dominate not just perspectives toward work but also broader social values, social orientations, self-conceptions, and intellectual functioning. The focus on disparity in self-direction is encouraged and rewarded at the higher end of the system but discouraged at lower levels where conformity is demanded and rewarded.

Lessons learned on the job are then generalized to nonwork situations. There is a direct relationship between social class and positive self-evaluations such as having "good sense and good judgment," "self-reliance" and "responsibility," all of which may be interpreted as consequences of having greater opportunities to wield responsibility on the job. There are also class differences in the characteristics people hope to instill in their children. Considerations of success, honesty, and happiness are widely defined as important, but other traits are apparently viewed differently. There is an inverse relationship between class and an emphasis on conformity to external standards of behavior—obedience, personal neatness and cleanliness, and having good manners. Thus, people at lower levels teach their children the kinds of traits that are demanded and rewarded by their class position. This pattern is replicated in other nations such as Australia, Italy, and Poland, suggesting that such value orientations may have their origins in industrial class systems (Kohn & Slomczynskai, 1990). It would seem that people's values are shaped by their work experiences, so that they come to value those traits which are attainable and subsequently attempt to inculcate them in their children.

LIFESTYLES OF THE OLD CAPITALIST ELITE

There can be little question that unusual wealth and the privileges that accompany affluence is the defining characteristic of the elite. There are, however, divisions within the elite. Members of the old capitalist elite are the individuals and families who possess significant economic assets in the form of money, property, and stocks and bonds. They enjoy inherited fortunes originally created by earlier generations. Consequently, they have grown up with a tradition of wealth and power, and their lifestyle is strongly influenced by a concern for the maintenance and perpetuation of the accumulated wealth and power of the family.

The Family and the Transmission of Privilege

The most enduring segment of the elite is born to wealth and power and dedicated to the maintenance of their advantaged social position through the preservation of the family, the elite class, and the economic and political system that supports both. Families play a central role in this process because the family line is both the source of position and the mechanism for transmitting social position to future generations. Consequently, they are socialized to think of themselves not so much as individuals, but as "a stage in the development of a historical family" (Caven, 1969: 85) Moreover, since the fortunes of specific families are linked to the survival of the elite class, they forge powerful allegiances with other members of the same class, as Max Weber noted.

The socialization of each new generation is organized around the perpetuation of family and class. Primary responsibility for teaching appropriate behavior and instilling proper attitudes falls to mothers (Domhoff, 1970). Children are, from the start, taught to believe that they are different from the children of other classes, and a clear element of moral superiority is instilled (Ostrander, 1984). Socialization means immersion in the elegant lifestyle that wealth offers, with a strong emphasis on appropriate elite behavior. This includes the need for sons to follow parents in careers as business and governmental leaders. The daughters' responsibilities include participation in community affairs (Daniels, 1987). For both there is great stress on the importance of "good marriages," which means a union with a member of another elite family. Good marriages are facilitated by limiting children's circle of acquaintances to other members of the elite. This is accomplished through an intricate system of informal social activities, private schools, exclusive clubs, and debutante activities.

Children are expected to assume positions of influence and work to maintain family fortunes, but they also face some unique problems. One of the most troublesome is that their privilege denies them the opportunity to prove their own self-worth through individual accomplishment (Ostrander, 1984). Many Americans seek to validate themselves in the occupational world, often measuring success by income. The children of wealth are denied that opportunity because not only are they born to wealth, their route to future positions of influence is virtually guaranteed. Consequently, some are destined to forever wonder how well they might have fared on their own merits.

A different challenge emerges in social relationships since there is always the underlying suspicion that people around them are attracted to their wealth and position, not to them as individuals. Thus, in every generation a few renounce their wealth or change their names to disassociate themselves from their wealth, and a few are driven to seek psychiatric help to cope with the need to create a meaningful life.

It has long been noted that upper-class families tend to be conservative and emphasize traditional values (Warner & Lunt, 1941; Blood & Wolf, 1960). Families tend toward patriarchy, with husbands and fathers controlling major decisions within the context of the family—decisions about jobs, housing, and major expenditures. Patriarchy prevails despite the fact that most wives possess substantial wealth inherited from their own families. This pattern is inconsistent with the experience in families in other classes, where the relative income of spouses influences the distribution of authority. Although it is an apparent source of marital dissatisfaction among elite wives, it seldom produces open challenges to husbands' authority.

It is believed that several factors contribute to the survival of the capitalist elite tradition of patriarchy. One factor is that upper-class women derive their social identities from their class position and their community work, not their family roles, thus rendering them less important. But perhaps the major reason is the economic and political position of upper-class men outside the family where they dominate their businesses, communities, and the society. They are men accustomed to control and unlikely to voluntarily relinquish power in any area.

Noblesse Oblige

A recurrent theme running through both the socialization of children and the activities of capitalist class families is an emphasis on responsibility for the less advantaged members of society, the concept of **noblesse oblige**. A member of the Rockefeller family recalls, "My mother and father's greatest fear was that their children might take their wealth for granted and grow up spoiled and arrogant. They wanted us to learn that with wealth comes responsibility" (*The New York Times,* 1989: 4F). It was a pattern set by the business leaders of the nineteenth century. It is estimated that oil man John D. Rockefeller, Sr., donated over $500 million to charity in his lifetime, an amount equivalent to $5.4 billion in current dollars (Tanaka, Branscum & Borsook, 1996). Paul Mellon, heir to a banking fortune, has donated at least a billion dollars over his lifetime.

Members of the elite are also active in countless national and local benevolent activities that range from fund-raising for charitable causes to acting as caretakers for vast international philanthropic organizations. The Rockefeller Foundation alone has assets of $2 billion, which is used to support higher education, the arts, and environmental causes. Heirs to some of the major fortunes in America such as Pillsbury and Oscar Mayer work through a group called the Funding Exchange to funnel money into social reform efforts such as nuclear disarmament and voter registration (Neuborne, 1990).

Noblesse oblige activities serve different motives. Some members of the upper class sincerely accept this idea as a moral obligation that accompanies inherited wealth. Critics point out that philanthropy also serves less noble purposes. It is a matter of control, a means of moving into positions of authority where they can direct organizations' resources in ways they see as most appropriate. For example, members of urban elites often control fund-raising for metropolitan orchestras and opera houses, and although these organizations give public performances, it is largely members of the elite who fill the audience (Arian, 1971). There is also the matter of justifying and legitimizing privileged position. The devotion of time, money, and effort to public service helps to deflect potential criticism and as such is a way of perpetuating the position of their family and class.

The financial contributions of the very rich are often quite large, involving millions of dollars. However, on the whole, the rich tend to contribute a smaller proportion of their wealth than ordinary upper-middle-class Americans. It is estimated that the "very rich" (with assets over $1.3 million) donate about one-half of one percent (0.5 percent) of their fortunes to charity annually, but those with assets of $40,000 to $1.3 million give between 0.8 and 1.5 percent (Fabrikant & White, 1995). Moreover, charitable gifts are often contingent upon public display of family names on buildings or monuments.

An African-American Elite

A small number of free blacks lived in the South prior to the Civil War. They were forced to carry identification papers proving their freedom, but unlike slaves, they enjoyed the right to work for pay and own property. This small group of families were the first black Americans able to accumulate some modest level of wealth, and eventually they came to form a black elite (Graham, 1999). The emergence of the group was fostered by the creation in the 1860s and 1870s of black colleges like Howard, Fisk, and Spelman, where their children could receive an education and gain access to professional careers or move into a black-oriented business in newspaper publishing, banking, or insurance. This led to the emergence of a group of wealthy families who developed their own churches, debutante balls, exclusive social clubs, and private vacation areas not unlike their white counterparts. They provided generous financial support for the NAACP, the Urban League, the Negro College Fund, and other groups that helped to fuel the Civil Rights movement of the 1960s and 1970s.

LIFESTYLES OF THE NEW CAPITALIST ELITE AND THE INSTITUTIONAL ELITE

Members of the new capitalist elite and the institutional elite are newcomers to wealth, power, and status. The new capitalist elite is made up of the new millionaires and multimillionaires created by e-commerce, the entertainment industry (including films, books, and television), and professional sports. They are joined by an institutional elite of corporate leaders and political figures. Their wealth and social standing is more uncertain than that of the old capitalist elite because it is built on their own efforts and contingent upon continued success. Show business personalities are only as good as the most recent ratings, politicians must worry about the next election cycle, and corporate leaders must monitor their most recent quarterly earnings reports. The new capitalist/institutional elite displays two different lifestyles, the highly visible conspicuous consumption of the rich and famous generation and the much more private and sedate world of the quiet millionaires.

Conspicuous Consumption

There are some wealthy people who deliberately participate in an extravagant lifestyle, sometimes actually encouraging television and the tabloids to peek into their homes, their lavish parties, and their personal lives (Taylor, 1989). Thorstein Veblen's (1899) insights into the behavior of the newly rich capitalists at the end of the nineteenth century continues to have contemporary relevance. He interpreted their ostentatious and extravagant expenditures as **conspicuous consumption**, the open and public display of luxury for the express purpose of flaunting their vast wealth.

Conspicuous consumption often takes the form of lavish parties and celebrations. For example, it is estimated that the November 18, 2000, wedding of Michael Douglas and Catherine Zeta-Jones may have cost $1 million to entertain a guest list that included Jack Nicholson, Art Garfunkle, Martha Stewart, Qunicy Jones, and Ed Bradley (Williams, 2000). And there is no shortage of luxuries to attract today's millionaires. They can, for example, take a theme tour of Polynesia or the Brazilian rain forest for $34,950 per person, which coincidentally surpasses the average income of an American worker for a whole year (MacNeille, 2000). They can check the time on a Minute Repeater Tourbillon 5850 RMT wristwatch that sells for $233,000, which is more than the average cost of a home in the United States (Kuczynski, 1998). They can snack on caviar that costs $1,150 for 500 grams, which is about three hundred dollars more than the average monthly social security payment ($845) to people who worked their whole adult lives (Yazigi, 1999).

The children of the new rich also live in pampered elegance. Alison, 13, for example, calculates the numbers of her personal staff in Hollywood:

> I have a personal trainer, I have a counselor, I have a nutritionist, I have a singing coach. And I think that's it. Oh, yeah, I have a driver, too (Greenfield, 1997).

Wendy, 23, laments her graduation gift:

> When I graduated from college, my dad wanted to buy me a new car. . . . Because he has two Mercedes he has a very good relationship with the Mercedes people. I had wanted a BMW really badly, and I was really uncomfortable about getting a Mercedes, but I didn't have a choice. . . . I just didn't think it was an appropriate car for a 21-year old. It's the stigma attached to a Mercedes (Greenfield, 1997).

The Quiet Millionaires

Not all of the newly rich choose extravagant lives. The largest segment of the institutional elite is made up of self-employed businesspersons who built their fortunes in conventional businesses such as fast-food franchises, auto dealerships, or software. They, along with some entertainers and business leaders, prefer more private, relatively frugal lives (Stanley & Danko, 1996). A look at the lives of America's millionaires shows that more drive Fords than any type of car, few have ever spent more than $600 for a suit of clothes or paid more than $250 for a wristwatch. Warren Buffet, worth over $12 billion dollars, still lives in the same home he bought for $31,500 in 1958 (Lewis, 1995)

Their working lives are consistent with their spending habits. Most continue to work long hours at their businesses, and place a major share of their earnings into savings and investments rather than conspicuous consumption. In a very real sense they continue to pursue the American Dream of hard work and thrift long after having achieved it. Microsoft's Bill Gates, the richest American, still puts in 70 hour work weeks and doesn't worry about financial failure. "I would," he claims, "still eat the same hamburgers" if his fortune collapsed.

Some members of the newly wealthy institutional elite are devoting a portion of their wealth to philanthropic endeavors, not unlike the traditional capitalists, Bill Gates (Microsoft) and Ted Turner (CNN) among them. Gates has donated over $200 million to bring the internet to libraries, and Turner pledged $100 million a year for ten years to the United Nations.

THE UPPER MIDDLE CLASS

The upper middle class of experts occupies an advantaged position in the occupational sphere and class structure. It is not uncommon for the upper middle class to have responsibility for organizing and directing the activities of large numbers of subordinates. In fact, some occupations (e.g., paralegals, hygienists) have evolved as structurally subordinate to established professions, and the parameters of their work is set by these professions. In a larger sense the upper middle classes organize and direct both the work and the *nonwork* lives of those below them in the class structure—the lower middle class, the working class, and the poor. Relations between the upper middle class and the bulk of society are a one-way dialogue, with managers

CASE STUDY
New Wealth in the Silicon Valley

The contemporary center of vast new wealth created by the digital revolution is the fifty-mile corridor in northern California running north from San Jose to San Francisco, now called the Silicon Valley for the silicon chip that fuels the digital revolution. It is here that one out of five of the one hundred largest electronics and software companies such as Intel originated. The industry has created many multimillionaires, and pay for its rank-and-file workers is well above earnings elsewhere. Consequently, it is a magnet for those seeking to join or begin a high-tech firm and become a millionaire on stock options when it goes public. They live the American Dream.

There are, however, heavy social, psychological, and financial costs associated with the quest. Stress is prevalent because workers must plan on working long hours, easily reaching 55 to 60 hours per week, with night and weekend work common. Firms such as Intel, Sun Microsystems, and Hewlett-Packard are forced to experiment with flexible hours and telecommuting to help alleviate some of the work-related stress.

The stress of work spills over to the family. Relationships are frayed, and family lawyers report that divorces are increasing (Swartz, 2000). Divorces can create difficult child custody problems because the high cost of living can force the lower wage earner to leave the Valley. A different form of family problem arises among those spouses who commute to the Valley from as far away as Salt Lake City (764 miles). The lure of riches attracts one person while family responsibilities or family ties keeps the other in place. It is a choice based on the belief that workers will have abundant free time once they strike it rich.

Housing is scarce, and competition for homes means an inflationary housing market where the median price of a Valley home reached $505,000 in 2000 (Swartz, 2000). A two-bedroom, one-bath ranch house in San Carlos that listed for $599,000 actually sold for $797,000 (Ritter, 2000). Prices in that range exclude the middle class of city workers, police officers, and school teachers. California pays its teachers well, the average of $45,000 ranks it tenth in the nation, but it is not nearly enough in a housing market that can increase by one-third in a year. It means that these communities are unable to recruit middle-income workers to teach the schools and police the streets. As the quality of services declines, these municipalities run the risk of losing the key industries that originally fueled their prosperity.

and supervisors, journalists and teachers, social workers and judges, physicians and lawyers controlling the flow of information, making judgments, and issuing commands and instructions to subordinate classes (Ehrenreich, 1989).

Their work usually offers high levels of both autonomy and opportunity. Most are freed from routine and direct supervision, granted wide latitude in the conduct of their work, and allowed to establish their own schedules within broad limits. Most occupy career paths that offer opportunities for upward mobility, and a small number may realistically look forward to movement into the institutional elite. However, although they enjoy significant authority, it must be remembered that they lack ultimate decision-making responsibility since they are organizational employees who carry out decisions enacted by the institutional elite at the highest organizational levels. As Eric Olin Wright points out, they occupy a structurally ambivalent position, simultaneously *bourgeois* in exercising control over others and *proletariat* by being subject to the control of others (Wright, 1997). Consequently, they have something in common with all employees in the lower-middle and working classes.

Some segments of the upper middle class do have economic worries. While free from the worry of unemployment that constantly threatens the lives of the poor and the working class, the upper middle class do face the consequences of the globalization of the economic system that has led to downsizing and corporate restructuring. Broad levels of middle managers must face the possibility of being displaced.

Most members of this class have succeeded on the basis of educational attainments. However, claims to upper-middle-class position—skill and knowledge—cannot, unlike real capital, be hoarded or preserved or bequeathed to their children (Ehrenreich, 1989). Consequently, their legacy to their children must be in the form of accessibility to the best possible educational credentials. In extreme cases, parents endure high taxes so that their children have access to quality public schools and expend large amounts of money on private tutors and test-preparation courses. Teachers in the greater New York City area can easily earn an extra $50,000 tutoring students on nights and weekends (Gross, 1997). Unfortunately, this exposes upper-middle-class children to high expectations of success, and intense stress.

Members of the upper middle class earn salaries that allow them a very comfortable lifestyle. They are partial to expensive sport utility vehicles and sheltered suburban communities, and they are likely to be active in local politics and community activities. Despite the highly rancorous rhetoric of liberals and conservatives, most upper-middle-class people are political and social moderates (Wolfe, 1998). Support for women's rights, civil rights, and aid for the poor is strong, as is a general tolerance for diversity and religious differences.

THE LOWER MIDDLE CLASS

The lower middle class includes people in a variety of work settings and situations. There are clerical or administrative workers (secretaries, bookkeepers, shipping clerks, insurance policy processors, bank tellers, data entry operators, timekeepers, postal service workers, dispatchers, stock clerks), retail sales and service workers (cashiers, clerks), some salaried professionals (paralegals, nurses, physical therapists, teachers, social workers) and technicians (drafters, dental hygienists). Despite the diversity, several common themes define their situation.

Most members of the lower middle class tend to have a high school education and some university credits or community college degrees. Salaried professionals are the exception, filling jobs that require college degrees. Earnings are moderate when judged against the standards of the upper middle class, and in many instances fall below that of blue-collar craft workers and operatives. Moreover, although some proportion of lower-middle-class workers can look forward to rising to first-line supervisory positions, careers are largely blocked beyond that level because of the increasing demand for advanced education for middle-management positions. There are thus some real limits on the potential for advancement and making major gains in earnings, meaning that lower-middle-class workers can anticipate performing the same routines over the course of their careers.

The work of the lower middle class allows little room for personal discretion or grants much in the way of authority, rather, their work is more likely to be defined for them by strict job descriptions or administered by upper-middle-class professionals and managers. They are people who have large segments of their work lives directed by others. Even professionals with college degrees, such as nurses and teachers, occupy clearly subordinate positions in the organizational hierarchy. Subordination is most pronounced among office workers. Supervisors oversee them, and in extreme cases their activities are monitored by electronic surveillance devices that observe and record virtually every aspect of workers' behavior. Electronic surveillance includes video cameras overseeing workspaces and rest areas, audio tapes of the length and content of telephone conversations, and software programs embedded in computers that record the interval between keystrokes and measure the length of rest periods. Consequently, there is the risk of a reprimand if coffee breaks extend beyond the norm or if there are unexplained breaks in the rhythm of typing. It is even alleged that one company used special chairs with sensors in the seats to measure movements, using the rationale that "wigglers" are not working efficiently (Rothfeder & Galen, 1990). Employees may not even be aware of the surveillance. Workers complain that electronic surveillance is an invasion of their privacy and that constant monitoring is extremely stressful. Comparisons of monitored and unmonitored workers often reveals stronger feelings of anxiety, tension, fatigue, and anger among those under surveillance (Smith, et al., 1992). One of the major sources of stress is that workers constantly being monitored feel pressure to work harder and worry that they risk punishment for tiny deviations in productivity. In short, electronic surveillance contributes to feelings of powerlessness and loss of control over their own work.

Thus, although the work of the lower middle class is important and essential to the functioning of society, it is not work that yields major rewards or supports claims to social status at work or in the larger society. In fact, the gap between the rewards of the upper middle class and the lower middle class is sizable, and it seems to be increasing as the rewards of high-tech jobs increase. Moreover, adhering to the work habits of effort and dedication endorsed by the ideology of individualism do not offer much chance for major advancement.

Class and Status in the Lower Middle Class

Most analysis of the lower middle class suggests that they are sensitive to the fact that their accomplishments seem modest compared to those of the upper middle class (Mills, 1951; Gans, 1967; Hamilton, 1972). There is often dissatisfaction with their standard of living, but they are not poor and take pride in their ability to acquire consumer goods that are the visible announcements of purchasing power—furnishings, homes, and cars—and validate a measure of economic success. Obviously, the consumer goods they purchase cannot approach the quantity and quality of the more affluent (Case Study).

Despite relatively modest accomplishments, there is a strong emphasis on standards of behavior that exemplify the ideology of the American Dream—hard work and individual effort. Lower-middle-class families tend to be strongly family-oriented and child-oriented, especially in the field of education where they encourage strong aspirations in their children, which reflects their recognition of the importance of education in the success of their children (Gans, 1967).

CASE STUDY
Two-Tier Marketing

Americans at all class levels are tempted by consumer goods. Clothing, cars, and electronic gadgets make life more amenable, but are also an important and readily visible claim to social status. Not everyone can afford to shop in Beverly Hills, but virtually anyone can display a Rodeo Drive credit card. Retailers respond to the lure of prestige-enhancing impulses with a two-tier marketing strategy that offers similar products or name brands to two quite different income groups. Marketing people call it the "Tiffany/Wal-Mart" strategy (Leonhardt, 1997).

Two-tier marketing is readily evident in cars and designer jeans. At the top end of the automotive market are luxury cars and lavish sport utility vehicles, and Lexus offers both with price tags over $50,000, but an ES300 series sedan costs about half that. People who are satisfied with a new car that does not have the status of the Lexus name can turn to General Motors and buy a basic Saturn for under $11,000. Gap Inc. sells jeans for $58 at its Banana Republic stores, or for about $22 at Old Navy stores. Those content with generic jeans find even better bargains at Wal-Mart.

Another aspect of two-tier marketing is found in the resale of used products. There has always been a market for pre-owned cars and homes, but the sale of used clothing, furniture, and electronics doubled between 1987 and 1997. Name brand merchandise is cleaned and refurbished and sold at a fraction of the original cost. One clothing store even repackages its items in shrink wrap to convey the image of newness.

Religion also plays a central role in their lives, and there is some indication that lower-middle-class families are more likely to adhere to more conservative standards of morality in areas such as personal honesty and modesty in sexual behavior. One interpretation that has gained some attention is that concern with traditional standards of respectability is also a claim to social status. Consequently, their ambiguous accomplishments in the economic sphere are translated into concern with social status and social respectability in their personal and social lives (Mills, 1951).

THE WORKING CLASS

The working class has two segments. On the one side are the skilled craft workers such as automotive technicians, machinists, and electricians, and on the other are factory workers who operate machines, work the assembly lines, or drive trucks for a living. All employees face the threat of joblessness, but unemployment rates for the less-skilled segment of the working class consistently stands above that of white-collar workers. Some joblessness is temporary, but thousands of jobs are permanently lost to globalization and technology. Globalization results in the displacement of manufacturing jobs to developing nations, and technological developments, especially automation, take a toll by using machines to replace people. The working class has been especially hard hit in autos, textiles, and steel production. Thus, while the lives of high-tech workers are enriched by the digital revolution the lives of the working class are made more insecure and precarious.

Large-scale layoffs lead workers to believe that employers think of them as no more than a disposable commodity. Not surprisingly, there is bitterness and dread. The words of a young father of three are telling:

> It's like they don't see you like a person. Like you don't have bills and kids. They don't need you any more, so they toss you out like you're not a real human being. I've been looking for steady work for eight or nine months, but there ain't none, least none I can get. So me and my wife, we live scared (Rubin, 1997).

Consequently, economic insecurity is a major concern, and the sight of the homeless is a constant reminder of their own anxiety.

The Segregation of Work and Social Roles

Much manual work is intellectually uninteresting, offers few opportunities for innovation or creativity, and holds little chance of winning meaningful promotions. In addition, blue-collar workers face strong pressure for productivity. Assembly line workers must struggle to keep pace with the unremitting tempo of the line, while others work under piece-rate systems that link wages to output. Supervisors regularly and continuously monitor their levels of effort. Consequently, it is not uncommon for blue-collar workers to tend to segregate their work from their social lives and seek fulfillment in leisure activities (Shostak, 1969; Halle, 1984). Large blocks of free time are devoted to active participation in softball, bowling, hunting and fishing, and attendance at spectator sports such as football and baseball games. There is a strong sense of neighborhood or community, and as a result local bars, taverns, and clubs are often the center of social life in the form of watching television sports, gossip, and socializing. There is also a powerful loyalty to the community, sometimes at the cost of self-advancement.

Blue-collar men often express a preference for male companions, and there is a tendency for leisure activities such as hunting to be segregated along gender lines. This is not a firm line, and many activities involve both spouses, with some wives involved in sports, while visiting among family and friends is a shared activity. The origins of segregated activities probably has its roots in the gender segregation of jobs that prevailed for most of the twentieth century. Whole categories of skilled craft and factory jobs were men's work, and lower-white-collar jobs were women's jobs, meaning that people spent their workday in the company of people of the same sex. It is logical that friendships forged at work would be extended to leisure activities. Many marital disputes apparently have their origins in a conflict over the division of time between male friendships and marital and family activities (Halle, 1984: 55).

The Working-Class Family: Husbands and Wives

The division of labor and power within blue-collar families has long been divided along gender lines. Husbands filled the role of provider in the paid labor force while wives assumed responsibility for the home, although many also held jobs outside the home. Accompanying this was the location of authority in the family with male superiority legitimized on the grounds that the husband provided the major economic support for the family unit. At least some blue-collar husbands, especially poorer ones, became quite authoritarian, imposing severe restrictions on the lives of their wives, attempting to dictate how they could spend their time and money, and even whom they could visit (Rubin, 1976).

As more and more women in blue-collar families become critical financial contributors and as traditional gender roles weaken in the larger society, there is some significant renegotiating of authority and roles within the family (Rosen, 1987; Earle & Harris, 1989). Wives' financial contribution to families plagued by economic insecurity allows them to resist their husbands' preference for a nonworking spouse. Major decisions are more likely to be joint endeavors, and husbands assume a somewhat larger (albeit not large) role in domestic chores once delegated almost exclusively to wives. Thus, although there is still a tendency for working-class males to hold to the idea of husband-centered decision making, there is also support for women's careers and shared household tasks.

Blue-collar women are sensitive to the fact that the role of "provider" is still a powerful aspect of defining and validating the male role at work and in the larger society. Hence, while negotiating a larger role in decision-making and shared domestic tasks they continue to publicly define their husbands as the major provider or "breadwinner," and devote their paychecks to "extras" such as consumer goods that enrich their lifestyles and verify their status in society. It is a social fiction that avoids marital conflict.

It should be noted that blue-collar women, like wives at all class levels, assume a disproportionate share of domestic tasks. This exacts a heavy toll in time and effort, but working-class women value both paid employment and unpaid home and family activities (Ferree, 1987). Paid work offers economic rewards that grant a degree of financial security and an enhanced standard of living, but work relationships are often seen as impersonal and exploitative. The family may be hierarchical, but simultaneously offers support, intimacy, and love. Thus, each role offers what the other cannot. Domestic life permits a partial escape from the inhumane demands of factory work while paid work allows temporary escape from patriarchal domination (Rosen, 1987).

Gender distinctions between provider and homemaker roles are generally not as rigid in black families as in white families (Taylor, et al., 1990). A key factor underlying this pattern is the fact that African-American women have historically been more likely to be in the paid labor force because of the depressed earnings of black men. Despite this, married African-American women also perform a majority of domestic tasks in the home.

THE POOR

The poor occupy the lowest levels of the stratification system. The poor includes several different groups. There are, first, the working poor who work on a regular or periodic basis, but in jobs that are part-time or offer marginal wages. People in this category are laborers, unskilled factory workers, domestics, and some service workers. Racial and ethnic minorities have been concentrated in these forms of work at every stage of the industrialization process in the United States. The poor also includes those not currently working—the unemployed, the unemployable, and the discouraged. At one extreme are the short-term jobless who are displaced but are subsequently reemployed and are able to survive with the aid of unemployment insurance and welfare payments. At the other extreme are the long-term unemployed who lack the skills or training to be permanently attached to the labor force.

Life at the bottom of the stratification system is overshadowed by financial deprivation and economic insecurity. Many work, but the pay is low and the threat of unemployment is a common and constant reality. To illustrate, in any given year less than 10 percent of the unemployed voluntarily leave jobs; the majority (about 60 percent) are displaced due to plant closings and industrial transformations that eliminate jobs (textiles are a prime example) and temporary or seasonal layoffs (agricultural workers, construction laborers). Thus a large part of unemployment can be traced to the vagaries of the economic system. The remainder are young people entering the workforce for the first time or older workers attempting to reenter the workforce. Adult women are overrepresented, attempting to rejoin the paid labor force because of a change in family status or at the conclusion of child-care responsibilities.

The marginal economic situation of the poor is reflected in their lifestyles and life chances (Exhibit 9.1). Less than half enjoy home ownership, and while things such as cars and telephones are taken for granted by most middle-class Americans, sizable proportions of the poor lack them. The lack of a phone or car is more than an inconvenience, it is also a barrier to finding steady work. Employers have more difficulty reaching potential employees without phones, and the lack of a vehicle makes it more difficult for city dwellers to take jobs across town or in the suburbs.

Certain health risks among the poor are also evident. Fewer have health insurance, which contributes to inadequate prenatal care, which in turn, shows up in significantly higher infant mortality rates. The poor are also more susceptible to violence. Residents of poorer neighborhoods with concentrations of substance abuse problems show a much greater likelihood of being the victim of a violent crime. The stresses of life on the underside is summarized in the number of deprivations they face. Deprivations include burdens such as eviction; discontinuation of telephone, gas ,or electricity; lacking sufficient food within the last four months; crowded liv-

EXHIBIT 9.1   Living Poor in the United States

	Nonpoor families	Poor families	Poor single-parent families	Welfare families
Total income	$55,394	$8,501	$6,794	$12,678
Own a home	77.6%	40.8%	24.3%	24.9%
Own a car	97.2	76.8	64.1	66.3
Have a phone	97.2	76.7	69.9	67.5
No health insurance	12.1	26.8	18.0	n/a
Infant mortality (per 1,000 births)	8.3	13.5	14.6	14.3
Violent crimes (per 1,000 people)	26.2	53.7	87.5	n/a
Two or more persons per room	4.2	19.2	16.7	24.9
Deprivations:				
at least one	13.0	55.1	56.8	65.4
three or more	1.0	11.8	12.9	14.6

Definitions: Poor are people in families with incomes below the poverty threshold. *Poor single-parent families* have an unmarried head of household and at least one child under age 18. *Welfare families* include families with children under 18 receiving some welfare assistance. *Deprivations* include the following: eviction, discontinuation of gas or electric service, lacking food, crowded living conditions, and no refrigerator, stove, or phone.

Source: Mary Federman, et al. "What does it mean to be poor in America?" *Monthly Labor Review* 119 (May, 1996), pp. 3–17.

ing conditions; and no refrigerator, stove or phone that families experience in the course of a year.

The problems of economic insecurity are compounded by the social and political position of the poor in American society. The work they do carries little prestige, and the individualistic themes that dominate society mean that some segments of their society hold them in disrepute, believing that they are largely responsible for their own plight. One consequence is that social welfare programs designed to buffer the effects of economic deprivation—unemployment insurance, minimum wage laws, social welfare programs—typically encounter opposition in the political arena, so that benefits often fail to achieve their goals. Minimum wage legislation is a good example. Congressional debates over raising the rate are always protracted and contentious. Ironically, the twenty-first century began with the rate set at $5.15 per hour, but a full-time worker with a family of three earns less than the official poverty level even at that rate.

Considering the social and economic handicaps encountered by the poor it might be anticipated that they would have lost faith in the dominant ideology of hard work and open opportunity. In fact it has long been known that this is generally not the case (Goodwin, 1972; Kozol, 2000). Some do express less optimism about the system and their chances in it than do the more affluent, but a majority believe in an open opportunity structure and are optimistic about their own chances for success. For example, despite the obvious limits on opportunities for those without a high school degree, surveys show only about one-fifth feel they have a less than average chance for success (Kluegel & Smith, 1986: 68–72). Women generally see the system as less open, perhaps reflecting an awareness of the more limited occupational chances for females. African Americans at all levels have a less favorable assessment of the opportunity structure, and among the poor a large majority feel they have not had a fair chance to succeed.

Growing Up Poor

One of the largest segments of the poor in many rich nations are infants and children. About one in every five children in the United States (over 15 million children under age 18) is growing up poor, including nearly 6 million under the age of 6. This includes over 45 percent of all black children and 39 percent of Hispanic children. It is a situation that ranks the United States at the bottom of international comparisons of child poverty in industrial nations (UNICEF, 2000). To illustrate, child poverty is 22 percent in the United States, 16 percent in Canada, 13 percent in Australia and Japan, 11 percent in Germany, and less than 5 percent in Sweden, Norway, Belgium, and Luxembourg. Child poverty is the result of a combination of factors: the magnitude of economic inequalities, the proportion of single-parent families, and the scope of governmental social-welfare programs.

The long-term educational prospects for poor children seem dismal by all standards. Their living conditions are more precarious and their neighborhoods less safe; they have fewer educational resources (books or computers) at home, are more likely to be detached from school and homework, and lack a regular medical provider. Despite the handicaps imposed by poverty, most parents strive to create a supportive home life and sustain positive aspirations for their children (Weil, 1999). Two out of five parents read to their children almost every day (compared to 56 percent of higher-income parents), and most do religious or volunteer activities. As a result, the children of the poor are likely to be imbued with aspirations and hopes not unlike more advantaged youngsters. Nine out of ten school children living in poverty plan on continuing past high school, and four out of five believe they will graduate from college (Federman, et al., 1996). Admittedly, their goals are different—their aspirations often center on stable blue-collar work, manufacturing, construction, or the military—certainly not the lofty professional and business careers held by the children of the middle class but a secure and constructive place in the class system. For example, a poor urban teenager rehearses a future that is not unlike the aspirations of children of the more advantaged, "I'll have a regular house, y'know, with a yard and everything. I'll have a steady job, a good job. I'll be living the good life, the easy life" (MacLeod, 1987: 5).

CONCLUSION: HUNGER IN THE WORLD, HUNGER IN AMERICA

In 1974 Secretary of State Henry Kissinger vowed that world hunger would be eradicated "within ten years" (Owen, 1996). More than two decades later the proportion of chronically undernourished has been reduced by only one-fifth, leaving 840 million people worldwide facing hunger on a continuing basis. Hunger has been alleviated largely by improvements in food production that have tripled the output of rice, grains, and other staple crops. The most dramatic progress has been made in East Asia, but the problem has actually worsened in sub-Saharan Africa where the number of undernourished has doubled to over 200 million. Nations such as Zaire are the most dramatic examples of mass starvation.

A lack of nutrition endangers everyone, but children and pregnant women face the greatest risks. Undernourished expectant mothers risk anemia and expose the child to a whole range of deficiencies, not the least of which is low birth weight. Frail infants have a much higher infant mortality rate, and those that survive are more likely to have growth and development problems later. Hunger causes weakness and lethargy; thus, hungry children in the schools have more difficulty concentrating and seem to fall behind their peers. Chronic nutritional problems also have physiological consequences. Iron deficiency, for example, causes cognitive disabilities.

The problem of hunger has not even been eliminated in the United States, one of the richest nations in the world, and it touches many more people than is generally understood. Dependable data on the extent of hunger are limited because of debate over the measurement of hunger. Problems with measuring hunger led to the idea of food security as an alternative way of focusing on the issue. **Food security** means having a "culturally acceptable, nutritionally adequate diet, through *non-emergency* food sources at all times" (U.S. House of Representatives, 1990). The advantage of this approach is that it focuses on the context of hunger in the sense that it takes account of individual resources such as personal income and access to transportation as well as competitively priced food and local availability of stores and other sources of food. The U.S. Department of Agriculture found that 31 million people (12 million of them children) were food insecure—they did not have assured access to enough food—and 3.5 percent of households actually experienced hunger in 1999 (Andrews, 2000).[1]

Other research shows that 21 million Americans turned to emergency food programs in a recent year, and they came from all parts of society (Second Harvest, 1998). More than one-half were minorities and 62 percent were women. Unemployment or disability was a factor in many cases, but one recipient in five (21 percent) were employed and 39 percent lived in a household where someone worked. They turn to these sources because of unemployment or family crisis, or simply because their regular diet is inadequate. One-third of those served by Second Harvest had to choose between paying their rent or mortgage and buying food at least once, and 28 percent had to chose between medicine and food. A significant number of the people who turned to soup kitchens or food pantries missed meals (27 percent of adults and 9 percent of children), and one-quarter survived on a regular basis with no stove or no refrigerator. Despite the strong economy of the 1990s, a survey of twenty-seven cities in 1999 by the U.S. Conference of Mayors (2000) found an 18 percent increase in appeals for emergency food assistance, and 21 percent of the requests went unfilled in the richest country in the world!

KEY CONCEPTS

conspicuous consumption	learning-generalization	lifestyles
food security	hypothesis	noblesse oblige

SUGGESTED READING

MAYA ANGELOU. *I Know Why the Caged Bird Sings*. New York: Bantam, 1970. A poignant remembrance of rural poverty in Arkansas by this world-famous African-American author and poet.

JILL DUERR BERRICK. *Faces of Poverty: Portraits of Women and Children on Welfare*. New York: Oxford University Press, 1995. Welfare mothers struggle to survive and support their children in the face of poverty.

---

[1]Scientists think of hunger as the chronic lack of nutrition needed for good health, but research on hunger must typically depend upon subjective judgments. In this study, hunger means at least one person in the household reported they experienced hunger pangs once a month for at least three consecutive months.

K. Edin and L. Lein. *Making Ends Meet: How Single Mothers Survive Welfare and Low-Wage Work*. New York: Russell Sage Foundation, 1997.

Lawrence Otis Graham. *Our Kind of People: Inside America's Black Upper Class*. New York: HarperCollins, 1999. The little-known history and lifestyles of a wealthy black society in America by a member of the group.

David Halle. *America's Working Man*. Chicago: University of Chicago Press, 1984. A rich and detailed account of the lives of members of the working class and their image of their place in the class system.

LeAlan Jones and Lloyd Newman with David Isay. *Our America: Life and Death on the South Side of Chicago*. New York: Scribner, 1997. Two inner-city Chicago teenagers confront a world of poverty, drugs, and crime, but their deep humanity survives in this chronicle told in their own words.

Frank McCourt. *Angela's Ashes*. New York: Scribner, 1996. This account of the world of a poor Irish family in Limerick in the 1930s and 1940s earned the 1997 Pulitzer Prize.

C. Wright Mills. *White Collar*. New York: Oxford University Press, 1951. The pioneering analysis of class and status among lower-middle-class workers.

Susan A. Ostrander. *Women of the Upper Class*. Philadelphia: Temple University Press, 1984. A detailed account of the world of elite women whose lives center on the transmission of privilege.

USEFUL WEB SITES

The Center for Working Class Studies at Youngstown State University (**www.as.ysu.edu/~cwcs/**) conducts research on the social and political lives of blue-collar workers and families.

The World Hunger Program at Brown University (**www.brown.edu/Departments/World_Hunger_Program**) focuses on the hunger in the world and policy issues related to the eradication of the problem.

America's Second Harvest, a network of food assistance agencies (**www.secondharvest.org**) conducts surveys of homelessness and hunger.

The U.S. Department of Agriculture (**www.usda.gov**) publishes annual reports on hunger in the United States.

CHAPTER TEN

Class Consciousness

SUBJECTIVE PERCEPTIONS OF INEQUALITY AND STRATIFICATION

Marx and Engels visualized class consciousness as the engine of revolutionary social change as members of the working class became aware of their subordinate position in the economic system. There is not much question that Americans are sensitive to the magnitude of economic, social, and political inequality in their society. In fact, when asked if there is anything they are not particularity proud of about the United States, a full one-third volunteer the words "inequality" or "poverty" (Robinson, 1983). Such responses are not unexpected, because it is difficult to discount the homeless or ignore the cars, homes, and jewelry of the very wealthy. Even the more comfortable suburban middle classes, often socially insulated from direct contact with other classes, cannot escape the magazines and television programs that glorify the lifestyles of the rich and famous or show graphic images of the plight of the poor and homeless.

The presence of hierarchies of income and wealth, social status, and political power raise the question of how people view the stratification system and their place in it. As Marx observed in making the distinction between *klasse an sich* and *klasse fur sich*, classes are no more than aggregates of people in the same market position unless those distinctions shape their awareness, attitudes, and behavior. He saw conflicts between classes as the driving force in historical change, and at some places in his writings he argued for the inevitability of class conflict because members of the

196

emerging urban industrial proletariat would develop a collective consciousness and take action to overthrow the ruling bourgeois. The United States is certainly not on the verge of armed class conflict, nor do Americans exhibit the same level of allegiance to trade unions or class-based political parties common in western European nations, but that does not mean that Americans do not visualize a society divided into classes and express some feelings of rapport with others at the same level.

The term **class consciousness** is now frequently used as a general or generic term that includes several different subjective perceptions of the class system. (It is important to make this distinction to emphasize that this is not the way in which Marx or other social theorists use the term.) It is useful to think of class consciousness as ranging from the most basic and minimum acknowledgment that there is a hierarchy of social classes to participation in overt action to enhance shared class-based interests. For analytic purposes it is possible to identify, as shown in Exhibit 10.1, four different forms of class consciousness. **Class awareness** is the weakest level of class consciousness and involves recognition of the partition of society into two or more classes. Because people may be aware of class divisions but unwilling or unable to locate themselves in that system, the term **class identification** is used for taking the step of self-placement in a specific class. Class identification also presupposes recognition of other classes. **Class solidarity** implies a sense of unity with, and sharing values and interests with other members of the same class. Class solidarity involves a perception of other classes with divergent values and interests. **Class action** means taking, or at least being willing to take, some overt action to further the perceived interests of one's class. This level of consciousness implies a degree of confrontation or conflict with other classes.

Subjective perceptions of the class system are dynamic and can change in response to changing conditions. Moreover, class consciousness may be enhanced or weakened by a number of other factors such as race, ethnicity, gender, employment or unemployment, working conditions, and marital status that represent alternative forms of identity.

EXHIBIT 10.1   Types of Subjective Awareness of Social Stratification

Concept	AWARENESS	IDENTIFICATION	SOLIDARITY	ACTION
Dimensions	Cognitive	Cognitive Attitudinal	Cognitive Attitudinal	Cognitive Attitudinal Behavioral

Measurement	Verbalization	Verbalization
		Self-placement
			Verbalization
			Self-placement
			Reference group
			Differential
			  association
				Verbalization
				Self-placement
				Reference group
				Differential
				  association
				Behavior

Conceptualizing Class

A key issue in the examination of class consciousness is the question of the criteria people use to define social class membership. It is easy to think of class in strictly economic terms because Americans tend to rely on words such as "rich," "million-aires," "poor," and "average" to describe members of different classes. Moreover, when forced to mention one single factor Americans will usually choose income. However, more detailed analysis shows that class has a much more complex meaning to people. Class encompasses a complex of factors with lifestyles (73 percent), beliefs and attitudes (69 percent), occupation (68 percent), income (60 percent), education (59 percent), and family background (49 percent) all being rated as either "very important" and "somewhat important" (Jackman & Jackman, 1983: 37). There is a tendency to believe these factors are interrelated, suggesting that people have multidimensional concepts of class, not a single, unidimensional one. In contrast, occupation seems to play a much greater role in defining classes in countries such as Canada and Britain (Pammett, 1987; Johnston & Baer, 1993).

CLASS AWARENESS

The idea that the United States is a classless society, or that if classes exist they are not particularly important, is consistent with the ideology of individualism in the United States that emphasizes individual performance rather than social structure. Moreover, denying class also deflects attention away from the advantages of inherited wealth and privilege, or the handicaps of poverty. The idea of a classless society is encouraged by politicians, the media, and the popular culture (DeMott, 1990). Media coverage of the pregnancies of television and entertainment personalities such as Madonna and Connie Chung emphasize their problems as "working mothers," somehow implying that these multimillionaire celebrities face the same dilemmas in finding quality child care as working-class mothers. The message is that although class differences in wealth and social status do exist, all people have the same problems and rewards. Hollywood is famous for its use of love stories to perpetuate the myth that no social barriers separate the rich from people below them socially or economically.(Case Study).

The claims of functionalist theorists are, to some extent, supported by surveys that reveal that many members of society feel social class differences have positive implications. When people are asked to react to this statement, "Only if differences in income and social standing are large enough is there an incentive for individual effort," just over 50 percent agree, and about 38 percent disagree (Ladd & Bowman, 1999). Going a step farther, 70 percent agree with the statement that no one would devote the years of study necessary to become a lawyer or doctor unless they could anticipate earning much more than ordinary workers. This view prevails because people also believe that there is plenty of opportunity for ambitious workers.

Systematic studies of sensitivity to class divisions date back to the 1940s (Cen-

CASE STUDY
Class and Love in Hollywood

American filmmakers like to craft love stories that have happy endings. It is a simple and effective story line; true love between partners prevails over all obstacles. One of the more popular and enduring versions of the Hollywood romance begins with encounters between young men and women from dissimilar class backgrounds, but any social class differences have faded into insignificance by the end of the film (McDonald, 1997).

The classic love story that announced class did not matter is appropriately titled *Love Story* (a 1970 release), where a baker's daughter and an aristocrat's son learn that love means you never have to say you're sorry. More recently, in *Pretty Woman*, a wealthy and ruthless businessman and a warm-hearted street prostitute ultimately find happiness, and in the process he is transformed into a compassionate and caring person. In *Titanic,* Hollywood turns a tragedy at sea into a love story between a penniless artist and a young society woman. And in *Fools Rush In* the issue of class is compounded by ethnicity because he is a rich, white junior executive and she is the daughter of a working-class Mexican-American family who works in a gambling casino. In one revealing scene the man's elite parents mistake her for his housekeeper.

It is not only Hollywood that perpetuates this idea. The familiar television series *Frasier* carries the same message (Gates, 1998). In it, the genteel psychotherapist Niles Crane is enamored with the British working-class woman Daphne Moon. Interestingly, this sitcom is a spin-off from the enormously popular *Cheers* in which the snobbish brother Frasier Crane was able to socialize with working-class postal workers and waitresses at the famous Boston tavern.

To some this is harmless fantasy, pure entertainment that no one believes or takes seriously. Other observers argue that Hollywood is guilty of trivializing the implications of differences in background. Social class differences in attitudes and perspectives developed during infancy and childhood demand accommodations if meaningful long-term relationships are to survive. "In the movies you get the feeling that . . . it doesn't matter that you went to Utica State and your wife went to Wellesley," when it fact it makes a great deal of difference (MacDonald, 1997). At a more abstract level, it may be argued that Hollywood plays a major role in perpetuating a myth of an open and classless society without barriers to advancement. That is an idea that can be traced to Karl Marx, who suggested that the major cultural images of society are perpetuated by those who benefit the most from them.

ters, 1949). All attempts to measure class awareness raise complex methodological problems. The major problem is that the very act of posing questions about classes can alert people to the issue and cause them to think about matters not previously considered relevant (McFarland & Lew, 1992). Or, they may feel pressure to give a particular response because they believe that it is appropriate or socially acceptable.

Some researchers have attempted to deal with this problem by determining if people will spontaneously raise the issue of classes when discussing inequality. The paradox is that the failure to volunteer class-based answers does not guarantee that people are unaware of them, merely that they did not volunteer them.

With these limitations in mind there is consistent evidence that most Americans visualize a society divided into social classes. More than nine out of ten people acknowledge classes. Only a very tiny proportion—usually less than 2 or 3 percent—assert that the United States is a classless society (Zeller, 2000). Some manual workers tend to emphasize a two-class model with a basic cleavage between blue-collar work and white-collar work, but most people spontaneously visualize a minimum of at least three levels, the wealthy, the poor, and a broad middle class (MacKenzie, 1973). However, many people also identify a fourth group—a working class—and some make a distinction between upper and lower levels within the middle class.

CLASS IDENTIFICATION

The vast majority of Americans identify themselves as members of a particular social class (Exhibit 10.2).[1] Well over 95 percent are willing to locate themselves in the stratification system, and when presented with four choices overwhelmingly identify with either the middle class (45 percent) or the working class (45 percent), with the remainder divided between poor (6 percent) and upper class (4 percent) (Smith, 1996). Moreover, most people report strong attachment to their class. When questioned about the intensity of their feelings, a full one-half report feeling "very strongly" about their membership in that class. Another 28 percent report "somewhat strong" feelings, and only one in five define their attachment as "not too strong" (Jackman, 1979).

The most obvious feature of class identification in the United States is the tendency of Americans to ignore extremes of class. One-third of people earning less than $15,000 think of themselves as middle class, and 71 percent of those with incomes over $75,000 do, too (Smith, 1996). Many factors contribute to this pattern. Language is an obvious one, for many class terms have disagreeable connotations that people prefer to avoid, "poor" and "rich," "upper class" and "lower class" are not neutral terms. Working class has connotations of manual work. More important than semantics is recognition of the fact that most people are, in fact, neither very rich nor exceedingly poor.

Therefore, when prompted, Americans are willing and able to locate themselves within a more complex class system. The data on class identification reported in Exhibit 10.2 are organized by occupation and show a pronounced correspondence between structural position and subjective evaluation, emphasizing the importance

---

[1]The number of options that are presented to people influences the distribution of responses. Most working-class and upper-middle-class people will choose middle class if they have only three options.

EXHIBIT 10.2   Occupation and Class Identification

| | | Class Identification | | |
Occupation	Poor	Working	Middle	Upper Middle	Upper
Professional	<1%	17%	62%	20%	<1%
Managerial	<1	20	59	18	2
Sales	3	22	61	12	1
Clerical	7	43	41	9	0
Craft workers	5	53	39	3	<1
Operatives	10	53	35	<1	1
Service	22	46	30	2	<1
Unskilled	17	51	30	1	0
Totals	8	37	43	8	1

Note: Class identification is reported for those who responded to the following question: "People talk about social classes such as the poor, the working class, the middle class, the upper-middle class, and the upper class. Which of these classes would you say you belong in?"

Source: Mary R. Jackman and Robert W. Jackman, Class Awareness In the United States. Berkeley: University of California Press, 1983, Table 4.1, p. 73. Copyright © 1983 by the University of California Press.

of work in shaping the broad outlines of the stratification system. Most professionals and managers think of themselves at the upper end of the stratification system, favoring the middle-class or upper-middle-class label. Sales workers tend to make the same distinctions, while clerical workers typically divide themselves between middle class or working class. A much clearer pattern is found in blue-collar occupations where a majority of manual workers place themselves in the working class, although about one-third do favor the middle-class designation, and some see themselves among the poor. Service workers and the unskilled are the most likely to identify themselves as the poor.

As would be expected, education and income modify class identification. People with less formal education and lower incomes place themselves at lower levels. This is apparent among that segment of blue-collar and service workers who identify with the poor and among the better-educated and better-paid clerical workers who identify with the middle-class. Thus, the link between occupation and class is well established in people's minds, but gains in income and education can cause people to place themselves in a higher class, just as lower pay can cause reduced self-placement.

Racial Identity

Race and gender compete with class as a source of subjective identification. Minorities frequently encounter subtle forms of racial profiling or outright discrimination that is a constant reminder of the importance of skin color in their lives. This would be more salient to those mired at the bottom of the stratification system, who could feel that their race hindered their educational and occupational attainments. A comparison of middle-class and poor African Americans shows that poor black Americans emphasize race more than class as a form of self-identification (Durant & Sparrow, 1997). This suggests that less advantaged blacks see race as a more decisive factor in their social and economic lives than social class. In contrast, although middle-class African Americas are not insensitive to racial prejudice, they are more likely to identify with their class position.

Moreover, as the assimilation model loses salience and is replaced by a multicultural model of society, more minorities are likely to have ties to two cultures and hence two racial or ethnic identities as well as a class identity. While prior to the 1960s black children's preferences often tended toward white images, they now favor black forms (Cross, 1991). This bicultural identification is more pronounced among more recent immigrants where it is easier to retain a native identity at the same time that a separate new American identity develops.

CLASS SOLIDARITY

The idea of class solidarity moves beyond self-identification and focuses on the extent to which people feel they share values and interests with other members of the same class and feel a sense of unity with them. Although there is some sense of compatibility with members of the same social class, who are perceived as sharing similar values and lifestyles, this perspective does not widely extend to feelings that higher or lower classes have *conflicting* economic and political interests. Rather, people are more likely to feel that classes have divergent but not incompatible interests. Thus, blue-collar workers might agree that manual workers have different interests than managers but simultaneously feel that all classes are members of a "team" in which each makes an essential contribution (MacKenzie, 1973). It is very uncommon for Americans to see different classes as "enemies." This holds true despite the fact that there are strong feelings among the middle and lower levels of society that the political and economic system is tilted in favor of the wealthy. For example, surveys show that a majority of Americans believe owners and corporate executives have disproportionate influence on the government (Kluegel & Smith, 1986: 120).

It is believed that one of the major reasons that individuals do not develop a sense of solidarity with other members of their class is that potential class loyalties are overwhelmed by internal divisions based on income, race, ethnicity, gender and other factors which serve to divide rather than unite. Race appears to be among one of the most salient sources of diversity. One survey revealed only 19 percent of whites and 26 percent of blacks thought they shared "a lot" of common interests with members of the other race in the same social class (Colasanto & Williams, 1987).

CLASS ACTION

This form of class consciousness exists when overt action is contemplated or under-taken in an attempt to further the interests of one's own class or inhibit the interests of some other class. This form of behavior is rare in the contemporary United States, which is not surprising considering that few people see classes separated by vastly divergent interests. Only small numbers of workers, for example, express much interest in joining with others in picketing or other actions (Leggett, 1968). Labor unions and political parties are two of the organizations that articulate the interests of the social classes, especially the working class, and they have different histories in the United States and Europe.

The Role of Labor Unions

Nineteenth-century workers responded to industrialization in different ways. Some, such as printers, formed unions that sought to protect the wages and working condi-tions of members of their own occupation. Others attempted to develop broadly based labor unions that united *all* workers. The Knights of Labor recruited at the class level, seeking to unite all working people—skilled and unskilled, women and men, white and black—except for liquor dealers, professional gamblers, bankers, and stockbrokers, under the slogan that "an injury to one is the concern of all" (Bai-ley, 1956: 538). At its peak in the 1880s the Knights claimed a membership of one million workers out of an urban labor force of ten million. Still others challenged the very foundations of capitalism. In the United States the Western Federation of Min-ers was one of the groups that sought to "abolish the wage system" (Dubofsky, 1969).

Most employers staunchly resisted the labor union movement, and the gov-ernment often came to the aid of employers, as for example when federal troops were used to quell railroad strikes in 1877 and again in 1894. Over the course of the first two decades of the twentieth century the Knights, along with other more radi-cal unions such as the Western Federation of Miners, were superseded by the Amer-ican Federation of Labor, representing only the skilled trades. The AFL took a more moderate and less confrontational stance and was able to win important concessions on wages, hours, and working conditions for members of craft occupations.

Unskilled and semiskilled factory workers were largely ignored by the AFL, in part because such jobs tended to be filled by racial and ethnic minorities that sep-arated them from craft workers who were typically native-born (Mink, 1986). The devastating economic dislocation of the 1930s stimulated successful attempts to unionize whole industries—auto workers, steel workers—represented by the rival Congress of Industrial Organizations. The unionization of these industries was not accomplished without strikes and violence, but it did finally establish the right of unions to exist and collectively bargain for their members. They won significant wage concessions for members of some industries such as the auto industry, but in the process increased the economic discrepancy between the top and bottom of the working class (Form, 1985).

Union membership began to decline soon after, and at the beginning of the twenty-first century membership continues in decline—standing at about 15 percent of the workforce. In contrast, union membership approaches 30 percent in Germany, 40 percent in Ireland, and 90 percent in Sweden. Contracting membership reflects a number of factors, including the erosion of traditional blue-collar industries such as steel and automobiles combined with limited success in unionizing white-collar and service workers. Organized labor today acts as an interest group in Washington (and the state capitals) lobbying for workers' interests in things such as occupational health and safety, worker privacy, and minimum wage legislation and supporting pro-labor candidates for political office, but it has not been as successful as union movements in other nations. Moreover, although unions are able to exert some influence on the voting choices of its members, it is very modest (Juravich & Shergold, 1988), meaning that they cannot deliver blocks of votes for candidates as they once could.

Political Parties

Political parties in some industrial democracies have come to be explicitly aligned with the interests of different classes. This is most evident in Western European nations that have parties such as Labour (Britain) or Social Democratic (Germany or Sweden) that expressly pursue working-class interests. In contrast, political parties in the United States have typically been loose coalitions of voting blocks rather than ideological groups. The Republican party is divided into a more liberal Northeastern wing and a more conservative Midwestern wing and is typically identified with the interests of the more affluent segments of society on economic issues and the more conservative on social issues. The Democratic party as we know it was created in the 1930s as a coalition of workers, immigrants, and racial and religious minorities and has traditionally favored governmental action to buffer the worst effects of capitalism, and it has won the allegiance of minorities through its support for civil rights.

The links among social class, labor unions, and political parties is less pronounced in the United States than in Europe, but there is a strong tie between unions and the Democrats. Almost all (over 90 percent) of unions' political contributions go to Democrats, and the Democratic party is favored by blue-collar workers, union members, and the poor, but it has never been an exclusively partisan working-class party, nor has it ever held a monopoly of working-class votes. About one in three union members vote Republican in most years, and support for Republicans is even more pronounced at the Presidential level, where more than 40 percent of union members voted for Nixon, Reagan, and Bush during the 1970s and 1980s (Greenhouse, 1997). George W. Bush won 37 percent of the vote in union households in 2000. Consequently, both major parties are better understood as coalitions rather than rigidly ideological groups.

Despite its orientation toward workers, the modern Democratic Party was formed by a representative of the capitalist elite (Franklin Roosevelt) and later chose another member of the elite as its national standard-bearer (John F. Kennedy) and long depended upon the financial support of wealthy contributors, even before the proliferation of "soft money" contributions in the 1990s (Ferguson & Rogers, 1986). Therefore, American political parties do not offer voters a clear choice along economic or class lines. Some interpret the notoriously low voter turnout rates in the United States to this: Voters choose not to vote rather than support a party that fails to articulate their interests (Vanneman & Cannon, 1987).

In fact, when political candidates attempt to articulate differences between the needs of different classes, opponents successfully silence them with charges of "class warfare." When candidate Al Gore suggested the 2000 election was a choice between advocates of "the people" and "the powerful" he was publicly chastised by his opponents. Gore was denounced as a "candidate who wants to wage class warfare to get ahead" (Safire, 2000a). The charge was enough to force the Vice President to back away from openly advocating populist ideals.

The Interplay of Unions, Parties, and Class Solidarity

The link between class consciousness, union membership, and political strength is more pronounced in European nations (Kautsky, 1996). Those nations had aristocratic traditions that highlighted social differences between nobles and the rest of society and excluded workers from participation in major social and political institutions. Working-class solidarity emerged from their vulnerability and fostered the creation of unions and political parties pursuing workers' interests. Large and powerful unions are able to exert influence on the political process and win legislation benefiting workers, and political success in turn reinforces the sense of class solidarity. Four out of five voters in Britain believe that a "class struggle" is going on in their nation (*The Economist,* 1997c). Sweden is probably the best example of a nation with a large and powerful union movement (90 percent of salary and wage workers are union members), political dominance by a working-class-oriented Social Democrat party, and an extensive social welfare program that includes generous heath care and retirement benefits (Johnston & Baer, 1993).

CLASS CONSCIOUSNESS AND THE WORKING CLASS

Social scientists have traditionally devoted more attention to class consciousness among blue-collar workers, in large part because of the major historical role assigned to this group by Karl Marx. It is an interesting irony that members of the working class in some eastern European nations were in the forefront of challenges to communism, with shipyard workers in Gadanz, Poland, the most visible case. It is clear that a certain configuration of characteristics that are consistent with Marx's reasoning tend to increase working-class identification among manual workers. Union members and the youngest, least educated, lowest paid, most dissatisfied manual workers with the least autonomy on the job are the most likely to locate themselves in the working class (Zingraff & Schulman, 1984). Thus, as a general rule it is the most disadvantaged blue-collar workers that identify with the working class while the more advantaged are more likely to see themselves as middle class.

Sociologists have long sought to understand why blue-collar manual workers in the United States fail to develop a broader sense of working-class solidarity with lower-middle-class white-collar workers and the working poor, who typically encounter the same experiences on the job (low pay, a lack of autonomy and responsibility, sometime harsh supervision), and why members of the working class seldom press for dramatic changes in the political economy despite the belief that the economic and political system is biased in favor of a wealthy minority.

Studies of male blue-collar workers in stable, well-paying jobs suggest that part of the answer may be found in the fact that they perceive more than one stratification criterion and simultaneously locate themselves on two quite different hierarchies (MacKenzie, 1973; Halle, 1984). One identity, based on the characteristics of their work, leads them to divide the world into four classes—the rich; the poor; a broad middle class of professionals, managers, and clerical workers; and the working class. Blue-collar workers perceive a definite and fundamental distinction between those who are working people and those who are not. One important feature is the characteristics of the work—productive, manual, strenuous, difficult, and dangerous (Halle, 1984). The other feature is control and authority, or more accurately, the lack of it. Thus their work and their class position are determined by the type of work they do and their subordination to the orders of organizational superiors. Managers certainly do not work, merely hiring others to work. Other white-collar workers are often characterized as consisting of little that is productive and meaningful—"shuffling papers" or "working with their mouths," even literally doing nothing, "They just sit on their butts all day." For these workers, working-class identification is likely to be limited to those who engage in certain kinds of productive manual labor.

The concept of "working man" also includes considerations of class, color, and gender (Halle, 1984). The poor are not working people for they are believed to be unable or unwilling to work. An emphasis on working-class tasks as strenuous, dirty, and dangerous has traditionally also made them *men's* tasks in the minds of many, just as clerical work is defined by them as women's work. The recent movement of increasing numbers of women into blue-collar work is contributing to a reevaluation of the concepts of both class and gender. A person's race and ethnicity are also important, apparently more important than any definition of social class. Therefore, blacks or Latinos may do the same kind of work or have similar lifestyles, but they tend not to be accepted as members of the same class. Peoples' race or ethnicity is powerful enough to divide them from other blue-collar workers.

A second blue-collar perspective on the class system is based on education, income, and material possessions. Working-class families tend to have education comparable to that of lower-middle-class workers, and their income allows them to enjoy consumer goods and live in pleasant neighborhoods with lower-middle-class and some upper-middle-class families. Hence they also identify themselves as "middle class," a very broad and amorphous group based largely on similar lifestyles. There is such diversity in this group that it is difficult to draw a line between the middle class and the rich at the top of the system and the poor at the bottom.

The workers also reveal another facet of the situation. Confrontational class action does not develop because there is strong commitment to American democracy as a system of government superior to all others. Although there is widespread belief in corruption among politicians and control of the government by economic interests, this rarely translates into attraction for radical restructuring of society. For one thing, the basic system is believed to be sound, but it has been subverted by the actions of individuals. Moreover, the lure of alternative political systems is dampened by the belief that reform could only be accomplished at the expense of individual liberty and freedom.

FAMILY, GENDER, AND CLASS CONSCIOUSNESS

The question of the formation of class consciousness is made more complex by the fact that many families include spouses occupying different class levels. Using occupation as the measure of social class reveals that somewhere between one-half and two-thirds of all employed husbands and wives are in occupations that would place them in different classes. This fact has its origin in the gender segregation of occupations with women concentrated in clerical jobs, retail sales work, and service occupations, compared to the overrepresentation of men in blue-collar jobs. Moreover, even spouses in the same occupational category can be separated by a number of gender-based forms of inequality; women earn less (the earnings gap), are less likely to exercise workplace authority, and have limited mobility opportunities because of the glass ceiling. In short, spouses at the same class level may very well have very different experiences at work.

Class consciousness is also influenced by differences in the way men and women think about social class, especially in making the distinction between working class and middle class (Robinson & Kelly, 1979; Vanneman & Cannon, 1987; Simpson, Stark & Jackman, 1988). The most important factors contributing to women's identification with the working class are employee status (as opposed to self-employed), full-time rather than contingent employment, being in a female-dominated job, and being a member of a union. The lack of authority which is so important in fostering working-class identification among men is somewhat less important for women. One interpretation is that blue-collar women are not insensitive to their subordination, merely that they are more willing to accommodate to it than to focus on it as a major source of potential conflict (Rosen, 1987: 72).

The question of how members of families define their individual class standing is an intriguing one. One of the most common responses to disparate class positions is the idea of **status maximization,** the strategy of claiming the highest class level possible to optimize social status (Davis & Robinson, 1988). This is the tendency of people to "borrow" the best attributes of their spouse in locating themselves in the system. Blue-collar husbands might, for instance, emphasize the white-collar occupation of their schoolteacher wives in defining their social class position (Baxter, 1994). Borrowing thus allows people to elevate their class level beyond their own accomplishments. This process happens among both women and men, but is most common among married women not in the paid workforce, who must almost of necessity rely on their husband's class in defining their class placement because the role of unpaid homemaker occupies an ambiguous place in the class system. Moreover, this way of thinking about class is also grounded in the tradition of a male head of household and implies that they use the family as the unit of analysis in locating themselves in the stratification system.

However, the situation is more complicated for married women in the paid workforce because they possess their own claims to class standing. In such situations it appears that both spouses consider the others' class in defining their own class, but the husbands' class has a greater impact (Baxter, 1994; Zipp & Plutzer, 1996). Women are more likely to elevate or depress their own class identification on the basis of their spouses' occupation than are men. This pattern holds generally in Australia, Norway, and Sweden as well as the United States.

Dependence upon husbands' occupation in wives' class placement is reduced in some situations, but the magnitude of the change is unclear (Davis & Robinson, 1988; Zipp & Plutzer, 1996). Wives' class identification is now, compared to the 1970s and earlier, somewhat more likely to be based on their own occupational and educational accomplishments. Full-time employment, higher levels of education and pay, and contributing a greater share of the family's income have all been shown to increase reliance upon their personal situation in subjective definitions of class. Therefore, it can be predicted that as women move into jobs that offer greater rewards and contribute ever greater proportions of family income, they will develop more individualized conceptions of their class position.

CONCLUSION: FACTORS MITIGATING AGAINST CLASS CONSCIOUSNESS

The vast majority of Americans recognize significant social, political, and economic inequalities and a hierarchy of classes and their position in the larger system. Social class is definitely a conscious factor in social relationships and lifestyles, but class consciousness does not extend to the belief that social classes are at odds with each other or that major structural changes or a massive redistribution of resources is necessary. Marx was, during his own lifetime, acutely aware of the failure of Americans to develop a sense of *klasse fur sich*. A number of factors combine to explain the absence of clearly articulated feelings of class consciousness in American society, even among the less advantaged segments of that society, who do not enjoy major benefits (Lipset & Marks, 2000).

History. It is important to recognize that the history of the United States was, in some important ways, unique. Forged as a new nation in the eighteenth and nineteenth centuries, it lacked the feudal tradition of a hereditary aristocracy so common to many European nations. In addition, it was founded on abstract principles of democracy and equality before the law and voting rights. They were not rights that extended to all people at the outset—slaves, women, and the propertyless were not included—but the legal guarantees incorporated in the Bill of Rights were eventually extended to ever-greater segments of the population, albeit slowly and only under political pressure. It was a nation that flourished under industrial capitalism and produced widespread prosperity that made it possible for large numbers of blue-collar workers to enjoy a relatively high standard of living. Thus, it is argued that American society did not produce the widespread deprivation likely to foster broadly based discontent and anger.

Immigration. America, being a nation of immigrants, continually accommodates waves of immigrants from all corners of the world. Immigrants are often relegated to the lowest levels of the stratification system, but differences among them hinder the development of class solidarity with other disadvantaged members of society. Their religious, cultural, and linguistic diversity impedes communication and often generates hostility and antagonism. Such antagonisms frequently have an economic as well as a cultural basis since minorities often compete for the same jobs. Employers have been known to actively exploit ethnic and gender divisions in battles against unions, using women and members of minority groups as strikebreakers (Foner, 1964). Consequently, the potential for solidarity based on common economic position is subverted by the disintegrating factors of race and ethnicity.

Gender. Gender has often operated in the same way as race and ethnicity in driving a wedge between workers in the same class by objective criteria. Print shop owners in the nineteenth century recruited unskilled women workers from the clothing and textile industries to undermine the strength of the trade union by training the women to perform some of the tasks that master printers controlled. The women were attracted to opportunities in the printing business because of the notoriously poor pay and working conditions in the textile factories (Baron, 1980). In other cases, women were employed as strikebreakers at newspapers in Boston, New York, and Chicago. Today, men and women workers are still separated by the earnings gap that disadvantages women.

Another aspect of gender that serves to divide members of the working class is occupational segregation. Large numbers of women and men labor in different jobs, work different hours, and have different experiences. All of these factors serve to separate rather than integrate workers.

Social Mobility. The characteristic belief in an open opportunity structure and the chance for individual mobility that permeates all levels of the society is another factor inhibiting the development of group consciousness. Polls indicate a majority of Americans believe there is plenty of opportunity for those with ambition who are willing to work hard. These beliefs are, to some extent, supported by their own experiences because many are the children or grandchildren of immigrants who were able to significantly improve their relative position in society. The consequence is that less-advantaged Americans are able to think of their position as temporary rather than as permanent membership in a particular class.

Multiple Hierarchies. Americans, most notably the working class, employ a number of factors to define subjectively their class position—type of work, authority or lack of it, income and wealth, manual or mental work, and a behavioral dimension—lifestyles. Consequently, class location on one dimension need not coincide with class position on other dimensions. Occupationally defined classes may, for example, include families with very different incomes. Work in factories is "working class" by any standard, but it encompasses women and men who are skilled craft workers, first-line supervisors, janitors, machine operators, and laborers, all of whom may earn very different incomes and have very different lifestyles. In fact, many better-paid blue-collar workers see themselves as having a middle-class lifestyle.

The Ethos of Individualism. The dominant ideology of individualism leads most Americans to believe they are just about where they belong in the system considering their talents and efforts. Blue-collar workers typically explain their position in personal terms, rather than in terms of their modest origins or the workings of the system (Halle, 1984: 169). They are likely to cite their intellectual limitations, lack of effort in school, or that they lacked the boldness to set up their own business. Thus, Americans are constrained to think in personal terms rather than structural terms.

Cross-national differences in adherence to the value of individual effort is strong. Citizens of several nations were asked to locate their beliefs on a ten-point scale from 1 ("In the long run, hard work usually brings a better life") to 10 ("Hard work doesn't generally bring success; it's more a matter of luck and connections"). Just under 60 percent of Americans strongly agreed with the individualist approach by placing themselves at one to three on the scale, compared to only 38 percent of the British and 33 percent of Japanese who took this view (Ladd & Bowman, 1999).

KEY CONCEPTS

class action
class awareness

class consciousness
class identification

class solidarity
status maximization

SUGGESTED READING

DAVID HALLE. *America's Working Man*. Chicago, IL: University of Chicago Press, 1984. An in-depth analysis of working-class conceptions of the stratification system and their place in it.

MARY R. JACKMAN and ROBERT W. JACKMAN. *Class Awareness in the United States*. Berkeley: University of California Press, 1983. This study of class consciousness in America remains one of the most thorough analyses of the subject despite the fact that it is somewhat dated.

SEYMOUR MARTIN LIPSET and GARY MARKS. *It Didn't Happen Here: Why Socialism Failed in the United States*. New York: Norton, 2000. The authors include the lack of class consciousness among the major reasons why socialism never gained a foothold in America.

REEVE VANNEMAN and LYNN WEBER CANNON. *The American Perception of Class*. Philadelphia, PA: Temple University Press, 1987. This approach to class consciousness emphasizes the way that class is experienced.

DANIEL J. WALKOWITZ. *Working With Class: Social Workers and the Politics of Middle Class Identity*. Chapel Hill: University of North Carolina Press, 1999. This historical analysis of social work professionals focuses on the contradictions of class identity they face.

USEFUL WEB SITES

The AFL-CIO (**www.aflcio.org**), the largest labor organization in the United States maintains this web site, which contains a wealth of information about the labor movement.

A number of Marxist, socialist, and egalitarian organizations seek to promote a sense of solidarity among members of the working class around the world. Their web sites seek to convince and recruit with their message. Among them are the League of Revolutionaries for New America (**www.lrna.org**), Workers Liberty (**www.workersliberty.org**), and the Anarchist Federation (**burn.ucsd.edu/~acf/org**).

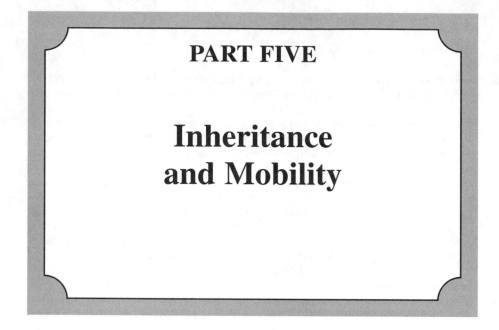

PART FIVE

Inheritance and Mobility

A key feature of the ideology of individualism affirms that upward social mobility is based on individual effort and ability, unfettered by modest social class origins, race, or gender. It is a perspective that has attracted and sustained generations of immigrants. Yet parental location in the stratification system is not irrelevant, influencing the educational and occupational attainments of their children. This chapter explores the direct and subtle ways that class, race, and gender can facilitate or hinder movement across class lines.

CHAPTER ELEVEN

Patterns of
Social Mobility

SOCIAL MOBILITY: OPEN AND CLOSED SYSTEMS

Children invariably inherit their place in the stratification system from their parents. Each infant begins life with the economic resources, social rank, and lifestyles of their parents. In some stratification systems parental position has fixed and permanent consequences for subsequent generations, confining them to the level of their birth. Feudal societies were, for example, rigidly divided between three estates—peasants, clergy, and aristocracy. In the Hindu caste system of the nineteenth century, caste membership was hereditary, and it was virtually impossible for individuals to hope to succeed by their own efforts. Societies in which positions in the stratification system are inherited and permanent are described as **closed systems**.

Closed systems are organized to perpetuate privilege and inequality. Structural barriers are erected in law or custom, enforced by coercion to ensure that access to the higher classes is closed to all except the children of the advantaged. Educational systems such as those in India were segregated along caste lines, denying lower-level children access to the skills and credentials that might allow them to challenge authority for more advantageous positions. Such practical barriers are legitimized by prevailing sociocultural ideas and beliefs. A common ideology posits some intrinsic divisions along class lines. Theories of genetic inferiority (e.g., ideological racism) claim the existence of inherent biological differences among the classes that predispose members of those groups for certain levels at birth. Aristocracies usually claim the right to rule on the basis of a combination of breeding (biological) and training (social) disparities. Rulers in medieval estate systems sometimes declared divine support for their power. Each of these ideologies support the continuation of stable patterns of inequality over time, although there is always some social mobility, even in the most inflexible situations. Closed systems are much more likely to be found in stable agricultural societies and tend to be threatened by the process of industrialization.

In contrast, in completely **open systems**—admittedly an ideal type—there are no formal or ideological barriers to mobility and people rise or fall (relative to their parents) on the basis of their own abilities, efforts, and accomplishments. In short, there is no necessary link between the class levels occupied by parents and the ultimate class position of their children, although it turns out that parental class is seldom irrelevant. All democratic industrial class systems tend toward more openness than is found in agricultural societies because urbanization and the industrial transformation increase opportunities for social mobility. In the early stages of industrialization, for example, the most profound transformation is the shift from agriculture to manufacturing, and rural workers and small farm owners are able to move into the urban working class. The switch to factory work represents a dramatic improvement in earnings and working conditions for many propertyless rural farm workers. However, for others the pay and working conditions in urban sweatshops must be considered downward mobility because they suffer intolerable working conditions.

Thus, stratification systems differ in the extent to which one generation's accomplishments and opportunities are determined by the class level of their parents, and it is useful to visualize societies falling along a continuum from open to closed, although no actual society is at either extreme. Industrial democracies tend toward openness, and formal educational attainments are the single most important key to success.

Intergenerational and Intragenerational Mobility

Social mobility is formally defined as the movement of individuals and families from one level in the stratification system to another, either upward or downward. The study of social mobility focuses on experiences of individuals and is tracked in two different ways. **Intergenerational mobility** compares the social position of parents and their children and is considered the most basic measure of the openness of a society.[1] **Intragenerational mobility** traces changes occurring during the life cycle of individuals, from their first job to the end of their careers. Intragenerational

---

[1] There are a number of complex methodological and conceptual problems inherent in the study of intergenerational social mobility. The single most difficult issue is that of specifying the point in the life cycle of both generations (children and parents) at which to measure social class position because people experience changes in their situation over the course of their lives. A common way of handling this is to focus in on parental class when children are 14 to 18 years old, assuming that parents are established in their careers and children have embarked on educational or occupational paths.

Another issue is the question of determining the class position of the parental generation. Much older (pre-1980s) research focused on specific pairs of individuals, i.e., fathers to sons. This narrow

mobility involves movement among jobs or careers at different class levels and does not consider lateral moves among jobs that do not alter class position. Intragenerational mobility is studied as a separate topic and is also treated as a stage in the process of intergenerational mobility.

The Status Attainment Model of Social Mobility

Studies of intergenerational social mobility divide the process into three stages or steps. The first stage is the connection between social class origins and educational attainments, and the factors that influence educational success. The second stage is the link between social origins, educational attainments and first job in the adult labor market. The third stage focuses on social origins, education, and first job and how they are tied to employment later in the career. Research in this tradition, known as the **status attainment model**, began in the 1960s and clearly established the continuing impact of parental class location on their children's accomplishments (Blau & Duncan, 1967). The original research established empirical relationships among the basic variables in the process. Subsequent work added cognitive (ability measures) and social psychological factors (mobility aspirations) to the process (Sewell, et al., 1969).[2] Contemporary research focuses on the institutional arrangements that influence progress through educational systems and careers (Kerckoff, 1995). The status attainment model is clearly an oversimplification, but it remains a useful starting point for understanding intergenerational continuity and mobility (Exhibit 11.1).

The basic model has a clear logic to it, confirmed by a substantial body of empirical research.[3] In its most basic form, the model shows that in the first stage of the process, parental social class origins directly influence children's aspirations, academic ability, and level of educational attainment. Academic ability and aspirations have an independent impact on educational progress. In the second stage, social origins and years of education are directly correlated with the level of the first

---

approach ignored daughters and the role of mothers in the socialization process, typically based on the assumption that the husband was the "head of the household" or that his occupation determined the class position of the family. More recent studies are exploring four different combinations of individuals—fathers to sons and to daughters, mothers to sons and to daughters—and the interaction among the different combinations.

[2]This research project followed the careers of people in Wisconsin and is therefore sometimes referred to as the Wisconsin status attainment model.

3 The status attainment model has been widely criticized because it has a number of shortcomings. The links in the model are statistical correlations and do not necessarily explain how the links are articulated. Moreover, the statistical correlations explain less than one-half of the variance, meaning that important considerations beyond the variables contained in the model impinge upon the process. In addition, it must be emphasized that these relationships are more complex than suggested by this graphic representation. Most importantly, relationships are interactive. For example, while higher educational aspirations can inspire higher attainments, rising scholastic attainments can likewise encourage ever higher aspirations. Thus, continued academic success can stimulate a subsequent rise in aspirations, and likewise, repeated failure has the potential to dampen aspirations.

EXHIBIT 11.1   A Status Attainment Model

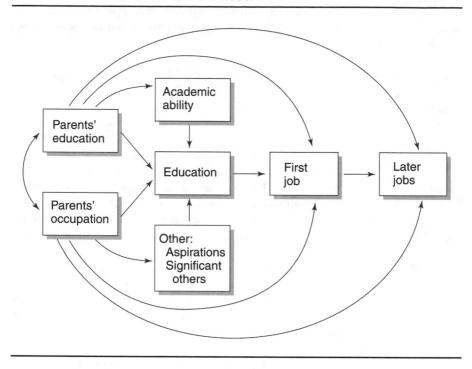

job. The third stage focuses on the second generation's later jobs, which are correlated with social origins, levels of education, and the level of the earlier job. Perhaps the key finding is that parental class has some impact on every factor in the process. In short, social class origins are never irrelevant!

Structural Mobility.   The opportunities for individual mobility and the total amount of mobility that occurs within societies is forcefully impacted by structural changes in the economic system of production and distribution. Shifts in the economy close out opportunities for some while opening them for others. A substantial number of people experience intragenerational downward mobility precipitated by the loss of a job followed by reentry into the labor market at a lower level in the system. Advanced stages of industrialization, for example, typically shrink the manufacturing sector and eliminate stable working-class jobs. The United States lost many working-class jobs in the steel and garment industries. At the same time the burgeoning of technologically based upper-middle-class occupations creates new channels of mobility for the better-educated children of lower-middle-class or working-class parents. These patterns are referred to as **structural mobility**, movement due to expansion and contraction of the underlying economic system.

INTERGENERATIONAL MOBILITY

America is celebrated as the epitome of an open system, a society in which individual effort and ability rather than family background determines location in the stratification system. This is, of course, the basic tenet of the "ideology of individualism," and it is relatively easy to find cases that validate the American Dream. For example, Mel Martinez, Secretary of Housing and Urban Development in the George W. Bush administration, came to the United States from Cuba in 1962, lived in a foster home for four years until the rest of his family could join him, and then worked his way through college and law school. However, moving beyond such anecdotal evidence suggests a more complex picture. A broader, more comprehensive view of the stratification system suggests that the United States is simultaneously an open system with people circulating between levels *and* a closed system with a sizable share of children inheriting the same class level as their parents (Rytina, 2000).

The mobility experiences of a sample of American males is reported in Exhibit 11.2, which illustrates some basic patterns of inheritance and mobility. There is inheritance at every level (indicated by bold type), but it is most pronounced among children of upper-middle-class white-collar and unskilled and semiskilled members of working-class fathers. White-collar parents are more affluent and are thus able to provide their children with educational and social resources that enable them to earn similar jobs. In contrast, the children of lower manual workers, many of whom are the working poor, are less likely to be able to facilitate the mobility of their children. The inheritance found in the upper reaches of blue-collar work reflects the fact that such occupations are perceived as desirable, and thus children often choose to fol-

EXHIBIT 11.2   Patterns of Intergenerational Mobility, Fathers to Sons, United States

Father's Position	Son's Class Position				
	Upper White Collar	Lower White Collar	Upper Manual	Lower Manual	Farm
Upper white collar	**58%**	18%	13%	12%	<01%
Lower white collar	42	**24**	16	18	01
Upper manual	28	16	**29**	26	01
Lower manual	22	15	25	**38**	<01
Farm	15	11	23	36	**14**

Note: Rows do not add to 100 percent due to rounding.

Source: Mark E. Sobel, Mark P. Becker, and Susan M. Minick. "Origins, destinations, and associations in occupational mobility." *American Journal of Sociology* 104 (November, 1998), Table 6, page 707.

low their parents. The handicaps for people at the bottom of the stratification system are more pronounced for African Americans, and the advantages for people at the top are more pronounced for whites.

The major path of upward mobility is from lower-middle-class into upper-middle-class white-collar jobs. Four in ten children move into higher level white-collar positions from other white-collar jobs. Significant numbers of children from other levels also succeed in reaching the better white-collar jobs. Clearly, formal education is the key to making this move since the boundary between managerial and professional jobs is expertise. To put it another way, the boundary separating the upper-middle-class from other class levels is "permeable," it is open to the combination of effort, achievement, and good fortune. There are differences in patterns of upward mobility in industrial nations, but education is always a primary route (Western & Wright, 1994; Ishida, Muller & Ridge, 1995). There is also a significant amount of downward mobility, with, for example, 40 percent of upper-white-collar children and 30 percent of lower-middle-class children failing to achieve that level in their own careers. Interestingly, there is some indication that all industrial democracies exhibit similar patterns of inheritance and mobility (Erikson & Goldthorpe, 1992). This challenges the idea that the United States alone is an open society and suggests that structural processes accompanying industrialization create mobility opportunities.

The class destinations of daughters suggest both differences and similarities between male and female patterns (Erikson & Goldthorpe, 1992). Comparing sons to daughters tends to show higher overall levels of mobility among females, but it is due to the fact that downward mobility exceeds upward mobility. Larger numbers of white-collar daughters than sons end up in the low-skill working class (downward mobility). In part this is a function of sex-segregated occupational opportunities, which means that a disproportionate number of women are likely to end up in lower-middle-class forms of work. Moreover, women experience more downward mobility resulting from the breakdown of families through death, divorce, or abandonment.

A Vicious Cycle of Poverty?

One of the most pressing issues facing industrial nations is the potential for a **vicious cycle of poverty**, the intergenerational transmission of poverty from parents to children. If the children of poor parents are themselves doomed to poverty, there is the risk of creating a permanent underclass of citizens mired in poverty, with children sentenced to a life of poverty and denied hope for a better life.

Although there is some opportunity for upward mobility, the children of poor parents do face a much greater likelihood of being poor as adults than are children of parents above the poverty threshold. When those in poor and nonpoor backgrounds are compared, children in poverty achieve less formal education, earn less, and are more likely to be poor as adults. To illustrate, white children raised in poverty averaged adult mid-1990s incomes of $22,141 compared to $33,655 for the nonpoor. African-American children raised in poor families are 2.5 times more likely to be poor as adults than black children raised in nonpoor families. The risk is even greater among white families, where poor children are 7.5 times more likely to be poor as adults than nonpoor children (Corcoran, 1995). Explaining the factors that contribute to the inheritance of poverty is difficult, and it appears that it is the result of the interaction of several different factors.

The Structure of Neighborhoods and Labor Markets.   The immediate physical and social environment in which poor children mature limits their opportunities and imposes upon them burdens not usually faced by the nonpoor. The poor are typically segregated in distressed neighborhoods that are isolated from the larger society. More than one in every four people below the poverty level lives in a neighborhood where 40 percent of the residents are also poor (Massey, 1996). Another 40 percent are in neighborhoods of 20 to 40 percent poor. It is a greater problem for minority youths because of the added burden of racial discrimination. Entry level jobs there are disappearing. The broad pattern of deindustrialization is constantly reducing the number of blue-collar manufacturing jobs available to youths with limited educational and occupational credentials (Wilson, 1987; 1996). These jobs are being replaced by jobs in service and retail sales, most of which offer low pay and limited career opportunities.

Families that are successful typically desert the inner cities for the more comfortable neighborhoods of the suburbs. The out-migration of better-educated middle class families deprives poor urban youths of role models that could foster hope and optimism. They are also deprived of links to the social networks that provide leads on jobs. Instead, ghetto residents are, "surrounded by failure and come to expect the same" (Ellwood, 1987). The loss of the middle class also has the potential to weaken important institutions—political machines, social clubs, and churches—that could offer links to the larger community.

Family Resources and Family Structure.   The modest financial resources of poor parents means they must allocate more of their income to current survival and less to investments in their children's education and schooling in the form of books and magazines, computers, visits to museums, and other educational experiences. These parents also have more limited residential options and are thus more likely to raise their children in areas with poorer schools.

Growing up in a single-parent or nonintact families is an additional risk factor for children, and a significant one. It doubles the danger that such youths will be high school dropouts, doubles their chances of being a teenage parent, and almost doubles the probability that they will enter adulthood without a job and not in school (McLanahan & Sandefur, 1994). This situation holds true regardless of race, ethnicity, or gender, although there are some differences among these groups.

The risks are produced by a combination of limited economic, social, and community resources. Nonintact families are poorer and thus have fewer financial resources to share with children for educational goals. Children growing up in married-couple families are also able to offer greater social resources in the form of time spent with their children, help with school work, parental supervision, and parental aspirations. Community resources are also entwined with family status in the sense that nonintact families reside in communities with poorer schools and fewer educational resources.

CLASS, RACE, GENDER, AND EDUCATION

The fundamental importance of educational credentials in advanced industrial nations is conclusive. Each major benchmark in the educational process (high school diploma, bachelor's and masters degree, and doctorate) is important, but the baccalaureate may be the most significant educational credential. It is readily apparent that access to virtually all positions in the institutional elite and upper-middle-class demand a minimum of a bachelor's degree, and those lacking the credentials are effectively barred from access. Moreover, the introduction of computer technology is imposing the same requirements on upper-level working-class jobs. Auto mechanics in the 1960s were able to repair most problems with hand tools. Today, they must be able to monitor and service the miniature computers that control most automotive functions. Advanced education is, of course, no guarantee of social mobility since many college graduates are "underemployed," working in jobs below their skill level. One estimate claims that 20 percent of college graduates are either unemployed or in "high school jobs" (Hecker, 1992). However, it remains a *prerequisite* to most of the better jobs.

Exhibit 11.3 demonstrates the importance of formal education by comparing the median earnings of full-time workers with different credentials. Each increment of formal education pays financial dividends, although the earnings gap means that women earn only about 70 or 75 percent of men's earnings. Workers—either men or women—with only an elementary school education are stalled at or near the poverty level, and have little chance of ever improving their status. Moreover, they suffer unemployment rates more than four times that of college graduates. A high school diploma is worth $7,000 a year for a male and $6,000 for a female. A bachelor's degree pays much more significant benefits, about $13,000 for women and $19,000 for men. People with master's and professional degrees, the credentials of the upper-middle-class, have the highest median earnings of any group.

The link between parental social class and their children's educational attainments is unequivocal; the higher the class of parents the greater the educational attainments of children. It is a connection that shows up in the United States and in many other industrial societies including Great Britain, France, Israel, and the Netherlands (Shavit & Blossfeld, 1993). There are two major factors that combine to explain this link between social class and educational accomplishments. Not only

EXHIBIT 11.3   Median Earnings and Educational Attainment

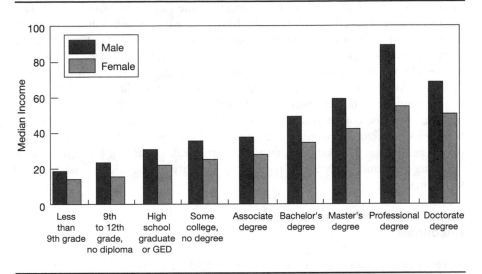

Note: Median earnings (thousands of dollars) for full-time, year-round workers, age 25 and older.

Source: U.S. Bureau of the Census, *Money Income in the United States, 1998.* Current Population Report P60–206. Washington, DC: U.S. Government Printing Office, 2000. Table 8.

do children from higher-class backgrounds have broader access to the academic tools that money can buy, they also have the advantage of subtle social resources that support them in school.

Social Class and Academic Resources

Parents at higher levels in the stratification system are able to furnish their children with several different advantages that facilitate progress through the educational system. The advantages bestowed by parental finances are not trivial. There are, first, material things in the form of computers, Internet access, educational videos, books, and tutors, all of which can improve educational performance.

In addition, their children's schools are also differentiated by class. The impact of social class emerges early in the education process in the form of inequities among schools. American public schools rely heavily on property taxes to support a large proportion—about 40 percent—of their budgets. States contribute somewhat more than half, and the federal government furnishes the remaining 6 to 8 percent. Deteriorating property values in poorer areas, especially inner cities and depressed rural areas, have contracted the tax base in many areas. The consequence is that poorer districts have less money to devote to the schools, and less money translates into lower teacher salaries, larger class size, and fewer enrichment activities. Low-income schools, for example, need more renovation of buildings, have fewer computer and Internet resources and lack enough certified teachers (Wong, 2000). Two out of five teachers' aides, who typically have only a high school education, report they teach on their own without a teacher present at least half the time. In some instances the discrepancies are so dramatic that courts must intervene. To illustrate, the wealthy ski resort town of Stowe, Vermont, has enough money to spend 20 percent more per pupil and pay its teachers 30 percent more than the much poorer nearby community of Worcester (Burkett, 1998). Such discrepancies prompted the Vermont supreme court to order reform and equalization, but the process has not been smooth because it requires increased tax increases in richer districts to help poorer ones. Clearly, money isn't everything; research shows that increasing financial outlays produces only mixed results in the quality of education as measured by test scores.

Social Class and Social and Cultural Resources

More advantaged parents can also offer their children a different kind of dividend, something referred to as **cultural capital** (Bourdieu, 1977). Cultural capital is familiarity with and proficiency in the configuration of knowledge and social skills that place children at a distinct advantage in the school setting. Cultural capital includes linguistic styles, aesthetic preferences, and styles of social interaction. It is the result of exposure to a wide range of ideas and experiences over the course of the socialization process. It begins in infancy when parents begin to speak to their babies (Hart & Risley, 1995). Children of professional parents hear, on average, 2,100 words per hour during their first year of life, compared to 1,200 words per hour in working-class families and 600 words per hour in poor families. The number of words infants hear increases their ability to reason, think conceptually, and solve problems later in life. As they grow older, elite and upper-middle-class parents have the resources to provide more books and computers, visit more museums and galleries, travel, and attend more concerts and theater than parents at lower levels. These experiences combine to make their offspring conversant with the dominant ideas and values that are rewarded in most school systems. Consequently, their superior cultural literacy results in better grades and more schooling (DiMaggio, 1982; Aschaffenburg & Maas, 1997).[4] In contrast, children of the working class and the poor are less likely to possess significant cultural capital, contributing to lower subsequent academic and occupational success.

The concept of cultural capital has also been extended beyond academic literacy to a configuration of social skills, work habits, and styles (Lamont & Lareau, 1988). The reasoning is that educational attainments—and grades more specifically—reflect *both* a cognitive mastery of subject matter and the manner in which

---

[4]Empirical research on cultural capital has produced mixed results. Research in France (Robinson & Garnier, 1985) and Greece (Katsillis & Rubinson, 1990) did not support Bourdieu's formulation.

students behave in the context of the classroom; demeanor, level of effort, coopera-tion, and class participation are all aspects of cultural capital rewarded in the schools. Research in this area is not consistent, although there is some evidence that poor children, Hispanics, and African Americans are *perceived* as having poorer work habits and that such observations are associated with lower grades when con-trolling for performance on tests (Farkas, et al., 1990).

Class and Academic Test Scores

Academic and social and cultural resources combine with natural talent to shape something called "intelligence" or "IQ" or "academic ability." The idea of academic ability is an elusive concept, but for a variety of reasons educators depend on bat-teries of standardized tests to measure it. Schools administer millions of tests each year, starting as early as kindergarten or even preschool (Leslie & Wingert, 1990). Standardized tests are employed to decide admissions, allocate children among cur-ricula within schools, and advise students, and they are one factor in college (Scholastic Assessment Test (SAT) and American College Test(ACT)), graduate school (GREs) and professional school admissions (LSATs). Late in the 1990s these tests also became part of the "accountability movement," designed to use students' scores to measure the performance of individual teachers, schools, and whole dis-tricts. In some cases, school funding is linked to test scores.

Among the best-known tests are those used in college admissions. Two million youths take the SAT each year and one million the ACT, hoping to gain admission to the college of their choice (Lemann, 1999). The first paper and pencil tests of human intelligence were developed by French psychologist Alfred Binet in 1905. The idea of standardized testing entered American higher education in the 1930s through the efforts of Harvard University President James Bryant Conant (Lemann, 1999). Conant feared that the economic suffering of the Great Depression might encourage the growth of socialism among the impoverished. He believed that the best way to prevent that from happening was to open the channels of opportunity and social mobility to children of all classes. He was guided by the words Thomas Jef-ferson wrote in 1813, ". . . there is a natural aristocracy among men. The grounds of this are virtue and talents. . . . There is also an artificial aristocracy founded on wealth and birth, without either virtue or talents." He sought some way to discover natural talents and settled upon standardized testing as the answer. Ironically, many observers today believe standardized tests have become a structural barrier to equal educational opportunity. In response, a number of individual universities and two state public university systems (California and Texas) have dropped academic achievement tests.

There are now, and have been for decades, pronounced differences in scores associated with class level. Using either parental income as a measure of social class standing shows a dramatic 257-point difference in SAT scores! Specifically, the average combined math and verbal score of students with family incomes below $10,000—families living in poverty—is 872, compared to scores of 1029 for children of middle-income parents ($50,000 to $60,000) and 1131 for children in the wealthiest group ($100,000 and over).

There are both gender and racial or ethnic variations in average test scores. Scores for men and women are very similar on the verbal section, and there is a small gender gap in math, but the gap has been narrowing since the 1980s as more women participate in science and math courses. Although members of minority groups have made relatively large gains in recent years, all except Asian Americans on the math portion of the test continue to lag behind the white majority.

Such tests at best measure only certain types of abilities—verbal and mathematical skills—and ignore skills and abilities such as creativity, inventiveness, and imagination. In addition, critics have argued these tests are biased against the lower classes and minority groups who have acquired less cultural capital. Despite James Bryant Conant's optimism, such tests do not measure "innate intelligence" so much as they reflect the backgrounds, preparation, and training of students. An executive of one testing agency openly acknowledges that college entrance examination scores "reflect the inequities that continue to exist in our society (and) disparities in academic preparation" (Ordovensky, 1989). This point is best illustrated by the experiences of Asian Americans.

Asian Americans: Culture and Test Scores Asian Americans' college entrance test scores rival all other minority groups on standardized test scores, and both men and women consistently outrank other students on the math section of the SATs. Asian-American accomplishments can be traced to cultural traditions that stress effort and academic achievement. Asian-American success in higher education is illustrated by their registration at the elite schools (Fletcher, 2000). Asians, who make up 4 percent of the U.S. population, constitute 19 percent of the enrollment at Harvard, 28 percent at MIT, 39 percent at Berkeley, and 22 percent at Stanford.

Asian-American parents at all economic and social class levels seek to instill a high level of dedication to educational attainment in their children. At a general level this reflects the influence of Asian culture, specifically Confucian philosophy, which emphasizes self-discipline, hard work, and humility. For example, in a comparison of Chinese, Japanese, and American parents, Asian Americans place the strongest emphasis on the importance of hard work in school (Stevenson, 1982). They are likely to subscribe to the idea that anyone can do well if they study hard. In contrast, Americans are more likely to attribute school success to natural talent, thus de-emphasizing the importance of effort in the form of attendance and homework. This Asian attitude is translated into academic effort. In a survey of San Francisco-area high school students it was found that female Asian Americans spent an average of 12.3 hours per week doing homework, compared to 9.2 for blacks and 8.6 for whites (Butterfield, 1986). Comparable figures for males were 11.7 for Asian Americans, 6.3 for blacks, and 8.0 for whites. Moreover, Asian-American students had consistently better attendance records and cut classes less frequently.

Moreover, Asian culture emphasizes the importance of bringing honor to the family, and one way in which this can be done is through educational accomplishments. Still another aspect of this philosophy is that it encourages personal humility. When ratings of intellectual ability are compared, American parents give their children the highest ratings, and the children typically rate themselves as above average. It may be that this creates a sense of complacency which reduces the levels of effort. In contrast, Japanese and Chinese people are more likely to rate themselves average or below, thus instilling greater effort to achieve. Educational attainments have not yet translated into success in other areas. Asian Americans continue to be underrepresented in political office, university teaching posts, government jobs, and top corporate positions.

Social Class and College Attendance

The chances of a youth attending college are directly related to social class. As shown in Exhibit 11.4, increasingly larger proportions of children in each higher income bracket are currently enrolled in some form of higher education. Children of black and Latino parents are less likely to be attending college, but among those that do matriculate the same overall association between class and education is repeated. Even if there were no other factors at work, the sheer financial burden of higher education is prohibitive for some segments of society. One year of higher education in 2000 averages more than $10,000 at a public institution and over $25,000 at a private school. One way to measure the practical financial barrier of college is to focus on the share of annual family income required to pay college expenses (The College Board, 1999). College costs for the top-earning one-third of families take 14 percent of annual income for a private four-year college or 5 percent for a public college. In contrast, costs for families in the lowest one-third require 61 percent of their income for a public school or 162 percent for a private school!

Moreover, while tuition continues to rise, family incomes at lower ends of the

EXHIBIT 11.4   Family Social Class and Higher Education

Family Income	Percentage with Children in College
Under $10,000	16%
$10,000–$19,999	25
$20,000–$29,999	32
$30,000–$39,999	39
$40,000–$49,999	47
$50,000–$74,999	53
$75,000 and over	64

Note: Only families with college-age children included. Data include all forms of post-secondary education, including community colleges and four-year institutions.

Source: U.S. Bureau of the Census, Current Population Report P20–487, *School Enrollment—Social and Economic Characteristics—of Students: 1994.* Washington, DC: U.S. Government Printing Office, 1996. Table 19.

income hierarchy do not. Various forms of financial aid are designed to lessen the impact of class inequality, but do not eliminate it. Moreover, beginning in the 1980s federal aid for students declined in absolute dollars, although the number of students continues to increase and tuition to rise, meaning more students are competing for fewer dollars of financial aid. New money for scholarships tends to favor academic achievement over awards based on need (Burd, et al., 1996). In addition, there has been a shift in the pattern of financial aid away from grants to loans, which must be repaid. Low-income students with good test scores are much less likely to attend college than higher-income students with similar scores, and more than half cite lack of funds as the reason. Many low-income students are reluctant to accumulate large debts to attend college.

Children of the more affluent also have the resources to enlist the aid of private college counselors, private consultants, and educational therapists who work with individual students, offering lists of possible colleges, counseling—beginning as early as the eighth grade—on course selection, tutoring on improving admission test scores, and coaching and role playing on how to conduct campus visitations. Private tutoring starts at $25.00 per hour and can rise to $90.00 hourly, meaning that the total cost of these forms of guidance can cost thousands of dollars (Thomas, 1999). It should also be noted that the decline in the availability of student aid has a greater impact on minorities because their average family income is below that of whites.

CASE STUDY
Educational Networks Among the Elite

Breaking into the institutional elite of leadership positions in business, education, and government is the epitome of successful upward mobility. A review of the class origins of these men and women suggests that although the stratification system is open to people of modest social origins, it is heavily weighted in favor of those from more advantaged class backgrounds. A significant proportion of the elite are children of elite parents, and most who originate outside this class are recruited from the ranks of the upper middle class. The number of these persons who started life in the lower-middle or working class is small, and it is extremely rare for children of the poor to achieve such success.

Many of the advantages of the elite are articulated through a network of high-prestige schools that simultaneously prepare these children for future positions of leadership and virtually guarantee that they will achieve them by introducing them to a network of other children of the institutional and capitalist elites. For many children the first step is enrollment at a narrow circle of exclusive boarding schools (Cookson & Persell, 1985). Prep schools such as

Choate and St. Andrews provide a rigorous and sound academic preparation for future educational accomplishments and polish the social skills and values—the cultural capital of the elite—necessary for access to subsequent positions of power and influence. In addition, the students begin to associate with a network of other individuals who will also occupy such positions.

The process continues with enrollment at a small core of select undergraduate colleges—places such as Columbia, Harvard, Pennsylvania, Princeton, Stanford, and Yale (Useem & Karabel, 1986; Kingston & Lewis, 1990). Such schools are among the most exclusive and expensive, which narrows the pool of candidates although they are increasingly open to the general population. For example, about 10,000 high school seniors apply to Dartmouth College, but only 1,000 are accepted (Lee, 1999). Once there they participate in a structured series of group social events (Fall Bonfire, Winter Carnival) and rituals and are exposed to the college traditions that cement a permanent bond among them. By the time they graduate they are highly motivated, self-assured, socially well-rounded individuals who think of themselves as members of a special group, the "Dartmouth family," that will continue into their professional careers.

Moreover, many of these colleges grant preferential admission to the children of alumni, thus giving them an additional advantage. Alumni children typically comprise 12 percent of Harvard's entering class, and Notre Dame reserves 25 percent of its openings for alumni (Leslie, 1991). It is a practice not likely to change since all colleges and universities depend upon their wealthy alumni for donations, thus it will continue to give the children of the elite another advantage.

Nonelite students who are capable and fortunate enough to gain access to such schools dramatically increase their chances of upward mobility (Ishida, Spillerman & Su, 1997). One study of corporate executives showed that one-half had earned a B.A. from one of just eleven elite colleges (Useem & Karabel, 1986). It is at these schools that children of parents at lower levels in the stratification system can acquire the combination of skills, cultural capital, and social contacts that will help them later. The major organizations recruit from these schools, and research shows that the least able graduates (measured by standardized tests) of select colleges have a higher chance of economic success than the most able students from low-status schools (Kingston & Smart, 1990).

Possibly the most dramatic illustration of the role of elite schools can be seen in the U.S. government in the year 2000 (Karr, 2000). The controversial presidential election pitted George W. Bush (Yale) against Al Gore (Harvard). Bill Clinton's four top cabinet posts were held by Madeline Albright (Wellesley) at State, William Cohen (Bowdoin) at Defense, Robert Rubin (Harvard) at Treasury, and Janet Reno (Cornell) as Attorney General. Not one of the nine Supreme Court justices attended a public university or an obscure private school; their schools were Chicago, Cornell, Georgetown, Harvard, Holy Cross, and four graduated from Stanford.

Gender and the Science Pipeline.   Increasing numbers of upper-middle-class occupations depend on a firm grounding in science and mathematics. Engineering, medicine, academic science, system analysis are among the most obvious examples. Preparation for these careers can be visualized as forming a **science pipeline** of training, beginning with elementary school training in the basics and continuing through advanced university education to employment in these fields (Berryman, 1983). The number of students in the pipeline narrows over time because science is cumulative, and a lack of preparation at any one point excludes people from subsequent training. Following the experience of students in the pipeline reveals that women's participation declines more rapidly than men's beginning in the high school years. This holds true in the United States and Canada, Japan, and Sweden (Hanson, Schaub & Baker, 1996).

This is a puzzling development because girls, as a rule, tend to get better grades in all subjects (science and math included) beginning in the early school years and continuing into the first years of high school (Stockard & Wood, 1984). Younger girls (under age 14) outperform boys on both verbal and math standardized test scores, but male scores in math begin to outpace those of females in junior and senior high school (Wentzel, 1988). This manifests itself in an advantage of about 50 points on SAT tests by graduation from high school. Moreover, beginning in high school, girls express less interest and less confidence about their computer skills than boys (Krendl, Broihier, & Fleetwood, 1989). Thus, women and men have different experiences in the pipeline, suggesting the impact of socio-cultural factors.

Boys are very early subtly and directly encouraged in the direction of scholastic performance in mathematics, often because math skills are presumed to be more consistent with conventional sex-typed masculine traits such as "analytic ability." This shows up in the fact that parents and counselors tend to be more supportive of males following math-based careers. For example, parents are more likely to purchase personal computers for sons than daughters and enrollments at computer camps favor boys by a margin of three to one (Kiesler, Sproull & Eccles, 1983).

There are also differential experiences in the context of the classroom. Girls with high math aptitude are less likely to be assigned to "high ability" groups than boys (Hallinan & Sorensen, 1987). Teachers tend to initiate more academic contact with boys and give more attention to male students than female students. In addition, males who give incorrect answers are usually exhorted to greater effort while females are praised simply for trying. The experiences of black children in the area of math is not as well researched, but parallel those based on gender in other contexts. Teachers tend to devote more attention to white children, sometimes give more praise, and they are likely to grant only conditional praise for academic effort (e.g., "A good paper, for a change"), thus subtly suggesting a fundamental intellectual inferiority (Grant, 1984).

However, the inconsistency between grades and standardized test scores is perplexing (Kimball, 1989). It has been suggested that the higher grades earned by females may reflect the fact that social competencies as well as cognitive skills enter into the grading process. Females, on average, have an advantage in social competencies, being more cooperative and attentive and having more positive attitudes toward teachers. This leaves the decline in females test scores to be explained. One interpretation is that it is due to the increasing salience of conventional gender roles that surfaces in later adolescence. This is the age at which conforming to culturally defined gender roles looms large and subtly encourages females to underemphasize competence at cross-gender skills such as math, which is still being accepted as an area of male competence. The interaction between gender and math achievement is not fully understood, but the implications remain, especially among America's 2 million working engineers, where only about 8 percent are women.

Educational Attainments of Minorities. When asked to pick the one thing that can most help a young person succeed in today's world, 35 percent of parents of high school students choose education (Marklein, 2000b). Interestingly, minorities in America who face the greatest challenges are the most sensitive to the importance of education, with 47 percent of African-American parents and 65 percent of Latino parents mentioning it. Despite parental support for educational success African Americans and Hispanics have lower educational attainments than white students; they are less likely to finish high school and fewer of those with diplomas subsequently pursue higher education. Although minority enrollments in higher education continue to lag behind those of whites, the numbers show an encouraging upward trend over the last two decades.

High School Dropouts. African Americans and Latinos have high dropout rates from high school.[5] This is a troubling statistic because the decision to quit school effectively limits occupational careers. The myriad of causes for leaving school may be condensed into categories—background factors, social and psychological factors, and school based factors—that interact and reinforce each other. *Background factors* such as socioeconomic status and family structure are a central consideration. The financial resources of parents is a major factor because minorities form a disproportionate share of the working class and lower middle classes. Those from inner cities often start school lacking preschool and then attend underfunded and understaffed schools that are unable to meet student needs. Children in low-income households are often obliged to take jobs to help support the family. Recent immigrant children also have higher dropout rates than those who have longer residency, a problem associated with language barriers. *Social and psychological factors* such as parental support and academic aspirations also play an important role. The higher dropout rates of black male youth can in part be traced to the diminishing value placed on grades and academic performance as they progress through the grades. The sources of self-esteem shift from accomplishments in school to athletics and individual capacity. Finally, there are *school-related factors* such as

---

[5]There are differences within the Hispanic population, with Cuban Americans having the lowest dropout rate.

tracking, grades, and confrontations with authority. Both black and white students exhibit behavioral problems in school, but African Americans are subjected to harsher discipline in the form of suspensions and expulsions, and the frequency of punishment encourages leaving school.

Discrimination in Hiring

Educational attainments do not translate directly into occupational attainments because so many social factors influence the transition from school to jobs. One consistent pattern is that women and minorities do not earn the same benefits from additional education that white males do. This suggests that discrimination still haunts the marketplace. Law and custom have long combined to restrict employment opportunities for older applicants, women, and people of color, and the survival of outright discrimination cannot be ignored in the United States, even in the 1990s. New York City, for example, brought suit against several employment agencies for discriminating against African Americans and older people in making placements (Buder, 1990). They were accused of referring blacks and older citizens to fewer openings, less desirable jobs, and lower-paying work. Law suits in New York and elsewhere are typically based on the experiences of pairs of "testers," simulated candidates with similar qualifications who apply for the same jobs, a Hispanic and a white for example, or a man and a women. Because their qualifications are matched they should have roughly the same degree of success in finding jobs. Testers in Philadelphia found that men were twice as likely to get job interviews and five times as likely to be offered servers' jobs in expensive restaurants (Koretz, 1995).

DOWNWARD MOBILITY

Social origins initially determine peoples' place in the stratification system. Obviously, not all people remain at their original class level over the course of their entire lives and careers. While some people improve their situation, others experience **downward mobility**, temporary or more permanent movement to a lower social class level. Those most likely to experience downward mobility are the less educated and those in unskilled and manufacturing jobs (P. Smith, 1994). Mental illness is also a contributing factor (Rodgers & Mann, 1993). The precipitating event in most cases is the onset of illness, changes in family situation, or joblessness.

Catastrophic illness can easily devastate a family and quickly exhaust their resources. Changes in family situation is the decisive factor for many people, especially women. Death of a spouse, divorce or abandonment, responsibility for an aging parent, or the birth of a child are all factors that can initiate a move downward. And the one obvious event with the potential to impact the direction of careers is involuntary unemployment.

Joblessness and Downward Mobility

The very factors that have stimulated economic growth such as globalization, corporate restructuring, mergers and acquisitions, and the digital revolution have also rendered some workers vulnerable to being displaced. The risk of unemployment is inherent in the structure of industrial market economies, and workers are regularly displaced even in periods of prosperity. Businesses reduce their workforces through plant closings and large-scale layoffs prompted by economic considerations—rising costs, declining sales, mergers and acquisitions, global competition, cyclical business, languishing stock prices, or some combination of these problems.

Displaced workers are thrown into the labor market where they must compete for jobs, and some lose their place in the class system. Prolonged joblessness can cause people to fall into poverty. Even the threat of unemployment can be intimidating because few people are free of the worry that future developments will cost them their jobs and their future. Add to that the fact that remaining workers are usually expected to increase their own efforts in order to compensate for departed coworkers. Human resources professionals confirm that firms are understaffed (Olsten Corporation, 1996), and large proportions of corporate survivors feel overworked (Light & Tilser, 1994).

Those who survive corporate layoffs may also experience both short-term and long-term changes in perspective. Some survivors suffer survivor guilt, an uncomfortable feeling of remorse because they have jobs while friends and coworkers have lost theirs (Kirk, 1995). Not unexpectedly there is a heightened sense of anxiety and insecurity, even among survivors who do not face imminent job loss (Roskies & Louis-Guerin, 1990). Insecurity can erode the quality of work performance and contribute to negative attitudes toward management and a general decline in morale. There is an irony here because layoffs inspired by the need to improve the economic position of corporations can also set in motion attitudinal and behavioral changes that can weaken productivity and dilute loyalty to the firm.

Each year hundreds of thousands of people are displaced from their jobs and are compelled to seek to reestablish their careers, often at a lower class level. The experiences of displaced American workers during the 1990s reveals the scope and consequences of forced idleness (Gardner, 1995). In one two-year period about 5.5 million workers permanently lost their jobs to various forms of structural unemployment—plant closings, company failures, jobs abolished, or layoffs due to a lack of work. A follow-up of the displaced workers three to four years later showed that about three-quarters had found new jobs, but many settled for jobs that were inferior to those lost (Exhibit 11.5). About one-third (31.8 percent) were reemployed in full-time positions that paid the same or more than the jobs they lost. All the rest survived less well. About one-quarter were employed on a full-time basis but had taken a pay cut. (About one-third of this group took a pay cut of 20 percent or more.) Another 15 percent were earning less because they were in part-time work, self-employed, or had become unpaid family business workers. In a few cases involuntary unemploy-

EXHIBIT 11.5   Displaced Workers: Old Jobs and New

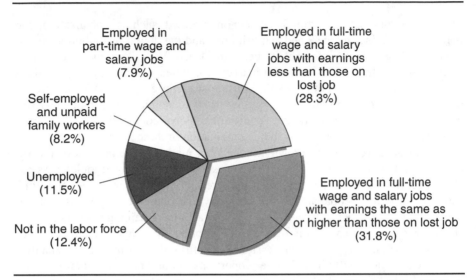

Employed in part-time wage and salary jobs (7.9%)

Employed in full-time wage and salary jobs with earnings less than those on lost job (28.3%)

Self-employed and unpaid family workers (8.2%)

Unemployed (11.5%)

Employed in full-time wage and salary jobs with earnings the same as or higher than those on lost job (31.8%)

Not in the labor force (12.4%)

Source: Jennifer M. Gardner, "Worker displacement: A decade of change," *Monthly Labor Review* 118 (April, 1995), Chart 1, page 50.

ment actually proved beneficial, although the trauma of unemployment is typically very painful. Some workers were freed from dead-end jobs and benefited from retraining programs that allowed them to secure better positions. For them, the ultimate outcome was upward mobility.

The remainder were less fortunate. More than one in ten was still unemployed, meaning that some had been without regular work for two or three years. The unemployment rate for Hispanic and African-American workers was much higher (18 percent) than for white workers (10 percent). Another 12.4 percent had left the labor force, some joining the ranks of "discouraged" workers, others accepting the role of "retired." Thus, not only did these 5.5 million people have to endure the shock of losing their livelihood, most were worse off financially than before.

The risk of downward mobility is greater for women, for minorities, and for people at lower levels of the stratification system (Flaim & Sehal, 1985). The threat of unemployment is greater in the jobs of the poor and the working class and thus also increases the risks for minorities, who hold a higher proportion of such jobs. These are the kinds of jobs that are lost to foreign competition or are rendered obsolete by technological change. Displaced black and Hispanic workers and women all experience longer periods of unemployment. Less affluent women typically have fewer options because child and elder care typically fall to them, necessitating more flexible schedules.

The Implications of Downward Mobility

Downward mobility carries with it the potential for personal stress as well as demanding significant readjustments in social relations and self-image. It may require a reorientation of lifestyles, especially when it is accompanied by financial loss. Moreover, it is not solely an individual experience because it impacts whole families, requiring spouses and children to reexamine lifestyles and long-term goals (Newman, 1988). Individuals socialized into the standards and values of one class during childhood can experience feelings of anxiety and isolation as they adjust to the situation of a different class. Some studies suggest a link between downward mobility and more serious forms of personal adjustment problems, mental illness, and even suicide (Kessin, 1971; Lopreato & Chafetz, 1970). Such problems prevail despite the fact that the sources of downward mobility can often be traced to structural sources beyond the control of the individual.

CONCLUSION: ENTREPRENEURS AND THE AMERICAN DREAM

Countless people aspire to begin their own business, and many risk it each year although the failure rate is high. Included in this category are software firms, e-commerce start-ups, grocery stores and restaurants, liquor stores and bars, consulting firms, small factories, fishing boats and taxicabs, service stations and dry cleaners. In many ways, the independent entrepreneur epitomizes the American Dream. These businesses are begun by people who believe in an idea and are willing to risk their savings, go into debt, and toil the long hours necessary to make a success of it.

Entrepreneurship has varied structural and individual origins. Many believe they have a new idea or product and are sustained by stories of the financial success of others. For example, Jerry Yang and David Filo, who perfected the search engine Yahoo!, were multimillionaires by age 30. Celebrated successes like theirs hold out the possibility that anyone with talent and initiative can prosper. Monetary rewards are only one enticement, and psychological factors may well outweigh the potential for making money. Some are attracted by the challenge of independent effort, seeing it as a chance to test their abilities. An important consideration for others is individual independence, the opportunity to exercise personal initiative and be free from supervision.

People are also propelled in the direction of independent businesses because of the lack of meaningful employment opportunities elsewhere. One group in this situation consists of people in jobs without realistic opportunities for career advancement. Members of the lower middle class and working class are often in this situation because their jobs offer limited promotion opportunities and are subject to strict authority on the job. More than anything else their own business offers these people personal independence. Limited mobility opportunities are also a salient factor. Women at all levels in the class system face limited mobility horizons because of glass ceilings, and in the 1990s women began to form small businesses at a rate twice that of men. A major motive is the limitations they experience in the workplace.

Racial and ethnic minorities also typically confront structural barriers. They face discrimination in the search for work and experience disadvantages in the labor market (Light, 1972). It is, for example, often difficult for professional and managerially trained immigrants to find employment in upper-middle-class jobs when they reach a new nation. Recent immigrants may also lack the communication skills necessary to compete for jobs. Therefore, minority groups show a penchant for small businesses in societies around the world: Greeks and Koreans in the United States, Indians and Turkish Cypriots in Britain, the Chinese in Southeast Asia (Cobas, 1986).

In some instances racial and ethnic minorities may be able to take advantage of opportunities not available to others (Cobas, 1986; Aldrich & Waldinger, 1990). New immigrants typically settle in older inner-city neighborhoods. The concentration of minorities in urban enclaves creates a situation called "protected markets," markets for goods and services that can best be met by minority business owners, who have special insight into cultural tastes and preferences. Ethnic restaurants and food stores are a good example of this. In addition, urban immigrants are often concentrated in geographic areas that large national firms such as supermarkets and banks abandon. Founding and operating small businesses within ethnic communities is in some instances enhanced by communal ties and networks. Some Asian immigrants, for example, bring with them the practice of informal community savings and loan arrangements that allow aspiring business persons to borrow money at low rates. This suggests that the success of immigrant entrepreneurs often is a group phenomenon that builds upon the social and economic resources of the community for employees and financing, and which provides a protected market sheltered from outside competition (Aldrich & Waldinger, 1990).

For some time it has been noted that the rate of entrepreneurship among African Americans is significantly lower than for whites and other minority groups, especially Asian Americans (Manning & O'Hare, 1988). One factor underlying this fact is that blacks have traditionally defined stable employment in the public sector as the route to middle-class status (Boyd, 1990). However, African Americans also face discrimination in the credit market (Koretz, 1998). Black enterprises have several financial disadvantages such as less business experience than whites and poorer credit records, and they are more likely located in central cities. Yet even when these factors and individual creditworthiness was considered, black-owned businesses were twice as likely to be denied loans as comparable white-owned businesses.

Small businesses do not necessarily bring great economic rewards, and the failure rate is daunting. However, entrepreneurship is an attractive alternative to organizational employment, especially for workers at the lower ends of the stratification system, women, and people of color. They offer opportunities for independence and autonomy, and a route for overcoming the social barriers that societies erect. Despite the risk and the heavy investment of effort, small businesses continue to have a powerful symbolic attraction.

KEY CONCEPTS

closed systems
cultural capital
downward mobility
intergenerational mobility

intragenerational mobility
open systems
science pipeline
social mobility

status attainment model
structural mobility
vicious cycle of poverty

SUGGESTED READING

PETER M. BLAU and OTIS D. DUNCAN. *The American Occupational Structure*. New York: Wiley, 1967. The original formulation of the status attainment model.

PETER W. COOKSON, JR. and CAROLINE HODGES PERSELL. *Preparing for Power: America's Elite Boarding Schools*. New York: Basic Books, 1985. A first-hand account of the schools where future members of the elite are socialized.

C.L. BARNEY DEWS and CAROLYN LESTE LAW, eds. *This Fine Place So Far From Home: Voices of Academics From the Working Class*. Philadelphia, PA: Temple University Press, 1995. College and university professors from working-class backgrounds reflect on their discomfort in the middle-class world of academics.

GREG DUNCAN. *The Consequences of Growing Up Poor*. New York: Russell Sage, 1997. The implications of poverty follow children into their adult lives.

ROBERT ERIKSON and JOHN H. GOLDTHORPE. *The Constant Flux: A Study of Class Mobility in Industrial Societies*. New York: Oxford University Press, 1992. A broad-based analysis of patterns of mobility among families in nine European nations.

ROBERTA FULGER. *Does Jane Compute? Preserving Our Daughters' Place in the Cyber Revolution*. New York: Warner Books. A practical examination of the ways in which society and the schools limit females' progress in math and the sciences.

KATHERINE S. NEWMAN. *Falling From Grace: The Experience of Downward Mobility in the American Middle Class*. New York: Free Press, 1988. A chronicle of the experiences of skilled blue-collar and white-collar workers coping with unemployment.

FREDERICK R. STROBEL. *Upward Dreams, Downward Mobility*. Lanham, MD: Rowman & Littlefield, 1993. A discussion of the economic and political factors that have contributed to the deterioration in earnings of the middle class. Suitable for advanced students.

WILLIAM JULIUS WILSON. *When Jobs Disappear*. New York: Knopf, 1996. An eminent sociologist explores the causes of inner-city poverty and offers some suggestions for dealing with it.

USEFUL WEB SITES

The U.S. Department of Education's National Center for Educational Statistics (**www.ed.gov/NCES/index.html**) is the source of a wealth of information on all aspects of the educational process.

Girl Tech (**www.girltech.com**) was founded in the 1990s to encourage young girls to fully participate in the digital revolution and offers practical advice to girls, teachers, and parents.

The College Board (**www.collegeboard.org**) is best known for administering tests, but also offers useful data on college costs and student performance.

Bibliography

ADAMS, THOMAS S., and HELEN L. SUMNER. 1985. *Labor Problems.* London: Macmillan.

ADLER, NANCY E., et al. 1993. "Socioeconomic inequalities in health." *JAMA* 269: 3140–3145.

ALDRICH, HOWARD E., and ROGER WALDINGER. 1990. "Ethnicity and entrepreneurship." *Annual Review of Sociology* 16: 111–135.

ALEXANDER, JEFFREY C., ed. 1985. *Neo-functionalism.* London: Sage.

———. 1998. *Neo-Functionalism and After.* Oxford: Blackwell.

ALEXANDER, KEITH. 1997. "American Airlines apologizes for manual." *USA Today* (August 21): 2B.

ALLEN, THEODORE. 1994. *The Invention of the White Race.* New York: Verso.

ANDERSEN, MARGARET L. 1997. THINKING ABOUT WOMEN. 4TH ED. BOSTON: ALLYN & BACON.

———, and PATRICIA HILL COLLINS, eds. 1992. *Race, Class and Gender.* Belmont, CA: Wadsworth.

ANDERSON, KAREN. 1988. "A history of women's work in the United States." Pp. 25–41 in Ann Helton Stromberg and Shirley Harkness, eds., *Women Working.* Mountain View, CA: Mayfield.

ANDREWS, MARGARET, et al. 2000. *Household Food Security in the United States, 1999.* U. S. Department of Agriculture. Washington, DC: Government Printing Office.

ANFUSCO, DAWN. 1994. "Deflecting workplace violence." *Personnel Journal* (October): 26–33.

APPLE, R. W. 1995. "Poll shows disenchantment with politicians and politics." *The New York Times* (August 12): 1–8.

ARIAN, EDWARD. 1971. *Bach, Beethoven, Bureaucracy: The Case of the Philadelphia Orchestra.* Tuscaloosa, AL: University of Alabama Press.

ARMOUR, STEPHANIE. 1998. "Workplace hazard gets attention." *USA Today* (May 5): 1–2B.

ARONSON, PETER, DAVID E. ROVELLA, and BOB VAN VORIS. 1998. "Jurors: A biased, independent lot." *The National Law Journal* (November 2): 1–25A.

ASCHAFFENBURG, KAREN, and INEKE MAAS. 1997. "Cultural and educational careers: The dynamics of social reproduction." *American Sociological Review* 62: 573–588.

AUERBACH, JERALD S. 1976. *Unequal Justice.* New York: Oxford University Press.

BACON, JOHN. 1997. "Uninsured kids." *USA Today* (March 28): 3A.

BAILEY, THOMAS A. 1956. *The American Pageant.* Boston, MA: D. C. Heath.

BALTZELL, E. DIGBY. 1958. *Philadelphia Gentlemen: The Making of a National Upper Class.* New York: Free Press.

———. 1964. *The Protestant Establishment: Aristocracy and Caste in America.* New York: Random House.

BANFIELD, EDWARD. 1970. *The Unheavenly City.* Boston, MA: Little, Brown.

BARNELLO, MICHELLE A. 1999. "Gender and roll call voting in the New York State assembly." *Women & Politics* 77–95.

BARON, AVA. 1980. "Women and the making of the American working class: A study in the proletarianization of printers." *Review of Radical Political Economics* 14: 23–42.

BARON, REUBEN M., DAVID Y. H. TOM, and HARRIS M. COOPER. 1985. "Social class, race and teacher expectations." Pp. 251–269 in Jerome B. Dusek, ed., *Teacher Expectancies.* Hillsdale, NJ: Lawrence Erlbaum Associates.

———, LINDA ALBRIGHT, and THOMAS E. MALLOY. 1995. "Effects of behavioral and social class information on social judgment." *Personality and Social Psychology Bulletin* 21: 308–315.

BARRETT, EDITH J. 1995. "The political priorities of African-American women in state legislatures." *Legislative Studies Quarterly* 20: 223–247.

BARRY, SKIP. 1996. "Rents out of reach." *Dollars & Sense* 208: 42–43.

BATES, TIMOTHY, and DARRELL L. WILLIAMS. 1993. "Racial politics: Does it pay?" *Social Science Quarterly* 74: 507–522.

BAXTER, JANEEN. 1994. "Is husband's class enough? Class location and class identity in the United States, Sweden, Norway and Australia." *American Sociological Review* 59: 220–235.

BEALS, GREGORY, and KAREN SPRINGEN. 1997. "Cracking a slavery ring." *Newsweek* (August 4): 39.

BELTON, BETH. 1997. "New chamber chief targets lawyers, unions." *USA Today* (June 12): 4B.

BENDIX, RINEHARD. 1962. *Max Weber: An Intellectual Portrait.* Garden City, NY: Doubleday.

BERGER, JOSEPH M., et al. 1977. *Status Characteristics and Social Interaction.* New York: Elsevier.

BERNSTEIN, AARON, 2000. "Too much corporate power?" *Business Week* (September 11): 144–158.

BERNSTEIN, JARED, et al. 2000. *Pulling Apart: A State-by-State Analysis of Income Trends.* Washington, DC: Economic Policy Institute.

BERRYMAN, S. E. 1983. *Who Will Do Science?* New York: Rockefeller Foundation.

BERUBE, ALLAN, and FLORENCE BERUBE. 1997. "Sunset Trailer Park." Pp. 16–39 in Matt Wray and Annalee Newitz, eds. *White Trash: Race and Class in America.* New York: Routledge.

BETEILLE, ANDRE. 1992. *The Backward Classes in Contemporary India.* New York: Oxford University Press.

BIANCHI, SUZANNE M., and DAPHNE SPAIN. 1997. "U. S. women make workplace progress." *Population Today* 25 (January): 1–2.

BIRNBAUM, JEFFREY H. 2000. *The Money Men: The Real Story of Fund-Raising's Influence on Political Power in America.* New York: Times Books.

BLAU, PETER M., and OTIS DUDLEY DUNCAN. 1967. *The American Occupational Structure.* New York: Wiley.

BLAUNER, ROBERT. 1972. *Racial Oppression in America.* New York: Harper & Row.

BLOCK, FRED L. 1992. "Capitalism without class power." *Politics and Society* 20: 277–302.

BLOOD, ROBERT O., and D. M. WOLF. 1960. *Husbands and Wives: The Dynamics of Married Life.* New York: Free Press.

BOBO, LAWRENCE, and FRANKLIN D. GILLIAM, JR. 1990. "Race, sociopolitical participation, and black empowerment." *American Political Science Review* 84: 377–393.

————, and CAMILLE L. ZUBRINSKY. 1996. "Attitudes on residential segregation: Perceived status differences, mere in-group preference or racial prejudice?" *Social Forces* 74: 83–910.

BONZCAR, THOMAS P., and ALEN J. BECK. 1997. *Lifetime Likelihood of Going to State or Federal Prison.* U.S. Department of Justice, Bureau of Labor Statistics. Washington, DC: Government Printing Office.

BORRUS, AMY. 1997. "The end of corporate welfare as we know it." *Business Week* (February 10): 36–37.

BOSE, CHRISTINE E. 1987. "Dual spheres." Pp. 267–285 in Beth B. Hess and Myra Marx Ferree, eds., *Analyzing Gender: A Handbook of Social Science Research.* Newbury Park, CA: Sage.

————, and PETER H. ROSSI. 1983. "Gender and jobs: Prestige standings of occupations as affected by gender." *American Sociological Review* 48: 316–330.

BOURDIEU, PIERRE. 1977. "Cultural reproduction and social reproduction." Pp. 487–511 in J. Karabel and A. H. Halsey, eds., *Power and Ideology in Education.* New York: Oxford University Press.

BOWLER, MARY. 1999. "Women's earnings: An overview." *Monthly Labor Review* 122 (December): 13–21.

BOWLES, SCOTT. 2000. "Bans on racial profiling gain steam." *USA Today* (June 2): 3A.

BOYD, ROBERT L. 1990. "Black and Asian self-employment in large metropolitan areas: A comparative analysis." *Social Problems* 37: 258–274.

BRADDOCK, DOUGLAS. 1999. "Occupational employment projections." *Monthly Labor Review* 122 (November): 51–77.

Bradwell v. Illinois. 1873. (83 U.S. 16 Wall 141).

BRAGG, RICK. 1996. "Just a grave for a baby, but anguish for a town." *The New York Times* (March 31): 14.

BRAVERMAN, HARRY. 1974. *Labor and Monopoly Capitalism.* New York: Monthly Review Press.

BRENNER, O. C., JOSEPH TOMKIEWICZ, and VIRGINIA ELLEN SCHEIN. 1989. "The relationship between sex role stereotypes and requisite management characteristics revisited." *Academy of Management Journal* 32: 662–669.

BRINK, WILLIAM, and LOUIS HARRIS. 1967. *Black and White.* New York: Simon & Schuster.

BRINKLEY, JOEL. 2000. "Vast trade in forced labor portrayed in C.I.A. report." *New York Times* (April 3): 20.

BRODER, JOHN M., and DON VAN NATTA. 2000. "Perks for biggest donors, and pleas for more cash." *The New York Times* (July 30): 1–16

BROWN, PHIL, and FAITH I. T. FERGUSON. 1995. "Making a big stink: Women's work, women's relationships, and toxic waste activism." *Gender & Society* 9: 145–172.

BUDER, LEONARD. 1990. "Employment agency accused of bias." *The New York Times* (February 21): 3B.

BURD, STEPHEN, et al. 1996. "The widening gap in higher education." *The Chronicle of Higher Education* 62 (June 14): 10–12A.

BURKETT, ELINOR. 1997. "God created me to be a slave." *The New York Times* (October 12): 56–60.

————. 1998. "Don't tread on my tax rate." *The New York Times Magazine* (April 26): 42–45.

BURRIS, VAL. 1986. "The discovery of the new middle class." *Theory and Society* 15: 317–349.

BURT, MARTHA R., and LAUDAN Y. ARON. *1999. Homelessness: Programs and the People They Serve.* Washington, DC: The Urban Institute.

BUTTERFIELD, FOX. 1986. "Why Asians are going to the head of the class." *The New York Times* (August 3): 18–22.

CAMPELL, JENNIFER. 1998. *Health Insurance Coverage.* Current Population Reports, P60-208. Washington, DC: U.S. Government Printing Office.

CARSON, IAIN. 1998. "The world as a single machine." *The Economist* (June 20): 4–18.

CASPER, LYNN, SARA S. McLAHANAHAN, and IRWIN GARFINKLE. 1994. "The gender-poverty gap: What we can learn from other countries." *American Sociological Review* 59: 594–605.

CAUCHON, DENNIS. 1999. "Indigents' lawyers: Low pay hurts justice." *USA Today* (February 3): 4A.

CAVEN, RUTH. 1969. *The American Family.* New York: Crowell.

CENTER FOR RESPONSIVE POLITICS. 1999. "Former members turned lobbyists." www.opensecrets .org/pubs/lobby98/formerreps.htm.

CENTERS, RICHARD. 1949. *The Psychology of Social Classes.* Princeton, NJ: Princeton University Press.

CHAMPION, DEAN J. 1989. "Private counsels and public defenders: A look at weak cases, prior record, and leniency in plea bargaining." *Journal of Criminal Justice* 17: 253–163.

CHANDLER, SUSAN. 1995. "Look who's sweating now." *Business Week* (October 16): 96–98.

CLANCY, PAUL. 1988. "Camel companions." *USA Today* (December 28): 2A.

CLARK, TERRY NICHOLES, and SEYMOUR MARTIN LIPSET, eds. 2000. *The Breakdown of Class Politics: A Debate on Post-Industrial Stratification.* Baltimore, MD: Johns Hopkins University Press.

CLAWSON, DAN, ALAN NEUSTADTL, and DENISE SCOTT. 1992. *Money Talks: Corporate PACs and Political Influence.* New York: Basic Books.

COBAS, JOSE A. 1986. "Paths to self-employment among immigrants: An analysis of four interpretations." *Sociological Perspectives* 29: 101–120.

COCKERHAM, WILLIAM, et al. 1986. "Social stratification and self-management of health." *Journal of Health and Social Behavior* 17: 1–13.

COHEN, WARREN, and MIKE THARP. 1999. "Fed-up cities turn to evicting the homeless." *U. S. News & World Report* (January 11): 28–30.

COLASANTO, DIANE, and LINDA WILLIAMS. 1987. "The changing dynamics of race and class." *Public Opinion* 9: 50–53.

COLEMAN, RICHARD P., and LEE RAINWATER. 1978. *Social Standing in America: New Dimensions of Class.* New York: Basic Books.

THE COLLEGE BOARD. 1999. *Trends in College Pricing.* New York: The College Board.

THE COLLEGE BOARD. 2000. *College Bound Seniors, 2000.* New York: The College Board.

COLLINS, CHIQUITA A., and DAVID R. WILLIAMS. 1999. "Segregation and mortality: The deadly effects of racism." *Sociological Forum* 14: 495–523.

COLLINS, CHRIS. 2000. "Why so many young adults won't vote Tuesday." *USA Today* (November 6): 19A.

COLLINS, RANDALL. 1986. *Weberian Sociological Theory.* New York: Cambridge University Press.

———, and MICHAEL MAKOWSKY. 1984. *The Discovery of Society.* 3rd ed. New York: Random House.

CONNELLY, MARJORIE. 2000. "Who voted: A portrait of American politics, 1976–2000." *The New York Times* (November 12): 4WK.

COOKSON, PETER W., JR., and CAROLINE HODGES PERSELL. 1985. *Preparing for Power: America's Elite Boarding Schools.* New York: Basic Books.

COOPER, KENNETH J. 1997. "Free, but bound by their past." *Washington Post* (August 14): 1–27.

COOPER, MARC. 1997. "The heartland's raw deal: How meat packing is creating a new immigrant underclass." *The Nation* (February 3): 11–17.

CORCORAN, M. 1995. "Rags to rags: Poverty and mobility in the United States." *Annual Review of Sociology* 21: 237–268.

COYLE, MARCIA, FRED STRASSER, and MARIANNE LAVELLE. 1990. "Fatal defense." *The National Law Journal* 13 (June 11): 30–44.

CROOK, CLIVE. 1997. "The future of the state." *The Economist* 344 (September 20): 1–48S.

CROSS, HARRY, et al. 1990. *Employment Hiring Practices: Differential Treatment of Hispanic and Anglo Job Seekers.* Washington, DC: Urban Institution.

CROSS, WILLIAM. 1991. *Shades of Black: Diversity in African American Identity.* Philadelphia, PA: Temple University Press.

CROSSETTE, BARBARA. 1996. "U. N. survey finds world rich-poor gap widening." *The New York Times* (July 15): 3a.

CRULL, SUE R., and BRENT T. BRUTON. 1985. "Possible decline in tolerance toward minorities: Social distance on a Midwest campus." *Sociology and Social Research* 70: 57–60.

CRUTCHFIELD, R.D., G.S. BRIDGES, and S. R. PITCHFORD. 1994. "Analytic and aggregation bias in analysis of imprisonment: reconciling discrepancies in studies of racial disparity." *Journal of Research in Crime and Delinquency* 31: 166–183.

———, and S. R. PITCHFORD. 1997. "Work and crime: The effects of labor stratification." *Social Forces* 76: 93–118.

DAHL, ROBERT A. 1958. "A critique of the ruling elite model." *American Political Science Review* 52: 463–469.

DANIELS, ARLENE KAPLAN. 1987. *Invisible Careers: Women Civic Leaders in the Volunteer World.* Chicago, IL: University of Chicago Press.

DAVIS, KINGSLEY. 1953. "Reply to Tumin." *American Sociological Review* 18: 394–397.

———, and WILBERT E. MOORE. 1945. "Some principles of stratification." *American Sociological Review* 10: 242–249.

DAVIS, NANCY, and ROBERT V. ROBINSON. 1988. "Class identification of men and women in the 1970s and 1980s." *American Sociological Review* 53: 103–112.

DEAR, MICHAEL J., and JENNIFER R. WOLCH. 1987. *Landscapes of Despair: From Deinstitutionalization to Homelessness*. Princeton, NJ: Princeton University Press.

DEAUX, KAY, and MARY E. KITE. 1987. "Thinking about gender." Pp. 92–116 in Beth B. Hess and Myra Marx Ferree, eds., *Analyzing Gender: A Handbook of Social Science Research*. Newbury Park, CA: Sage.

———, and LIONEL L. LEWIS. 1984. "Structure of gender stereotypes: Interrelationships among components and gender label." *Journal of Personality and Social Psychology* 46: 991–1004.

DEL PINAL, JORGE, and AUDREY SINGER. 1997. *Generations of Diversity*. Washington, DC: Population Reference Bureau.

DEMOTT, BENJAMIN. 1990. *The Imperial Middle: Why Americans Can't Think Straight About Class*. New York: Morrow.

DEPARLE, JASON. 1991. "New rows to hoe in the 'Harvest of Shame.'" *The New York Times* (July 28): 3E.

DICKEY, CHRISTOPHER, and JEFFREY BARTHOLET, 2000. "The new people trade." *Newsweek* (July 3): 32–36.

DIMAGGIO, PAUL. 1982. "Cultural capital and school success: The impact of status culture participation on the grades of U. S. high school students." *American Sociological Review* 47: 189–201.

DOMHOFF, G. WILLIAM. 1970. *The Higher Circles*. New York: Vintage.

———. 1984. *The Bohemian Grove and Other Retreats: A Study in Ruling Class Cohesiveness*. New York: Harper & Row.

———. 1998. *Who Rules America? Power and Politics,* 3rd ed. Mountain View, CA: Mayfield.

DREW, CHRISTOPHER, and DAVID CAY JOHNSTON. 1996. "For wealthy Americans, death is more certain than taxes." *The New York Times* (December 22): 1–30.

DRUMMOND, ANDREW, and DOMINIC KENNEDY. 2000. "Runaway London sex slaves expose Thai vice ring." *The Times of London* (July 8): 5.

DUBOFSKY, MELVYN. 1969. *We Shall Be All: A History of Industrial Workers of the World*. Chicago, IL: Quadrangle.

DUGAS, CHRISTINE. 1997. "Nationwide settles redlining charges." *USA Today* (March 11): 1B.

DUNCAN, GREG J., J. BROOKES-GUNN, and P. K. KLEBANOV. 1994. "Economic deprivation and early-childhood development." *Child Development* 6: 296–318.

DURANT, THOMAS J. JR., and KATHLEEN H. SPARROW. 1997. "Race and class consciousness among lower- and middle-class blacks." *Journal of Black Studies* 27: 334–346.

DUSTER, TROY. 1990. *Backdoor to Eugenics*. New York: Routledge.

DYE, THOMAS R. 1990. *Who's Running America? The Bush Era*. Englewood Cliffs, NJ: Prentice Hall.

———. 1995. *Who's Running America? The Clinton Years*. Sixth ed. Englewood Cliffs, NJ: Prentice Hall.

EARLE, JOHN R., and CATHERINE T. HARRIS. 1989. "College students and blue-collar workers: A comparative analysis of sex role attitudes." *Sociological Spectrum* 9: 45–466.

The Economist. 1997a. "Homelessness and race: Black hole." *The Economist* 342: (January 18): 30–31.

The Economist. 1997b. "Politicians for rent." *The Economist* (February 8): 23–25.

The Economist. 1997c. "Fighting the class war." *The Economist* (September 27): 63.

The Economist, 2000a. "A continent on the move." *The Economist* (May 6): 25–27.

The Economist, 2000b. "GM's motor man." *The Economist* (March 18): 69.

The Economist. 2000c. "Dead man walking out." *The Economist* (June 10): 21–23.

EDITORS. 1988. "Developments in the law—race in the criminal process." *Harvard Law Review* 101: 1520–1532.

EHRENREICH, BARBARA. 1989. *Fear of Falling*. New York: Pantheon.

ELIAS, MARILYN. 1997. "Academics lose relevance for black boys." *USA Today* (December 2): 1D.

ELLWOOD, D. 1987. *Understanding Dependency: Choices, Confidence, or Culture?* U. S. Department of Health and Human Services. Washington, DC: U. S. Government Printing Office.

ENGELS, FRIEDRICH. 1972. *The Origin of the Family, Private Property, and the State*. New York: International Publishers.

ERIKSON, ROBERT, and JOHN H. GOLDTHORPE. 1992. *The Constant Flux: A Study of Class Mobility in Industrial Societies*. New York: Oxford University Press.

ETAUGH, CLAIRE, and PATRICIA POERTNER. 1991. "Effects of occupational prestige, employment status and marital status on perceptions of mothers." *Sex Roles* 24: 345–353.

FABRIKANT, GERALDINE, and SHELBY WHITE. 1995. "Noblesse oblige . . . with strings." *The New York Times* (April 30): 3F.

FARKAS, GEORGE, et al. "Cultural resources and school success: Gender, ethnicity, and poverty groups within an urban school district." *American Sociological Review* 55: 127–142.

FARLEY, REYNOLDS, and WILLIAM H. FRY. 1994. "Changes in segregation of whites from blacks: Small steps toward a more integrated society." *American Sociological Review* 59: 23–45.

———, et al. 1994. "Stereotypes and segregation: Neighborhoods in the Detroit area." *American Journal of Sociology* 100: 750–780.

FAUNCE, WILLIAM A. 1989. "Occupational status-assignment systems: The effect of status on self-esteem." *American Journal of Sociology* 95: 378–400.

FEAGIN, JOE R. 1972. "Poverty: We still believe that God helps those who help themselves." *Psychology Today* (November): 101–129.

———. 1984. *Racial and Ethnic Relations*. 2nd ed. Englewood Cliffs, NJ: Prentice Hall.

———, and CLAIRECE BOOHER FEAGIN. 1996. *Racial and Ethnic Relations*. 5th ed. Upper Saddle River, NJ: Prentice Hall.

FEC (FEDERAL ELECTION COMMISSION). 2000. "Congressional campaign receipts reach $653 million." www.fec.gov/press/can1800text.htm.

FEDERMAN, MARY, et al. 1996. "What does it mean to be poor in America?" *Monthly Labor Review* 119 (May): 3–17.

FERGUSON, THOMAS, and JOEL ROGERS. 1986. *Right Turn: The Decline of the Democrats and the Future of American Politics*. New York: Hill and Wang.

FERREE, MYRA MARX. 1985. "Between two worlds: German feminist approaches to working class women and work." *Signs* 10: 517–536.

FEUER, LEWIS S. 1959. *Marx and Engels: Basic Writings on Politics and Philosophy*. Garden City, NY: Doubleday.

FINDER, ALAN. 1995. "Despite tough laws, sweatshops flourish." *New York Times* (February 6): 1A–4B.

FISCHER, CLAUDE. 1982. *To Dwell Among Friends: Personal Networks in Town and City*. Chicago, IL: University of Chicago Press.

FISHER, GORDON M. 1992. "The development and history of the poverty thresholds." *Social Security Bulletin* 55: 3–14.

FITZGERALD, MARK. 1997. "Media perpetuate a myth." *Editor & Publisher* 130 (August 16): 13.

FLAIM, PAUL O., and ELLEN SEHAL. 1985. "Displaced workers of 1979–1982: How well have they fared?" *Monthly Labor Review* 108 (June): 3–15.

FLETCHER, MICHAEL L. 2000. "Asian Americans coping with success." *The Washington Post* (March 4): 3A.

FLOURNOY, CRAIG, and RANDY LEE LOFTIS. 2000. "Living in fear: Residents of projects find common neighbor: Pollution." *The Dallas Morning News* (October 3): 1–3.

FONER, PHILIP S. 1964. *History of the Labor Movement in the United States*. New York: International Publishers.

FORM, WILLIAM. 1985. *Divided We Stand: Working Class Stratification in America*. Urbana: University of Illinois Press.

FOSTER, JOHN BELLAMY. 2000. "Marx and internationalism." *Monthly Review* 52: 11–19.

FRANCIS, LESLIE J., and SUSAN H. JONES. 1996. "Social class and self-esteem." *The Journal of Social Psychology* 136: 405–407.

FRANKLIN, BENJAMIN. 1961. *Autobiography and Other Writings*. New York: New American Library.

GABLE, DONNA. 1993. "Series shortchange working-class and minority Americans." *USA Today* (August 30): 3D.

GAO (GENERAL ACCOUNTING OFFICE), 2000. *Better Targeting of Airline Passengers for Personal Searches Could Produce Better Results*. Washington, DC: Government Printing Office.

GALLUP POLL. 1991. "Americans say police brutality common." *The Gallup Poll Monthly* 306: 53–55.

GALLUP POLL. 1995. "Satisfaction with personal life, U.S." *The Gallup Poll Monthly* 357: 7.

GALLUP POLL, 1996. "Wealth distributed fairly?" *The Gallup Poll Monthly* 368: (May): 34.

GALLUP POLL. 1997. "Fund-raising ethics doubted." *USA Today* (October 8): 6A.

GANS, HERBERT. 1967. *The Levittowners*. New York: Random House.

GARCIA, JOHN A. 1997. "Latino national political survey." *ICPSR Bulletin* 18 (September): 1–5.

GARDNER, JENNIFER M. 1995. "Worker displacement: A decade of change." *Monthly Labor Review* 118 (April): 45–57.

GATES, ANITA. 1998. "Yes, America has a class system. See 'Frasier.'" *The New York Times* (April 19): 35–43AR.

GLASTER, GEORGE. 1990. "Racial steering by real estate agents: Mechanisms and motives." *The Review of Black Political Economy* 19: 39–62.

GLASTRIS, PAUL, et al. 1997. "Hang on to your wallet." *U. S. News & World Report* (April 14): 26–31.

GOLD, MARTIN. 1966. "Undetected delinquent behavior." *Journal of Research in Crime and Delinquency* 3: 27–46.

GOLDBERG, CAREY. 1996. "Asian immigrants help bolster U. S. economy, new report says." *The New York Times* (March 31): 32.

GONZALEZ, DAVID. 1992. "What's the problem with 'Hispanic'? Just ask a 'Latino.'" *The New York Times* (November 15): 6E.

GOODSTEIN, RENEE, and JOSEPH G. PONTEROTTO. 1997. "Racial and ethnic identity: Their relationship and their contribution to self-esteem." *Journal of Black Social Psychology* 23: 275–292.

GOODWIN, LEONARD. 1972. *Do the Poor Want to Work?* Washington, DC: The Brookings Institute.

GRABB, EDWARD G. 1997. *Theories of Social Inequality: Classical and Contemporary Perspectives.* 3rd ed. New York: Harcourt Brace.

GRAHAM, LAWRENCE OTIS. 1999. *Our Kind of People: Inside America's Black Upper Class.* New York: HarperCollins.

GRANT, LINDA. 1984. "Black females' place in the desegregated classroom." *Sociology of Education* 57: 98–110.

GRATTET, RYKEN. 2000. "Hate crimes: Better data or increasing frequency?" *Population Today* 28 (July): 1–4.

GRAY-LITTLE, BERNADETTE, and ADAM R. HAFDAHL. 2000. "Factors influencing racial comparisons of self-esteem: A quantitative review." *Psychological Bulletin* 126: 26–54.

GREENBERGER, ELLEN, et al. 1988. "Beliefs about the consequences of maternal employment for children." *Psychology of Women Quarterly* 12: 35–39.

GREENFIELD, LAUREN. 1997. *Fast Forward: Growing Up in the Shadow of Hollywood.* New York: Knopf/Melcher Media.

GREENHOUSE, STEVEN. 1997. "Debating union dues and political don'ts." *The New York Times* (October 12): 3WK.

GREIDER, WILLIAM. 1992. *Who Will Tell the People? The Betrayal of American Democracy.* New York: Simon & Schuster.

GROSS, JANE. 1997. "Stress on Wall Street? Try the eighth grade." *The New York Times* (October 5): 37–38.

GROVER, CHRIS, and KEITH SOOTHILL. 1996. "'A murderous underclass?' The press reporting of a sexually motivated murder." *The Sociological Review* 44: 398–416.

GRUSKY, DAVID B., and JESPER SORENSEN. 1998. "Can class analysis be salvaged?" *American Journal of Sociology* 104: 1187–1234.

HALLE, DAVID. 1984. *America's Working Man.* Chicago: University of Chicago Press.

HALLINAN, MAUREEN T., and AAGE B. SORENSEN. 1987. "Ability grouping and sex differences in mathematics achievement." *Sociology of Education* 60: 63–72.

HAMILTON, RICHARD. 1972. *Class and Politics in the United States.* New York: Wiley.

HANSON, SANDRA L., MARYELLEN SCHAUB, and DAVID P. BAKER. 1996. "Gender stratification in the science pipeline: A comparative analysis of seven countries." *Gender & Society* 10: 271–290.

HARRINGTON, MICHAEL. 1962. *The Other America: Poverty in the United States.* New York: Macmillian.

HART, BETTY, and TODD RISLEY. 1995. *Meaningful Differences in the Everyday Experiences of Young American Children.* Baltimore, MD: Paul H. Brookes.

HAUG, MARIE R., and HAROLD A. WIDDISON. 1975. "Dimensions of occupational prestige." *Sociology of Work and and Occupations* 2: 3–27.

HEALY, MICHELLE. 1999. "ERs less likely to treat pain of blacks, Hispanics." *USA Today* (December 29): 6D.

HECKER, DANIEL E. 1992. "Reconciling conflicting data on jobs for college graduates." *Monthly Labor Review* 115 (July): 3–12.

HEDDEN, SUSAN. 1993. "Made in the U.S.A." *U.S. News & World Report* (November 22): 48–55.

HENRY, TAMARA. 1999. "Is school desegregation fading?" *USA Today* (July 22): 1–2A.

HERO, RODNEY, et al. 2000. "Latino participation, partisanship, and office holding." *PS: Political Science and Politics* 33: 529–540.

HILL, ANN C. 1979. "Protection of women workers and the courts: A legal history." *Feminist Studies* 5: 247-273.

HILL, DEBBIE. 1996. "3m women below 'decency threshold.'" *The Times of London* (September 29): 1(5).

HIPPLE, STEVEN. 1997. "Worker displacement in an expanding economy." *Monthly Labor Review* 120 (December): 26–37.

———, and JAY STEWART. 1996. "Earnings and benefits for contingent and noncontingent workers." *Monthly Labor Review* 119 (October): 22–30.

HIRD, JOHN A., and MICHAEL REESE. 1998. "The distribution of environmental quality: An empirical analysis." *Social Science Quarterly* 79: 693–704.

HOBERMAN, JOHN. 1997. *Darwin's Athletes.* Boston: Houghton Mifflin.

HOCHSCHILD, JENNIFER. 1995. *Facing Up to The American Dream: Race, Class and the Soul of the Nation.* Princeton, NJ: Princeton University Press.

HOLMES, STEVEN A. 1997. "A rose-colored view of race." *The New York Times* (June 15): 4E.

HOOKS, BELL. 1984. *Feminist Theory From Margin to Center.* Boston: South End Press.

HOUT, MICHAEL, CLEM BROOKS, and JEFF MANZA. 1993. "The persistence of classes in post-industrial society." *International Sociology* 8: 259–277.

HOWLETT, DEBBIE. 2000. "Lawsuit claims black women targeted by customs agents." *USA Today* (April 11): 3A.

HRABA, JOSEPH, TIMOTHY RADLOFF, and PHYLLIS GRAY-RAY. 1999. "A comparison of black and white social distance." *The Journal of Social Psychology* 139 (August): 534–538.

HUBER, JOAN, and WILLIAM H. FORM. 1973. *Income and Ideology.* New York: Free Press.

HUDDY, LEONIE, and NAYDA TERKILDSEN. 1994. "The consequences of gender stereotypes for women candidates at different levels and types of office." *Political Research Quarterly* 46: 503–525.

HUDIS, PAULA M. 1977. "Commitment to work and wages: Earnings differences of black and white women." *Sociology of Work and Occupations* 4: 123–146.

ISHIDA, HIROSHI, WALTER MULLER, and JOHN M. RIDGE. 1995. "Class origin, class destination, and education: A cross-national study of ten industrial nations." *American Journal of Sociology* 101: 145–193.

———, SEYMOUR SPILLERMAN, and KUO-HSIEN SU. 1997. "Educational credentials and promotion chances in Japanese and American organizations." *American Sociological Review* 62: 866–882.

JACKMAN, MARY R. 1979. "The subjective meaning of social class identification in the United States." *Public Opinion Quarterly* 43: 433–462.

———, and MARY SCHEUER SENTER. 1982. "Different therefore unequal: Beliefs about trait differences between groups of different status." Pp. 123–134 in Donald J. Treiman and Robert V. Robinson, eds., *Research in Stratification and Mobility.* Volume 2. Greenwich, CT: JAI Press.

———, and ROBERT W. JACKMAN. 1983. *Class Awareness in the United States.* Berkeley: University of California Press.

JACOBS, JERRY A. 1989. *Revolving Doors: Sex Segregation and Women's Careers.* Stanford, CA: Stanford University Press.

JACOBSEN, JOYCE P., and LAURENCE M. LEVIN. 1995. "Effects of intermittent labor force attachment on women's earnings." *Monthly Labor Review* 118 (September): 14–19.

JAFFE, JIM, et al. 2000. *State Income Inequality Continued to Grow in Most States in the 1990s, Despite Economic Growth and Tight Labor Markets.* Washington, DC: Center on Budget and Policy Priorities.

JAMES, DAVID R. 1988. "The transformation of the southern racial state: Class and race determinates of local-state structures." *American Sociological Review* 53: 191–208.

JAYNES, GERALD D., and ROBIN M. WILLIAMS, eds. 1989. *Common Destiny: Blacks and American Society.* Washington, DC: National Academy Press.

JEFFRIES-FOX, SUZZANNE, and NANCY SIGNORIELLI. 1978. "Television and children's concepts of occupations." *American Journal of Sociology* 84: 53–77.

JOHNSON, DIRK. 2000. "Shoddy defense by lawyers puts innocents on death row." *The New York Times* (February 5): 1.

JOHNSTON, DAVID CAY. 2000. "I.R.S more likely to audit the poor than the rich." *The New York Times* (April 16): 1–24.

JOHNSTON, WILLIAM, and DOUGLAS BAER. 1993. "Class consciousness and national contexts." *Canadian Review of Sociology and Anthropology* 30: 271–295.

JURAVICH, TOM, and PETER R. SHERGOLD. 1988. "The impact of unions on the voting behavior of their members." *Industrial and Labor Relations Review* 41: 374–385.

KAHN, KIM F. 1992. "Does being male help? An investigation of the effects of candidate gender and campaign coverage on evaluations of U. S. Senate candidates." *Journal of Politics* 54: 497–517.

———, and EDIE N. GOLDENBERG. 1991. "Women candidates in the news: An examination of gender differences in U. S. Senate campaign coverage." *Public Opinion Quarterly* 55:180–199.

KALETTE, DENISE. 1991. "Swiss women strike for equal pay, benefits." *USA Today* (June 5): 6B.

KAPLAN, DAVID E., and LUCIAN KIM. 2000. "Nazism's new global threat." *U. S. News & World Report* (September 25): 34–35.

KARR, RONALD DALE. 2000. "Do elite colleges matter?" Posted to social class news group, listserve@listserv.uic.edu, August, 11.

KATSILLIS, JOHN, and RICHARD RUBINSON. 1990. "Cultural capital, student achievement, and educational reproduction: The case of Greece." *American Sociological Review* 55: 270–279.

KAUFMANN , KAREN M., and JOHN R. PETROCIK. 1999. "The changing politics of American men: Understanding the sources of the gender gap." *American Journal of Political Science* 43: 43–56.

KAUTSKY, JOHN H. 1996. "Contexts of conservatism, liberalism and socialism." *Society* 33 (March–April): 48–52.

KEEN, JUDY, JUDI HASSON, and TOM SQUITIERI. 1997. "Dinner raised $488,000, and questions." *USA Today* (February 7): 4A.

KEISTER, LISA A., and STEPHANIE MOLLER. 2000. "Wealth inequality in the United States." *Annual Review of Sociology* 2000: 63–81.

KENWORTHY, LANE, and MELISSA MALAMI. 1999. "Gender inequality in political representation: A worldwide comparative analysis." *Social Forces* 78: 235–256.

KEPHART, WILLIAM E. 1994. *Extraordinary Groups*. 5th ed. New York: St. Martin's Press.

KERCKHOFF, ALAN C. 1993. *Diverging Pathways: Social Structure and Career Deflections*. New York: Cambridge University Press.

————. 1995. "Institutional arrangements and stratification processes in industrial societies." *Annual Review of Sociology* 21: 323–348.

KESSIN, KENNETH. 1971. "Social and psychological consequences of intergenerational occupational mobility." *American Journal of Sociology* 77: 1–18.

KESSLER-HARRIS, ALICE. 1982. *Out to Work*. New York: Oxford University Press.

KIESLER, SARA, LEE SPROULL, and JACQUELYNNE S. ECCLES. 1983. "Second class citizens." *Psychology Today* 17: 40–48.

KILBORN, PETER T. 1995. "Up from welfare: It's harder and harder." *The New York Times* (April 16): 4E.

KIMBALL, MEREDITH M. 1989. "A new perspective on women's math achievement." *Psychological Bulletin* 105: 198–214.

KINGSTON, PAUL W., and LIONEL S. LEWIS, eds., 1990. *The High Status Track: Studies of Elite Schools and Stratification*. Albany: State University of New York Press.

————, and JOHN C. SMART. 1990. "The economic pay-off of prestigious colleges." Pp. 147–174 in Paul W. Kingston and Lionel S. Lewis, eds., *The High Status Track: Studies of Elite Schools and Stratification*. Albany: State University of New York Press.

KIRK, MARGARET O. 1995. "When surviving just isn't enough." *The New York Times* (June 25): 11F.

KLUEGEL, JAMES R., and ELIOT R. SMITH. 1986. *Beliefs About Inequality*. New York: Aldine de Gruyter.

KOHN, MELVIN L., and CARMI SCHOOLER. 1983. *Work and Personality: An Inquiry into the Impact of Social Stratification*. Norwood, NJ: Ablex Publishing.

————, and KAZIMIERZ M. SLOMCZYNSKAI. 1990. *Social Structure and Self Direction: A Comparative Analysis of the United States and Poland*. Cambridge, MA: Basil Blackwell.

KOLCHIN, PETER. 1988. *Unfree Labor: American Slavery and Russian Serfdom*. New York: Oxford University Press.

KORENMAN, SANDERS, JANE E. MILLER, and JOHN E. SJAASTAD. 1995. "Long-term poverty and child development in the United States: Results from the NLSY." *Children and Youth Services Review* 17: 127–155.

KORETZ, GENE. 1995. "Prejudice: Still on the menu." *Business Week* (April 3): 42.

————. 1998. "Wanted: Black entrepreneurs." *Business Week* (December 14): 26.

————. 1999. "Mean streets for the poor." *Business Week* (November 1): 32.

KOZOL, JONATHAN. 2000. *Ordinary Resurrections*. New York: Crown.

KRIEGER, NANCY, et al. 1993. "Racism, sexism, and social class: implications for studies of health, disease, and well-being." *American Journal of Preventative Medicine* 9: 82–122.

KUCZYNSKI, ALEX. 1998. "A Benz for the wrist." *The New York Times* (March 8): 1–3ST.

KUNEN, JAMES S. 1990. "Pop! Goes the Donald." *People* (July 29): 29–34.

LADD, EVERETT CARL, and KARLYN H. BOWMAN. 1999. "The nation says no to class warfare." *USA Today Magazine* (May): 24–27.

LAMBERT, BRUCE. 2000. "Analysis of home loan applications in New York shows racial bias." *The New York Times* (April 9): 26.

LAMONT, MICHELE, and ANNETTE LAREAU. 1988. "Cultural capital: Allusions, gaps and glissandos in recent theoretical developments." *Sociological Theory* 6: 153–168.

LARDNER, JAMES, 2000. "Give us your wired elite." *U.S. News & World Report* (July 10); 34–36.

LAREAU, A. 1989. *Home Advantage: Social Class and Parental Intervention in Elementary Education*. New York: Falmer.

LAUMANN, EDWARD O. 1966. *Prestige and Association in an Urban Community*. Indianapolis, IN: Bobbs-Merrill.

LAVELLE, MARIANNE. 1997. "EPA goes to bat for Native Americans." *The National Law Journal* (April 8): 12A.

LEE, BARRETT A., SUE HINZE JONES, and DAVID W. LEWIS. 1990. "Public beliefs about the causes of homelessness." *Social Forces* 69: 253–265.

LEE, DANIEL B. 1999. "College culture as cultural capital: Portrait of an elite college." Paper presented at the American Sociological Association meetings, Chicago.

LEE, JESSICA. 2000. "Energized black vote crucial to Gore's chances." *USA Today* (October 23): 14A.

LEE, SHARON M. 1998. *Asian Americans: Diverse and Growing*. New York: Population Reference Bureau.

LEEPER, MARK S. 1991. "The impact of prejudice on female candidates: An experimental look at voter inference." *American Politics Quarterly* 19: 248–261.

LEGGETT, JOHN C. 1968. *Class, Race, and Labor*. New York: Oxford University Press.

LEMANN, NICHOLAS. 1999. *The Big Test: The Secret History of the American Meritocracy.* New York: Farrar, Straus and Giroux.

LEMASTERS, E. E. 1975. *Blue-collar Aristocrats.* Madison: University of Wisconsin Press.

LEONHARDT, DAVID. 1997. "Two-tier marketing." *Business Week* (March 17): 82–90.

———. 2000. "In the options age, rising pay (and risk)." *The New York Times* (April 2): 1–17BU.

LEROY, GREG. 1999. "The terrible ten corporate candy store deals of 1998." *The Progressive* (May): 27–36.

LESLIE, CONNIE. 1991. "A rich legacy of preference." *Newsweek* (June 24): 59.

LEVELLE, MARIANNE. 1997. "A political elite joins lobby shop." *The National Law Journal* (August 4): 1–26A.

LEWCHUK, WAYNE A. 1993. "Men and monotony: Fraternalism as a managerial strategy at the Ford Motor Company." *Journal of Economic History* 53: 824–856.

LEWIS, MICHAEL. 1995. "The Rich." *The New York Times Magazine* (December 19): 65–135.

LEWIS, OSCAR. 1966. *LaVida.* New York: Random House.

LICHTER, ROBERT S., LINDA S. LICHTER, and STANLEY ROTHMAN. 1991. *Watching America.* Englewood Cliffs, NJ: Prentice Hall.

LIGHT, IVAN. 1972. *Ethnic Enterprise in America.* Berkeley: University of California Press.

LIGHT, LARRY, and JULIE TILSER. 1994. "The big picture." *Business Week* (November 7): 6.

LIGHTFOOT, SARAH LAWRENCE. 1983. *The Good High School.* New York: Basic Books.

LII, JANE H. 1995. "Week in sweatshop reveals grim conspiracy of the poor." *New York Times* (March 12): 1–40A.

LINDGREN, ETHEL J. 1938. "An example of culture contact without conflict: Reindeer Tungas and Cossacks of Northern Manchuria." *American Anthropologist* 40: 605–621.

LIPMAN-BLUMAN, JEAN. 1984. *Gender Roles and Power.* Englewood Cliffs, NJ: Prentice Hall.

LIPSET, SEYMOUR MARTIN. 1990. *Continental Divide: The Values and Institutions of the United States and Canada.* London: Routledge.

———, and GARY MARKS. 2000. *It Didn't Happen Here: Why Socialism Failed in the United States.* New York: Norton.

LOEB, PENNY, WARREN COHEN, and CONSTANCE JOHNSON. 1995. "The new redlining." *U.S.News & World Report* (April 17): 51–58.

LOGAN, JOHN. 2001. *Neighborhood Integration Is at a Standstill.* Lewis Mumford Center for Comparative Urban and Regional Research. Albany, NY: The University at Albany.

LOPREATO, JOSEPH, and JANET S. CHAFETZ. 1970. "The political orientation of skidders: A middle range theory." *American Sociological Review* 35: 440–451.

MACKENZIE, GAVIN. 1973. *The Aristocracy of Labor.* New York: Cambridge University Press.

MACKINNON, NEIL J., and TOM LANGFORD. 1994. "The meaning of occupational prestige scores." *The Sociological Quarterly* 35: 215–245.

MACLEOD, JAY. 1987. *Ain't No Making It.* Boulder, CO: Westview.

MACNEILLE, SUZANNE. 2000. "Nepal, Boreno and leg room, on thousands a day." *The New York Times* (August 20): 9BU.

MANNING, WILLIAM, and WILLIAM O'HARE. 1988. "The best metros for Asian-American businesses." *American Demographics* 10: 35–37.

MARCUS, STEVEN. 1998. "Marx's masterpiece at 150." *The New York Times Book Review* (April 26): 39.

MARKLEIN, MARY BETH. 1997. "SAT scores up, but so too is grade inflation." *USA Today* (August 27): 1A–4D.

———. 2000a. "Making them sweat." *USA Today* (April 13): 1–2D.

———. 2000b. "Those with the toughest path to college think it's critical." *USA Today* (May 3): 8D.

MARRIOTT, MICHAEL. 1997. "Black erotica challenges black tradition." *The New York Times* (June 1): 41–44.

MARTEL, JENNIFER L., and LAURA A. KELTER. 2000. "The job market remains strong in 1999." *Monthly Labor Review* 123 (February): 3–23.

MARTIN, PHILIP, and ELIZABETH MIDGLEY. 1999. *Immigration to The United States.* Washington, DC: Population Reference Bureau.

MARX, KARL, and FRIEDRICH ENGELS. 1959. *Marx and Engels: Basic Writings on Politics and Philosophy.* Lewis Feuer, ed. Garden City, NY: Doubleday.

———, and ———. 1964. *Selected Writings.* T. B. Bottomore, ed. New York: McGraw Hill.

MASLAND, TOM, et al. 1992. "Slavery." *Newsweek* (May 4): 30–39.

MASSEY, DOUGLAS S. 1996. "The age of extremes: Concentrated affluence and poverty in the twenty-first century." *Demography* 33: 1–26.

———. 2000. "Housing discrimination 101." *Population Today* 28 (August/September): 1–2.

———, GRETCHEN A. CONDRAN, and NANCY A. DENTON. 1987. "The effect of residential segregation on black social and economic well-being." *Social Forces* 66: 29–56.

MASTIO, DAVID. 1998. "Fewer and fewer pay taxes—that's not good news." *USA Today* (April 13): 17A.

MCALLISTER, IAN, and RHODA MOORE. 1991. "Social distance among Australian ethnic groups." *Sociology and Social Research* 75: 95–100.

MCCAFFREY, SHANNON. 2000. "Clinton-Lazio race most expensive." *USA Today* (December 13): 6A.

MCDONALD, MARCI. 2000. "Laughing all the way to the (phone) bank." *U. S. News & World Report* (May 29); 46–47.

MCDONALD, WILLIAM. 1997. "Movies find a way to close the class divide." *The New York Times* (April 6): 16–32H.

MCFARLAND, DAVID D., and VIVIAN LEW. 1992. "Social what? Some hypotheses and evidence on the salience of social class membership in the contemporary United States." Paper presented to the American Sociological Association, Pittsburgh, PA.

MCKEE, J. P., and A. C. SHERRIFFS. 1957. "The differential evaluation of males and females." *Journal of Personality* 25: 356–371.

MCLANAHAN, S. S., and GARY D. SANDEFUR. 1994. *Uncertain Childhood, Uncertain Future*. Cambridge, MA: Harvard University Press.

MCNAMEE, MIKE. 1998. "Job violence: A global survey." *Business Week* (August 17): 22.

MCQUILLAN, LAURENCE. 1999. "Study finds bias against female candidates in newspapers." *USA Today* (October 25): 8A.

MELICH, TANYA. 1996. *The Republican War Against Women: An Insider's Report Behind the Lines*. New York: Bantam.

MILKMAN, RUTH. 1983. "Female factory labor and industrial structure: Control and conflict over 'women's work' in auto and electrical manufacturing." *Politics and Society* 12: 159–203.

MILLAN, STAN. 1997. "Enviro-bias is hot topic in facility siting." *The National Law Journal* (June 23): 8–13B.

MILLER, BARBARA A. 2000. "Anchoring white community: White women activists and the politics of public schools." *Identities* 6: 481–503.

MILLS, C. WRIGHT. 1951. *White Collar*. New York: Oxford University Press.

———. 1956. *The Power Elite*. New York: Oxford University Press.

MINCEY, RONALD B., ISABEL SAWHILL, and DOUGLAS A. WOLF. 1990. "The underclass: Definition and measurement." *Science* (April 27): 450–453.

MINK, GWENDOLYN. 1986. *Old Labor and New Immigrants in American Political Development*. Ithaca, NY: Cornell University Press.

MINTZ, BETH. 1975. "The President's cabinet, 1897–1972: A continuation of the power structure debate." *Insurgent Sociologist* 5: 131–148.

MITCHELL, SUSAN, ed. 1996. *America's Attitudes*. Ithaca, NY: New Strategist Publications.

MONTEFIORE, SIMON SEBAG. 1996. "Black market." *The Times of London Sunday Magazine*. (November 17): 36–44.

MONTOYA, LISA J., CAROL HARDY-FANTA, and SONIA GARCIA, 2000. "Latina politics: Gender, participation, and leadership." *PS: Political Science & Politics* 33: 555–568.

MORE, DOUGLAS M., and ROBERT W. SUCHNER. 1976. "Occupational status, prestige, and stereotypes." *Sociology of Work and Occupations* 2: 3–27.

MORRISON, R. S., et al. 2000. "'We don't carry that'—failure of pharmacies in predominantly nonwhite neighborhoods to stock opioid analgesics." *The New England Journal of Medicine* 342: 1023–1026.

MOSS, DESDA. 1993. "American dream conquers troubles for the newcomers." *USA Today* (July 14): 6A.

———, and GORDON DICKSON. 1994. "Homeless remembered." *USA Today* (December 23): 3A.

Muller v. Oregon, 1908. (118 U.S. 465).

MYERSON, ALLEN R. 1996. "Executives are cradled while medical benefits are cut for rank and file." *The New York Times* (March 17): 1–13.

MYRDAL, GUNNAR. 1944. *An American Dilemma*. New York: McGraw-Hill.

NAGEL, JOANE. 1995. "Resource competition theories of ethnicity." *American Behavioral Scientist* 30: 442–458.

NAIFEH, MARY. 1998. *Trap Door? Revolving Door? Or Both?* U. S. Bureau of the Census, Current Population Reports, P-70-63. Washington, DC: U. S. Government Printing Office.

NAUGHTON, KEITH. 1999. "The global six." *Business Week* (January 25): 68–72.

NEUBORNE, ELLEN. 1990. "The young and wealthy take hands-on approach to philanthropy." *USA Today* (June 26): 6B.

The New York Times. 1988. "Philanthropy for the 21st century." *The New York Times* (July 12): 4F.

NEWMAN, KATHERINE S. 1988. *Falling from Grace: The Experience of Downward Mobility in the American Middle Class*. New York: Free Press.

NOCK, STEVEN L., and PETER H. ROSSI. 1979. "Household types and social standing." *Social Forces* 57: 1325–1345.

NORRIS, C., et al. 1992. "Black and blue: An analysis of the influence of race on being stopped by the police." *British Journal of Sociology* 43: 207–218.

NOTTINGHAM, ELIZABETH K. 1954. *Religion and Society.* New York: Random House.

OAKES, JEANNIE. 1985. *Keeping Track: How Schools Structure Inequality.* Santa Monica, CA: Rand Corporation.

O'HARE, WILLIAM P. 1992. *America's Minorities: The Demographics of Diversity.* New York: Population Reference Bureau.

———. 1996. *A New Look at Poverty in America.* Washington, DC: Population Reference Bureau.

OLSTEN CORPORATION. 1996. "Downsizing results." *USA Today* (April 16): 1B.

OLZAK, SUSAN. 1996. *The Dynamics of Ethnic Competition and Conflict.* Stanford, CA: Stanford University Press.

ORDOVENSKY, PAT. 1989. "Minorities gain, but gaps remain." *USA Today* (September 12): 5D.

OSTRANDER, SUSAN. 1984. *Women of the Upper Class.* Philadelphia: Temple University Press.

OWEN, RICHARD. 1996. "Seventies dream of world with no hunger destroyed by conflict." *The Times of London* (November 14): 23.

PAGE, SUSAN. 1997. "Poll: Fear of immigration eases." *USA Today* (October 13): 1–11A.

PALMER, PHYLLIS. 1989. *Domesticity and Dirt: Housewives and Domestic Service in the United States, 1920–1945.* Philadelphia, PA: Temple University Press.

PAMMETT, JON H. 1987. "Class voting and class consciousness in Canada." *Canadian Review of Sociology and Anthropology* 24: 269–290.

PARENTI, MICHAEL. 1995. *Democracy For The Few,* 6th ed. New York: St. Martin's.

PARSONS, TALCOTT. 1940. "An analytic approach to the theory of social stratification." *American Journal of Sociology* 45: 841–862.

———. 1953. "A revised analytic approach to the theory of social stratification." Pp. 395–415 in Rinehard Bendix and Seymour Martin Lipset, eds., *Class, Status and Party.* New York: Free Press.

PEAR, ROBERT. 1996. "Thousands to rally in capital on children's behalf." *The New York Times* (June 1): 10.

PEASE, JOHN, WILLIAM H. FORM, and JOAN HUBER RYTINA. 1970. "Ideological currents in American stratification." *The American Sociologist* 5: 127–137.

PEREZ-PENA, RICHARD. 1999. "Lawyers abandon legislatures for greener pastures." *The New York Times* (February 21): 3 WK.

PETERSON, ERIC, et al. 1997. "Racial variation in the use of coronary-revascularization procedures." *The New England Journal of Medicine* 336: 480–486.

PETERSON, KAREN S. 1997. "Interracial dating is no big deal for teens." *USA Today* (November 3): 10A.

PEYSER, MARC. 1997. "Question time: What will the 2000 census ask?" *Newsweek* (June 19): 14.

PILIAVIN, IRVING, and SCOTT BRIAR. 1964. "Police encounters with juveniles." *American Journal of Sociology* 70: 206–214.

———, MICHAEL SOSIN, and HERB WESTERFELT. 1987–88. "Tracking the homeless." *Focus* 10: 20–24.

PINES, DEBORAH. 1994. "Reebok gets the boot in its lawsuit against Kmart." *The National Law Journal* 16 (May 9): 27A.

POLIVKA, ANNE E., and THOMAS NARDONE. 1989. "On the definition of contingent work." *Monthly Labor Review* 112: 9–16.

POLLARD, KELVIN M., and WILLIAM P. O'HARE. 1999. *America's Racial and Ethnic Minorities.* Washington, DC: Population Reference Bureau.

POPE, HECTOR, et. al. 2000. "Missed diagnosis of acute cardiac ischemia in the emergency department." *The New England Journal of Medicine* 342: 1163–1170.

POPE, VICTORIA. 1997. "Trafficking in women." *U.S. News & World Report* (April 7): 38–44.

PRB (POPULATION REFERENCE BUREAU). 2000. *World Population Data Sheet, 2000.* Washington, DC: Population Reference Bureau.

POTOK, MARK. 1994. "Community, waste plant on common ground." *USA Today* (August 25): 8A.

———. 1996. "Immigration's other side: Interdependence." *USA Today* (September 30): 19–20A.

PRICE, HUGH B., ed. 2000. *The State of Black America, 1999.* Washington, DC: National Urban League.

PUENTE, MARIA. 1993. "Faces of nation's homeless take on a new look." *USA Today* (December 22): 3A.

———. 1995. "Immigrants eager to be called Americans." *USA Today* (July 5): 5A.

———. 2000. "Everyone wants a shot at being a millionaire." *USA Today* (August 16): 1–2D.

PURITZ, PATRICIA. 1995. *A Call for Justice.* Chicago, IL: American Bar Association.

PUTMAN, ROBERT, SUSAN PHARR, and RUSSELL DALTON. 2000. *What is Troubling the Trilateral Democracies?* Princeton, NJ: Princeton University Press.

RACHIN, JILL. 1989. "The label that sticks." *U.S. News and World Report* (July 3): 51–52.

RAEBURN, PAUL. 2000. "The perils of part-time for professionals." *Business Week* (March 6): 125.

RAMSEY, PATRICIA. 1991. "Young children's awareness and understanding of social class differences." *Journal of Genetic Psychology* 152: 71–82.

RANK, MARK R., and THOMAS A. HIRSCHL. 1999. "The likelihood of poverty across the American life span." *Social Work* 44: 201–216.

RATHOR, S. S., et al. 2000. "The effects of patient sex and race on medical students' ratings of quality of life." *American Journal of Medicine* 108: 561–566.

RATZAN, SCOTT C., GARY L. FILERMAN, and JOHN W. LESAR. 2000. *Attaining Global Health: Challenges and Opportunities*. Washington, DC: Population Reference Bureau.

RAUCH, JONATHAN. 1994. *Demosclerosis*. New York: Times Books.

REIMAN, JEFFREY. 1996. . . .*and the Poor Get Prison: Economic Bias in American Criminal Justice*. Boston, MA: Allyn & Bacon.

REINGOLD, JENNIFER. 1997. "Executive pay." *Business Week* (April 21): 58–66.

———. 2000. "Executive pay." *Business Week* (April 17): 100–142.

REMMINGTON, PATRICIA. 1981. *Policing*. Lanham, MD: University Press.

RESKIN, BARBARA, and IRENE PADAVIC. 1994. *Women and Men at Work*. Thousand Oaks, CA: Pine Forge.

RICHARDSON, JEREMY. 1993. *Pressure Groups*. New York: Oxford University Press.

RITTER, JOHN. 2000. "Priced out of Silicon Valley." *USA Today* (May 18): 1–2A.

ROBINSON, ROBERT V. 1983. "Explaining perceptions of class and racial inequality in England and the United States." *British Journal of Sociology* 4: 344–366.

———, and M. GARNIER. 1985. "Class reproduction among men and women in France: Reproduction theory on its home ground." *American Journal of Sociology* 91: 250–280.

———, and JONATHAN KELLEY. 1979. "Class as conceived by Marx and Dahrendorf: Effects on income inequality, class consciousness, and class conflict in the United States and Great Britain." *American Sociological Review* 44: 38–58.

RODGER, WILL. 2000. "Internet content, not access, creates the great divide." *USA Today* (December 21): 11D.

RODGERS, BRYAN, and SUSAN L. MANN. 1993. "Re-thinking the analysis on intergenerational social mobility." *Journal of Health and Social Behavior* 34: 165–172.

ROSEN, ELLEN ISREAL. 1987. *Bitter Choices: Blue-collar Women In and Out of Work*. Chicago: University of Chicago Press.

ROSENBAUM, JAMES E. 1975. "The stratification of the socialization process." *American Sociological Review* 40: 48–54.

ROSENBERG, MORRIS. 1989. "Self-concept research: A historical overview." *Social Forces* 68: 34–44.

———, and LEONARD I. PEARLIN. 1978. "Social class and self-esteem among children and adults." *American Journal of Sociology* 84: 53–77.

———, CARMI SCHOOLER, and CARRIE SCHOENBACH. 1989. "Self-esteem and adolescent problems: Modeling reciprocal effects." *American Sociological Review* 54: 1004–1018.

ROSENWASSER, SHIRLEY MILLER, and NORMA G. DEAN. 1989. "Gender role and political office." *Psychology of Women Quarterly* 13: 77–85.

ROSKIES, ETHEL, and CHRISTIANE LOUIS-GUERIN. 1990. "Job insecurity in managers: Antecedents and consequences." *Journal of Organizational Behavior* 11: 345–359.

ROSS, CHRISTINE, SHELDON DANZIGER, and EUGENE SMOLENSKY. 1987. "The level and trend in poverty in the United States, 1939–1979." *Demography* 24: 587–600.

ROTHFEDER, JEFFREY, and MICHELE GALEN. 1990. "Is your boss spying on you?" *Business Week* (January 15): 84–85.

RUBIN, LILLIAN B. 1976. *Worlds of Pain: Life in the Working Class Family*. New York: Basic Books.

———. 1997. "Family values and the invisible working class." In Steven Fraser and Joshua Freeman, eds., *Audacious Democracy*. New York: Houghton Mifflin.

RUNDEL, RHONDA. 1987. "New efforts to fight heart disease are aimed at blue-collar workers." *The Wall Street Journal* (March 16): 25.

RUSSELL, JAMES W. 1994. *Under the Fifth Sun: Class and Race in North America*. Englewood Cliffs, NJ: Prentice Hall.

RYTINA, STEVEN. 2000. "Is occupational mobility declining in the U.S?" *Social Forces* 78: 1227–1276.

SACHS, SUSAN. 1998. "The Marxist faithful celebrate their icon." *The New York Times* (November 1): 39.

SAFIRE, WILLIAM. 2000a. "On language." *The New York Times Magazine* (September 10): 28.

———. 2000b. "A new world of names before the dots." *New York Times* (April 9):34–36.

SALTZSTEIN, GRACE HALL. 1989. "Black mayors and police policies." *Journal of Politics* 51: 525–544.

SARGENT, ALLISON IJAMS. 1997. "The social register: Just a circle of friends." *The New York Times* (December 21): 1–2ST.

SCHEIN, VIRGINIA ELLEN. 1973. "The relationship between sex role stereotypes and requisite management characteristics." *Journal of Applied Psychology* 57: 95–100.

SCHULMAN, KEVIN, et. al. 1999. "The effect of race and sex on physicians' recommendations for cardiac catheterization." *The New England Journal of Medicine* 340: 561–566.

SCHWARZ, JOHN E. 1997. *Illusions of Opportunity: The American Dream in Question*. New York: W. W. Norton.

SECOND HARVEST. 1998. *Hunger 1997: The Faces and Facts*. Washington, DC: America's Second Harvest.

SEGAL, ELIZABETH A., and STEPHANIE BRUZY. 1995. "Gender and Congressional voting: A legislative analysis." *Affilia* 10: 8–22.

SEIDMAN, JOEL. 1942. *Needle Trades*. New York: Farrar and Rinehart.

SELTZER, RICHARD A., JODY NEWMAN, and MELISSA VOORHEES LEIGHTON. 1997. *Sex as a Political Variable*. Boulder, CO: Lynne Rienner.

SENNETT, RICHARD, and JONATHAN COBB. 1973. *The Hidden Injuries of Class*. New York: Vintage.

SEWELL, WILLIAM H., ARCHIBALD O. HALLER, and G. W. OHLENDORF. 1970. "The educational and early occupational status attainment process: A replication and revision." *American Sociological Review* 35: 1014–1027.

SHAVIT, YOSSI, and HANS PETER BLOSSFELF. 1993. *Persistent Inequality: Changing Educational Attainments in Thirteen Countries*. Boulder, CO: Westview.

SHEARER, GAIL. 2000. *The Health Care Divide*. Washington, DC: Consumers Union.

SHIBUTANI, TAMOTSU, and KIAN M. KWAN. 1965. *Ethnic Stratification: A Comparative Approach*. New York: Macmillan.

SHIHADEH, EDWARD S., and GRAHAM C. OUSEY. 1998. "Industrial restructuring and violence: The link between entry-level jobs, economic deprivation, and Black and White homicide." *Social Forces* 77: 185–204.

SHOSTAK, ARTHUR B. 1969. *Blue-Collar Life*. New York: Random House.

SIGELMAN, LEE, et al. "Making contact? Black-white social interaction in an urban setting." *American Journal of Sociology* 101: 1306–1332.

SIMMONS, ROBERTA, and MORRIS ROSENBERG. 1971. "Functions of children's perceptions of the stratification system." *American Sociological Review* 36: 235–249.

SIMPSON, IDA HARPER, DAVIS STARK, and ROBERT A. JACKMAN. 1988. "Class identification processes of married, working men and women." *American Sociological Review* 53: 284–293.

SINGH, G. K., K. D. KOCHANEK, and M. F. MACDORMAN. 1996. "Advance report of final mortality statistics, 1994." *Monthly Vital Statistics Report* 45: 19–20.

SIVARD, RUTH LEGER. 1995. *Women . . . A World Survey*. Washington, DC: World Priorities.

SKAFTE, DIANNE. 1989. "The effect of perceived wealth and poverty on adolescents' character judgments." *Journal of Social Psychology* 129: 93–99.

SMITH, CHRISTOPHER B. 1994. "Back to the future: The intergroup contact hypothesis revisited." *Sociological Inquiry* 64: 438–455.

SMITH, M. J., et al. 1992. "Employee stress and health complaints in jobs with and without electric performance monitoring." *Applied Ergonomics* 23: 17–28.

SMITH, PATRICIA K. 1994. "Recent patterns in downward income mobility: Sinking boats in a rising tide." *Social Indicators Research* 31: 277–303.

SMITH, STEVEN K., and CAROLE DEFRANCES. 1996. *Indigent Defense*. Washington, DC: U. S. Government Printing Office.

SMITH, TOM W. 1996. "Comment on 'Are you middle class?'" *American Demographics* 18: 56.

———. 1997. "Trends in confidence in government." *GSS News* 11 (August): 3.

SNIPP, C. MATTHEW. 1996. "A demographic comeback for American Indians?" *Population Today* 24 (November): 4–5

SOBEL, MICHAEL E, MARK P. BECKER, and SUSAN M. MINICK. 1998. "Origins, destinations, and association in occupational mobility." *American Journal of Sociology* 104:687–725.

SORENSEN, AAGE B. 2000. "Symposium on class analysis." *American Journal of Sociology* 105: 1523–1571.

SPOHN, C., and J. CEDERBLOM. 1994. "Race and disparities in sentencing: A test of the liberation hypothesis." *Justice Quarterly* 8: 305–327.

STANLEY, THOMAS, and WILLIAM DANKO. 1996. *The Millionaire Next Door*. New York: Longstreet.

STEARNS, LINDA BREWSTER, and JOHN R. LOGAN. 1986. "The racial structuring of the housing market and segregation in suburban areas." *Social Forces* 65: 28–42.

STEINHAUER, JENNIFER. 2000. "For some New York immigrants, a vast alternative health care system, underground." *The New York Times* (August 20): 24.

STEVENSON, HAROLD W. 1982. *School Experiences and Performances of Asian-Pacific American High School Students*. Washington, DC: U.S. Department of Education.

STOCKARD, J., and W. WOOD. 1984. "The myth of female underachievement: A reexamination of sex differences in academic underachievement." *American Educational Research Journal* 21: 825–838.

STOLBERG, SHERYL GAY. 1999. "Black mothers' mortality rate under scrutiny." *The New York Times* (August 8): 1–17.

STONE, ANDREA. 2000. "British female soldiers undergo battle trials." *USA Today* (July 17): 10A.

STRAUSS, GARY. 2000. "From public service to private payday." *USA Today* (April 17): 1–B.

STREITWEISER, MARY, and JOHN GOODMAN. 1983. " A survey of suburban areas." *Social Forces* 65: 28–42.

STRETESKY, PAUL, and MICHAEL J. HOGAN. 1998. "Environmental justice: An analysis of Superfund sites in Florida." *Social Problems* 45: 268–287.

STUDLAR, DONLEY T., IAN MCALLISTER, and BERNADETTE C. HAYES. 1998. "Explain the gender gay in voting: A cross-national analysis." *Social Science Quarterly* 79: 779–88.

SUMNER, WILLIAM GRAHAM. 1914. *The Challenge of Facts and Other Essays*. New Haven, CT: Yale University Press.

SWARTZ, JON. 2000. "High tech jobs put families in the long-distance business." *USA Today* (November 24): 1–2B.

SWEENEY, GAEL. 1997. "The king of white trash culture." Pp. 249–266 in Matt Wray and Annalee Newitz, eds., *White Trash: Race and Class in America*. New York: Routledge.

TANAKA, JENNIFER, DEBORAH BRANSCUM, and PAULINA BORSOOK. 1996. "The wealth and avarice of the cyber-rich." *Newsweek* (December 30): 48–51.

TAYLOR, HUMPHREY. 1996. "The problem of homelessness." Harris Poll No. 34. New York: Louis Harris Associates.

TAYLOR, JOHN. 1989. *Circus of Ambition*. New York: Warner.

TAYLOR, ROBERT JOSEPH, et al. 1990. "Developments in research on black families: A decade review." *Journal of Marriage and the Family* 52: 993–1014.

TERKEL, STUDS. 1972. *Working*. New York: Random House.

THOMAS, KAREN. 1999. "Tutoring's extra edge." *USA Today* (January 27): 1–2A.

THOMAS, SUE. 1994. *How Women Legislate*. New York: Oxford University Press.

THOMAS, WILLIAM I. 1928. *The Child in America*. New York: Knopf.

THOMPSON, EDWARD. 1963. *The Making of the English Working Class*. London: Allen Lane.

TILGHER, ADRIANO. 1930. *Homo Faber: Work Through the Ages*. New York: Harcourt Brace & World.

TITLE, CHARLES R., and ROBERT F. MEIER. 1990. "Specifying the SES/delinquency relationship." *Criminology* 28: 292–319. *Economist* 342: (January 18): 30–31.

TOMASKOVIC-DEVEY, DONALD. 1993a. *Gender and Racial Inequality at Work*. Ithaca, NY: ILR Press.

———. 1993b. "The gender and race composition of jobs and the male/female, white/black pay gap." *Social Forces* 72: 45–76.

TONER, ROBIN. 1989. "Americans favor aid for homeless." *The New York Times* (January 22): 1–21.

———. 1999. "Fevered issue, second opinion." *The New York Times* (October 10): 1–16 wk.

TONRY, M. 1994. "Racial disproportion in U. S. prisons." *British Journal of Criminology* 34: 97–115.

TURNER, FREDERICK JACKSON. 1920. *The Frontier in American History*. New York: Henry Holt.

UNDP (UNITED NATIONS DEVELOPMENT PROGRAMME). 1995. *Human Development Report, 1995*. New York: Oxford University Press.

UNICEF. 2000. *The State of The World's Children, 2000*. New York: United Nations.

U.S. BUREAU OF THE CENSUS. 1993. Current Population Reports P60–187. *Child Support for Custodial Mothers and Fathers, 1991*. Washington, DC: U.S. Government Printing Office.

———. 1997. *Historical Poverty Tables*. Washington, DC: U.S. Government Printing Office.

———. 1999. *Voting and Registration in the Election of November 1998*. Current Population Survey P20–523. Washington, DC: U.S. Government Printing Office.

———. 2000. *Money Income in the United States*. Current Population Reports P60–209. Washington, DC: U.S. Government Printing Office.

U.S. BUREAU OF LABOR STATISTICS. 1995. *Occupational Injuries and Illness*. Bulletin 2455. U.S. Government Printing Office.

———. 1999. "Contingent and Alternative Employment Arrangements." News release USDL 99–362, December 21. (http://stats.bls.gov/news.release/conemp.nws.htm) (September 6, 2000).

U.S. CONFERENCE OF MAYORS. 2000. *Hunger and Homelessness in America's Cities*. Washington, DC: U.S. Conference of Mayors.

U.S. CONGRESS. 1986. Joint Economic Committee. The Concentration of Wealth in the United States. Washington, DC: U.S. Government Printing Office.

U.S. HOUSE OF REPRESENTATIVES. 1990. Select Committee on Hunger. *Food Security in the United States*. Washington, DC: U.S. Government Printing Office.

USEEM, MICHAEL. 1983. *The Inner Circle: Large Corporations and the Rise of Business Activity in the U.S. and U.K.* New York: Oxford University Press.

———, and JEROME KARABEL. 1986. "Pathways to top corporate management." *American Sociological Review* 51: 184–200.

VANNEMAN, REEVE, and LYNN WEBER CANNON. 1987. *The American Perception of Class*. Philadelphia, PA: Temple University Press.

VEBLEN, THORSTEIN. 1899. *The Theory of the Leisure Class*. New York: Macmillan.

VERBA, SIDNEY, NORMAN H. NIE, and JAE-ON KIM. 1978. *Participation and Political Equality: A Seven-Nation Comparison*. New York: Cambridge University Press.

VERHOVEK, SAM HOWE. 1997. "Silent deaths climbing steadily as migrants cross Mexican border." *The New York Times* (August 24): 1–20

WARNER, W. LLOYD, and PAUL LUNT. 1941. *The Social Life of a Modern Community*. New Haven: Yale University Press.

WAYNE, LESLIE. 1997. "A special deal for lobbyists: A getaway with lawmakers." *The New York Times* (January 26): 1–16.

WEBER, MAX. 1946. *From Max Weber: Essays in Sociology*. H. Gerth and C. W. Mills (trans.). New York: Oxford University Press.

———. 1947. *Theory of Social and Economic Organization*. A. M. Henderson and Talcott Parsons (trans.). New York: Free Press.

WENTZEL, KATHRYN R. 1988. "Gender differences in math and English achievement: A longitudinal study." *Sex Roles* 18: 691–699.

WEST, CANDACE, and SARAH FENSTERMAKER. 1995a. "Doing difference." *Gender & Society* 9: 8–37.

———, and ———. 1995b. "Reply: (Re)doing difference." *Gender & Society* 9: 506–513.

WESTERN, MARK, and ERIK OLIN WRIGHT. 1994. "The permeability of class boundaries to intergenerational mobility among men in the United States, Norway and Sweden." *American Sociological Review* 59: 606–630.

WHITNEY, CRAIG R. 1998. "Paris transit halts in response to violence." *The New York Times* (November 1): 4.

WHYTE, MARTIN K. 1990. *Dating, Mating and Marriage*. New York: Aldine.

WILL, GEORGE. 1993. "A measure of morality." *The Washington Post* (December 16): 25A.

WILLIAMS, JEANNIE. 2000. "Douglas and Zeta-Jones tie the knot." *USA Today* (November 20): 2D.

WILLIAMS, JOHN E., and DEBORAH L. BEST. 1990. *Measuring Sex Stereotypes: A Multination Study*. Newbury Park, CA: Sage.

WILLING, RICHARD. 1997. "Courting the young and the rich." *USA Today* (March 17): 3A.

WILSON, WILLIAM JULIUS. 1987. *The Truly Disadvantaged*. Chicago: University of Chicago Press.

———. 1996. *When Work Disappears: The World of the New Urban Poor*. New York: Knopf.

WIRTH, LOUIS. 1945. "The problem of minority groups." Pp. 347–372 in Ralph Linton, ed., *The Science of Man in the World Crisis*. New York: Columbia University Press.

WOLF, CHRISTOPHER. 2000. "Blocks on 'hate-filled' web content are challenged." *The National Law Journal* (October 30): 12B.

WOLF, RICHARD. 2000. "Study finds large increase in extent of homelessness." *USA Today* (February 2): 6A.

WOLFE, ALAN. 1998. *One Nation, After All*. New York: Viking.

WONG, EDWARD. 2000. "Poorest schools lack teachers and computers." *The New York Times* (August 13): 14.

WRAY, MATT, and ANNALEE NEWITZ, eds. 1997. *White Trash: Race and Class in America*. New York: Routledge.

WRIGHT, ERIK OLIN. 1985. *Classes*. London: New Left Books.

———. 1997. *Class Counts*. Cambridge, MA: Cambridge University Press.

———, and BILL MARTIN. 1987. "The transformation of the American class structure, 1960–1980." *American Journal of Sociology* 93: 1–29.

YAZIGI, MONIQUE. 1999. "When you got it, flaunt it." *The New York Times* (December 26): 1–4 WK.

YBARRA, MICHAEL. 1996. "Don't ask, don't beg, don't sit." *The New York Times* (May 19): 5E.

ZELLER, TOM. 2000. "Calculating one kind of middle class." *The New York Times* (October 29): 5WK.

ZINGRAFF, RHONDA, and MICHAEL D. SCHULMAN. 1984. "Social bases of class consciousness." *Social Forces* 63: 98–116.

ZIPP, JOHN F., and ERIC PLUTZER. 1985. "Gender differences in voting for female candidates: Evidence from the 1982 election." *Public Opinion Quarterly* 49: 179–197.

———, and ———. 1996. "Wives and husbands: Social class, gender, and class identification in the United States." *Sociology* 30: 235–252.

Name Index

Subject Index